The Birmingham Rep
A City's Theatre 1962-2002

Claire Cochrane

For Henry

The Birmingham Rep: A City's Theatre 1962-2002
was first published by the Sir Barry Jackson Trust in 2003.

The Birmingham Rep: A City's Theatre 1962-2002
is published by the Sir Barry Jackson Trust, The Birmingham
Repertory Theatre, Broad St, Birmingham B1 2EP, a registered
charity set up by Sir Barry Jackson before his death
in 1961. The Trust administers schemes to promote touring
theatre, theatre training, theatre in education and the
development of the theatre arts in the West Midlands.

Designed by Ann-marie Comarsh. Graphic repro by Lithocraft Ltd,
Coventry. Printed by Edward Fox & Son Ltd.

Front cover photograph: Nobby Clark

Contents

Acknowledgements

It has taken a long time to research and write this book. I owe a great debt of gratitude to the many people who have shared their experiences and thoughts on Birmingham Rep with me. These include: John Adams, the late Sir Robert Aitken, Bill Alexander, Andy Allan, Sebastian Barnes, John Bettinson, Vanessa Booth, Susan Brock, Marjorie Brown, Paul Burley, the late Nancy Burman, David Buxton, June Callear, Jonathan Church, Anthony Clark, Andrew Coulson, Diana Dewes, the late Peter Dews, Simon Dormandy, David Edgar, the late Tom English, Mark Everett, Oliver Ford-Davies, Jane Freeman, Catherine Fudge, Margaret Gilham, John Greenwood, Alexander Hamilton, John Harrison, Carol Healas, Jennifer Hilary, Lucia Hogg, Christopher Honer, Kate Horton, Gwenda Hughes, Sally Isern, Russell Jackson, Gemma Jones, Trina Jones, Joel Kaplan, Rina Mahoney, Judith Mackay, Wiff Maton, Janice McKenzie, Ronnie Mulryne, Derek Nicholls, Sue Nightingale, Kate Organ, Mike Patch, Ben Payne, Clive Perry, John Pitt, Joanna Reid, Ros Robins, Stuart Rogers, Michael Simpson, John Stalker, Humphrey Stanbury, Bryan Townsend, the late J.C. Trewin, David Waine, Clive Wilkinson, David Williams, Dorothy Wilson, Graham Winteringham, Trevelyan Wright, and Mick Yates.

I would like to thank the staff of the Department of Arts, Languages and Literature of Birmingham Central Library for their unfailing patience and efficiency. Particular thanks, however, are due to the past and present custodians of the Barry Jackson archive and the archive of the Birmingham Repertory Theatre: Steve Haste, Diane Arnold, Niky Rathbone and especially, and most recently, Kathy Higgins who has worked tremendously hard on my behalf. Thanks are also due to the current press and marketing officer at the Rep, Clare Jepson-Homer, for her help.

I thank the members of the Sir Barry Jackson Trust, currently chaired by Roger Burman, who commissioned this work and who have patiently waited for its completion.

I thank my colleague at University College Worcester, Dr Catherine Neale, who has supported my research, and has recently read and commented on the first draft of the book. Thanks are also due to Gina Hansen for her work towards the publication of the book.

Finally I thank my husband John Cochrane and my son Tom Cochrane for their help and support.

List of illustrations

Abbreviations

Local and national newspapers which are the source of quoted press reviews and articles are represented by the following abbreviations:

BP	Birmingham Post	**CT**	Coventry Evening Telegraph
DM	Daily Mail	**EM**	Birmingham Evening Mail
FT	Financial Times	**G**	Guardian
I	Independent	**O**	Observer
PP	Plays and Players	**S**	Stage
SH	Stratford-upon-Avon Herald	**SM**	Sunday Mercury
ST	Sunday Times	**T**	Telegraph
TT	The Times	**W**	Walsall Observer
WO	What's On	**WES**	Wolverhampton Express & Star

Young people's companies or initiatives established by, or linked to the Rep; external theatre companies that have co-produced with the Rep or have presented in association with the Rep are represented in Appendix I by the following abbreviations:

BJT	Barry Jackson Community Tour	**BMT**	Black Mime Theatre
BRA	Birmingham Rep Alabama	**BYT**	Birmingham Youth Theatre
CAT	Cambridge Arts Theatre	**CT**	Crucible Theatre
CTC	Cambridge Theatre Company	**D**	The Drum
FA	Fifth Amendment	**FOCO**	Foco Novo
GRA	Graeae	**HAMP**	Hampstead Theatre
JS	Joint Stock	**LH**	Leicester Haymarket
MON	Monstrous Regiment	**MTJ**	Market Theatre Johannesburg
NP	Nottingham Playhouse	**OP**	Oxford Playhouse
PTW	Palace Theatre Watford	**RC**	Royal Court
REN	Renaissance Company	**RNT**	Royal National Theatre
RNTS	Royal National Theatre Studio	**RYW**	Rep Youth Workshop
SOHO	Soho Theatre	**ST**	Sphinx Theatre
TAM	Tamasha	**TC**	Theatre Clwyd
TEM	Temba Theatre Company	**TRP**	Theatre Royal Plymouth
WYP	West Yorkshire Playhouse	**YC**	Young Company
YR	Young Rep		

The Birmingham Rep

A City's Theatre 1962-2002

1. Introduction

The origins of the Birmingham Repertory Theatre Company can be traced back to a group of amateur actors performing plays in a large family home in a suburb of Edwardian Birmingham. The company is now the longest surviving of the building-based, English regional repertory companies set up in the early years of the twentieth century.[1] The last book-length, general history of Birmingham Rep was published by J.C Trewin in 1963,[2] two years after the death of its founder Sir Barry Jackson. My book picks up the record at that watershed in the company's history. After an analysis of the artistic and cultural reasons why the Rep was founded, and a short survey of its history up until 1961, I then explore the way the company responded to the challenge of modernisation in the rapidly changing theatrical climate of the following decade. This culminated in 1971 in the move from the old playhouse in Station Street, to a new, much larger building on Broad Street. The greater part of the book is devoted to the work of the company in the new theatre up until 2002.

The book bears the sub-title 'A City's Theatre' because after Jackson's death, what had been very much the product of one man's vision and tenacity of purpose, became closely tied to the City of Birmingham's cultural policy and financial management. Birmingham has suffered a reputation as a difficult city for theatre. In 1923, acknowledging the enthusiastic audience response to the ground-breaking British première of his epic *Back to Methusaleh*, Bernard Shaw asked:

> **whether, apart from a few personal friends of mine,**
> **there are any inhabitants of Birmingham in this house?**
> **This has been the most extraordinary experience of**
> **my life. I have had five magnificent performances in**

four days, and, what is more extraordinary, this has
been done in Birmingham. I remember it when it was
dramatically and theatrically, the most impossible place
in the world for work of this description.

This speech, reported in the *Birmingham Gazette* on 13 October 1923,[3] is a
significant document in the record of achievement of the Rep under Jackson. It is
also evidence of Shaw's own mischievous complicity in the idea that Birmingham
is a cultural desert and deserves to be held up as some sort of national joke. In the
nineteenth century Birmingham was dubbed 'the best governed city in the world'[4]
and has always been an ambitious, progressive city. Of course a concomitant
product of ambition can be arrogance and misjudgement and the city, together
with its most famous producing theatre, has, at times, suffered as a result. But
there is equally no doubt that civic will has kept the Rep afloat through some
difficult times.

The city is a complex construct of diverse communities of interest, and one
of the narrative strands in this book is to show how the Rep, post-Jackson, has
attempted to appeal more directly to those different communities. At the
ceremony which awarded him the freedom of the city in 1955, Jackson pointed
out the irony that such a great privilege should be given to a man 'looked upon
as a nuisance for forty years'.[5] It is clear he revelled in the epithet. The romantic
idealism, which created the Rep and other 'cultural' theatres like it, was a reaction
against the burgeoning, money-making ethos of the industrial city. That idealism,
which was characteristic of the repertory movement as a whole, can be seen to
be responsible for the problems, as well as the prestige of theatres like the Rep.
Jackson's famous statement, made in the introduction to the first history of the
Rep published in 1924 by Bache Matthews, that 'Art has no possible relation to
money; the spiritual cannot be estimated by the material',[6] would today provoke
a hollow laugh from the artists and managers who struggle to keep regional
producing theatres viable at the beginning of the twenty-first century.

No biography of the man whose personality shaped and dominated the Rep
for forty-eight years has been published. Born in Birmingham in 1879 the youngest
son of George Jackson, the Victorian grocer who founded the Maypole chain of
dairies, Jackson was very rich and very highly educated. He spoke several
languages, was widely travelled and had extensive knowledge of European culture
and theatre in particular. He was also homosexual at a time when open
acknowledgement would have brought opprobrium and possible prosecution.
Despite a public profile of elegance and urbanity, the combination of wealth and
sexual orientation made him intensely reserved and wary of close relationships. In
later life he disliked discussing money. And yet Jackson clearly inherited his father's

entrepreneurial energy which he then channelled into a capacity for considerable artistic risk based on an acute instinct for creative potential in others.

Peter Brook, who owed the launch of his directorial career in 1945 to Jackson, described him as 'an essentially simple direct man. An English gentleman of a kind that is now virtually extinct'.[7] That simplicity, however, also manifested itself in a singleness of purpose and decisiveness of taste which dominated his theatre's artistic policy. Certainly it could be argued that what was cultivated at Birmingham Rep was essentially a coterie audience, and that a consciously non-populist artistic policy led to a reputation for exclusiveness. That argument falters a little in the face of the fact that Jackson kept his companies going in the 1920s with endless revivals of Eden Phillpott's bucolic comedy, *The Farmer's Wife*, and was responsible for the stage première of the classic *1066 and All That*. But directors after Jackson have been compelled to broaden the base of the Rep's appeal and make it more inclusive.

What cannot be denied is that under Jackson the Rep was positioned at the centre of an important network of artistic influence that extended far beyond Birmingham. In his day Jackson challenged the commercial establishment and played his part in creating a new, flexible model of theatre which enabled artistic experiment and innovation. Shaw's speech in the little Station Street auditorium bears witness to a genuine, collective excitement about the possibilities of theatre which cannot be simplistically dismissed as narrow-minded elitism. After Jackson, as this book sets out to demonstrate, Rep directors took on that other more important legacy of challenge and commitment to innovation to enable theatre artists to develop their creativity and recapture that excitement for new generations of Birmingham audiences. It has not been easy in the economically turbulent years since 1971. While Jackson occasionally vented his spleen on the people of Birmingham when they left his theatre half-empty, he could (mostly) shrug his shoulders at deficit. His successors have not had that privilege and inevitably another major strand in the story is the struggle to survive.

Another difficulty, paradoxically, for the 'new' theatre, has been the legacy of love. 'Old' Birmingham Rep aficionados, who subscribe uncritically to the legend of the Station Street playhouse, have shied away from an acknowledgement of the considerable artistic achievements of Broad Street directorates. The old theatre inspired great love which has been hard to earn in the new. It is significant that while there are no less than four published histories (mine own included) of the work of Jackson's company, up till now there has been no considered account of the complex, equally ambitious period since his death.

The ecology of British theatre has changed to such an extent that it is no longer possible for young actors to be nurtured within a stable, building-based ensemble over an extended period of time as it was in Jackson's era. So the glory days of the old theatre linked to the stars of the past, are invoked to the detriment of the new.

The dominance of London as a centre for the acting profession, has if anything grown stronger. While this book explores the more obviously negative effects this has had on the Rep's recent artistic development, it will also become clear that the Rep has played a major role in redressing the imbalance of opportunity for actors who represent the wide cultural diversity of British society in general, and the Birmingham community in particular. An important, additional issue is the extent to which the achievement of metropolitan, and by extension national, prestige, which Jackson initiated in the 1920s, has diverted attention away from the needs of Birmingham audiences.

Ambition begets ambition, and the artistic endeavour of one generation continues to speak to the next. Barry Jackson founded Birmingham Rep not just for the sake of actors, but in order to introduce a new theatre aesthetic to classical drama, and prioritise the work of contemporary dramatists. Those fundamental priorities, combined with an emphasis on production values of the highest possible quality, have been maintained throughout the long life of the company, and continue to command respect amongst theatre practitioners. After Jackson's death, the need to address new trends in contemporary drama became even more pressing. In the new theatre, the periods of greatest artistic buoyancy have been characterised by a particular commitment to new writing which, in recent years, has made the Rep's studio space the most important developmental centre for new plays outside London.

David Edgar, the distinguished, Birmingham-born political dramatist is an interesting example of the way Jackson's legacy has borne fruit in ways that include, but go beyond, simple affection for the past, to produce drama of contemporary relevance within the mainstream British tradition which the Rep promoted from its earliest days. Edgar has family links to the Rep which go back to his grandmother Isabel Thornton who was a founder member of Jackson's first company. Edgar's parents met on the stage door steps (father Barrie an actor and stage manager, mother Joan an acting ASM). His aunt Nancy Burman became the Rep's administrator. His sister Kate has worked as an actor, musician and director in Broad Street. In 1972, when he was appointed playwright-in-residence at the new theatre, he spoke of his feelings in an interview published in the *Wolverhampton Express and Star*:

> **I feel a slight clutch in my throat about it.**
> **I've always thought of the Birmingham Rep**
> **as a great repertory theatre and a place one**
> **would want to get plays on at. I got my**
> **theatrical training at my parents' knees if you**
> **like. I saw at least the first three plays I ever**
> **saw at the Rep including my first Shakespeare.**

4

The trajectory of Edgar's sometimes turbulent professional relationship with the Rep is another strand threaded into this history.

A theatre as large as Birmingham Rep is a very complex organism not just because a large number of individuals contribute widely diverse skills to a collective endeavour, but because so many external cultural, political and economic factors impact on its operation. This book attempts to disentangle some of that complexity so that successive events and key individuals are explored within the context of the wider circumstances which influenced them. But hopefully the reader will never lose sight of the artistic product. Birmingham Rep has always aspired to be a great theatre, and the book also attempts to retrieve from the past those moments of artistic triumph and innovation which have made the struggle for survival worthwhile. Many plays, many artists and many shows are represented here. What began in a house in Moseley a century ago has come a long way.

1 Founded in 1911 the Liverpool Repertory Company ceased trading in 1998. In 2000 the Liverpool Playhouse and the Everyman Theatre were brought under one administration.

2 J.C.Trewin, The Birmingham Repertory Theatre 1913-1963 (Barrie & Rockcliff, 1963)

3 Bache Matthews, A History of the Birmingham Repertory Theatre (Chatto & Windus, 1924) pp.110-11

4 Claire Cochrane, 'Theatre and Urban Space: The Case of Birmingham Rep, New Theatre Quarterly, 62 (May, 2000) pp.137- 47

5 Film clip shown in 'The Quiet Pioneer', Central Independent Television, 1986

6 Barry Jackson in Matthews, p.xv

7 Quoted in Sally Beauman, The Royal Shakespeare Company: A History of Ten Decades (Oxford University Press, 1982) p.168

2. Contexts

Origins

On 11 February 1963, on the occasion of the fiftieth anniversary of the opening of the Birmingham Repertory Theatre, the critic Gareth Lloyd Evans wrote in the *Guardian* about the modest red-brick playhouse squashed amongst dingy buildings on Station Street:

> **Behind that flat façade which the theatre presents to its smoky zone of Birmingham there is a gutsiness of purpose which infects all who go inside. With its thrombotic stairs, its British Railways type dressing rooms, and its tiny foyers like igloos on a winter night, this theatre represents most of what is good about the British theatre. What is bad about the British theatre world is that it often fails to recognise the debt it owes to this place and a few others like it.**

In 1913 Birmingham Rep was the first purpose-built British repertory theatre. The repertory movement began to develop towards the end of the nineteenth century as theatre practitioners—playwrights, actors and critics—began to campaign for the kind of theatre which would offer not just more artistic opportunity, but would make the stage a platform for social and political change. Paradoxically it was a reaction against success. Theatre as an industry was hugely successful, generating a boom in theatre building which catered for mass audiences in the major cities across Britain and of course, pre-eminently, in London. In Birmingham by 1901 there were 10 theatres. The captains of the industry were the charismatic actor-managers like Herbert Beerbohm Tree and George Alexander, who operated as independent entrepreneurs from their own theatres in London's West End, and also toured their productions across the United Kingdom. However the power of the independent artist was beginning to wane as commercial theatre was passing out of the hands of individuals and becoming, instead, the focus of impersonal, speculative interests where financial rather than artistic criteria dominated policy.

The arguments about the role of theatre, which began to circulate in the first decade of the new century, reflected a much wider political debate. Increasingly the rising influence of socialism began to expose the social consequences of poverty and deprivation caused by the economic philosophy of laissez-faire which had assisted the growth of Britain's great empire. Just as the proponents of state intervention advocated centralised government policies which would provide a more equitable distribution of wealth and opportunity, so the advocates of a new kind of theatre began to discuss the possibility of state patronage which would release artists from the oppression of the profit motive or the instabilities of private patronage.

In addition to the economic constraints on theatre, there was the problem of stage censorship. For over 150 years the theatre had been subject to the Licensing Act of 1737 which meant that all new plays, both English and in translation, and indeed all new translations of ancient classical drama, had to be submitted to the office of the Lord Chamberlain for a performance licence. Any new play which attempted to address issues of serious social or political concern could either be refused a licence altogether—if the subject matter was deemed politically sensitive or offensive to public taste—or heavily cut. While changing societal mores gradually broke down the rigid attitudes which existed at the beginning of the century which meant, for example, that the plays of Ibsen and Strindberg were rarely seen before the 1920s, the system remained in place until 1968. Throughout his professional life, Sir Barry Jackson, like every other theatre manager, had to defer to the Examiner of Plays. The effect on the development of English drama, and the experience and expectations of mainstream British audiences in the first half of the century is incalculable

Between 1904 and 1911 companies established in Dublin, Manchester, Glasgow and Liverpool developed policies aimed at freeing serious young actors from the tyranny of long West End runs of commercially-popular plays and actor-manager dominated Shakespeare or, most crucially, the exhaustion of touring both. The ideal repertory company prioritised (circumspectly) new literary and polemical drama: plays of Irish culture and identity by the Abbey Theatre dramatists W.B. Yeats and J.M Synge; plays by Bernard Shaw, John Galsworthy, Harley Granville Barker and Elizabeth Robins which used the theatre to promote social and political reform, and, where possible controversial European drama. Regional dramatists like Harold Brighouse and Stanley Houghton in Manchester wrote for the potential new audiences in the rapidly-expanding industrial cities now conscious of the need to enhance cultural as well as economic status. Young actors were given opportunities in democratically-organised ensembles now often led by another new phenomenon: the director who did not dominate the company as the star actor.[1]

In Birmingham from about 1902, Barry Jackson began to gather around him a group of like-minded amateurs dedicated to serious play-making—initially in his family home. The wealth which Jackson inherited on the death of his father in 1906, permitted the further development of the group who now called themselves the Pilgrim Players. The company embarked on regular public performances: first in the dingy Mission Hall in Inge Street in the slum parish of St Judes, and then, more comfortably, in the Edgbaston Assembly Rooms. By 1912 the group was known as the Birmingham Repertory Company and Jackson (who had briefly trained as an architect) commissioned the building of his own theatre which was specifically designed to accommodate the values of the repertory movement and the new stagecraft.

Jackson's playhouse in Station Street was influenced by the small theatres recently built in Germany—then very much a powerhouse of theatrical innovation. Everything was geared towards an intimate, focused experience of the play. In complete contrast to the large Birmingham theatres such as the Theatre Royal and the Prince of Wales, which packed in audiences of more than two thousand in a lavishly-decorated ambience of plush and gilt, the Rep was consciously austere in brown wood and marble, and deliberately small. The total seating capacity of 464 was organised in the stalls and balcony in single, steeply-raked, straight-sided blocks. In the typical, curved horse-shoe circles of the Victorian theatre, audiences could relate, and indeed display, to each other as much as to the play. At the Rep, nothing was to distract from the play.

By contemporary standards, the stage was tiny: forty two feet deep and twenty eight feet wide. But combined with proscenium doors which opened onto a removable apron stage, it was perfectly adaptable for a wide range of drama. Rep audiences saw plays from the classical English canon, especially Shakespeare which was a Jackson passion, as well as modern naturalistic and verse drama. The company even staged chamber opera in the 1920s. When the theatre first opened, the then revolutionary Fortuny lighting system which reflected light through bands of coloured silk onto a forty feet high plaster cyclorama fixed to the back wall of the stage was an example of the company's determination to be in the forefront of technical innovation. Wrinkled painted back-cloths and an over-dependence on scenic-canvas wings and borders to create elaborate sets could be avoided in favour of uncluttered, elegant settings often designed by Jackson himself.

This was an enterprise of high artistic, even moral seriousness which was cushioned, unlike other pioneering repertory companies in the pre-state subsidy era which struggled financially or collapsed completely, by Jackson's personal wealth. The company could afford to refuse artistic compromise and stage plays which commercial managements could not contemplate. The Rep was not in fact a 'true' repertory theatre, that is a theatre which has a store of plays which can alternate within a season. Instead a 'short run' policy was operated where plays are performed for fixed periods. In the Rep's early years the pace was exhausting with weekly changes of bill. In 1914, for example, no less than thirty seven plays were mounted which meant that the principal qualities required of actors were versatility and sheer stamina. But those lucky enough to be taken into the company were eager for the opportunity to develop their skills and to benefit from the security and idealism promoted by the management.

After 1919, the pace slowed to fortnightly runs, but then major experiments, which included not only Shaw's *Back to Methusaleh* cycle, but also the first modern-dress productions of Shakespeare, began to attract national and international prestige. The Rep's founder and chief patron was knighted for his services to theatre in 1925 by which time Jackson's companies were performing under his management in London as well as Birmingham and out on tour. A formidable number of actors launched their careers in the company including Edith Evans, Gwen Frangçon-Davies, Cedric Hardwicke, Laurence Olivier and Ralph Richardson. John Gielgud played Romeo in the 1924 London revival of *Romeo and Juliet*. Even Peggy Ashcroft appeared briefly in Birmingham in 1927. In 1929 Jackson inaugurated the Malvern Festival initially to present the work of Bernard Shaw, but enlarged its scope to become a much wider celebration of theatre.[2]

When the twenty-year old Peter Brook was given the extraordinary opportunity to direct *King John*, *The Lady from the Sea* and *Man and Superman* in Birmingham in 1945, actors like Paul Scofield and Denis Quilley were in the company. Not long before Olivier and Richardson had invited Margaret Leighton to join the Old Vic Company. Jackson took Brook and Scofield with him to Stratford when he was invited to become Director of the Shakespeare Memorial Theatre. His refusal to allow the profit motive to dictate artistic policy, combined with a failure to recognise the prevailing trend towards high-gloss, star-led production values, resulted in his controversial resignation in 1948. But back in Birmingham in the early 1950s, his commitment to the principle of a young, vigorous company paid rich artistic dividends in the ground-breaking productions of Shakespeare's *Henry VI* trilogy staged in Birmingham and London by his dynamic director Douglas Seale. The new generation of Rep graduates included Eric Porter, Paul Daneman and Bernard Hepton. By the time Jackson died on 3 April 1961 his theatre had taken on legendary status.

The Theatre and the City

Legends, of course, aggrandize and smooth out the complex tangle of history. Birmingham Rep, like all theatres had its ups and downs. Indeed one reason why Jackson went into London management in 1924 was because he closed his Station Street theatre for eight months angered by the ingratitude of Birmingham audiences who failed to flock to some of his more radical experiments. Again in 1934, after a period when Emile Littler as theatre manager had attempted to put 'pep into Rep',

Jackson again threatened closure. He was ill and personal losses over twenty one years of not less than £100,000 had worn him down. The final result in 1935 was the effective gift of the theatre to Birmingham. The Rep became a limited company with all shares, property and assets transferred to the Sir Barry Jackson Trust which comprised various representatives of city institutions. Jackson remained as Governing Director on the understanding that the artistic policy remained unchanged.

Even so many Brummies remained suspicious of the temple of culture in their midst. In the late 1940s Birmingham Rep, at a time of proliferating commercial weekly reps, was one of the few regional theatres to enjoy the luxury of three to four week runs and relatively substantial rehearsal periods. But, as an article in the local *Evening Despatch* pointed out in 1948, there was a marked disjunction between the strength of the Rep's national and international status and the comparative weakness of its Birmingham support (18.11.48). While it was probably true as the journalist, Brian Harvey, suggested that no satisfactory policy had been devised to maintain solid support the problem lay much deeper. The company's origins could be traced back to the essentially patrician nature of the repertory ideal. While the repertory movement was for many of its proponents linked to the aspirations of socialism, the rejection of the profit motive and the concomitant disdain for the mass audience led to a reliance on the cultivation of a coterie audience, 'a compact majority', who would then educate the majority in the right artistic values.[3] In 1932 Jackson made this clear when he declared his opposition to giving the audience 'what it wants'. The public should be given 'what it ought to have' so it could wake up 'to new and hitherto undreamed of possibilities'. [4] What inspired deep love and loyalty and a rich artistic experience within the walls of the little playhouse did not necessarily reach out to engage with the complex concerns of the industrial city outside.

In 1957 a famous ex-Brummie, Kenneth Tynan, was very rude about the cultural climate of his home city. Reviewing a play by John Hall called *The Lizard on the Rock*, Tynan declared that the director Douglas Seale was 'working against the local grain; Birmingham is perhaps the only city on earth that has a population of more than a million and only two legitimate theatres' (*O*, 14.7.57) But, he conceded, it might be the right place for 'a potentially great actor to learn his craft unobserved'. Tynan had spotted Albert Finney—straight out of RADA, 'outrageously miscast' but performing with 'a square and solid authenticity'. The Rep was still a magical place to grow new actors. That 'gutsiness of purpose' which Lloyd Evans described continued to provide training and experience. In 1958 Seale directed Finney as Henry V. The following year not long before Charles Laughton whisked him off to London, Finney played Macbeth to June Brown's Lady Macbeth in a production directed by Bernard Hepton. In 1959 Hepton directed Ian Richardson as Hamlet. When Jackson died Derek Jacobi was in the company of *Antony and Cleopatra* which gave Elizabeth Spriggs her first important Shakespearean role as Cleopatra.

A New Era

But Lloyd Evans' 1963 article suggests that not only was the Station Street playhouse itself now shabby and inconvenient, but that at a more fundamental level what this theatre represented was beginning to seem outmoded. The fact was that the prestige of the Rep and other founders of the repertory theatre movement was in danger of being swept aside as a result of a further phase of revolution which was transforming British theatre. The great post-war social reforms which included the introduction of the National Health Service and the 1944 Education Act also saw the establishment of the Arts Council and the advent of state subsidy of the arts. The early twentieth-century dreams of a National Theatre supported by a subsidised network of regional theatres seemed about to come true. A new generation of artists, playwrights and actors from a far more diverse social background was changing the cultural face of Britain.

The English Stage Company's production of John Osborne's *Look Back In Anger* at the Royal Court Theatre in 1956 has passed into another legend as the first clear signal of a surge of new British theatre writing not seen since the beginning of the century. Two great national companies were born. Peter Hall founded the Royal Shakespeare Company in 1960, and in 1963, the National Theatre Company was inaugurated under the leadership of Sir Laurence Olivier. There was a parallel expansion in regional theatre. In 1958 the Belgrade Theatre in Coventry was the first new repertory theatre to be built since the Second World War, and the first civic theatre built specifically for repertory. The Chichester Festival Theatre where Olivier directed what became the National Theatre Company, followed in 1962. The new Nottingham Playhouse was opened in 1963, part financed by the City Council and part by funds raised by the Theatre Trust. In Birmingham there were hopes of a new building for the Rep. Before he died, Jackson spoke of dreams of a big, beautiful theatre in a green setting which provided not just plays but food and drink in a comfortable elegant environment. But in other respects he was living in the past.

When challenged in an interview in 1956 about the absence of important new plays in the Rep's programme Jackson replied blandly that there weren't any. He described a recent visit to the Royal Court, the scene, over thirty years before, of his modern-dress productions of Shakespeare:

> It was very noisy. Young people shouting and
> behaving in a most extraordinary fashion.
> It left me completely cold. Before the play I
> looked round the audience. Girls with pale
> emaciated faces and long, black hair. Young
> men in dirty slacks and pullovers and beards
> with pipes. No, I think there is something more solid

in the theatre than the type of play I saw there.
Fantasy, profundity, particularly profundity.
I think there is something deeper to people than
a lot of modern playwrights realise. (*WES*, 24.5.56)

One Court play obviously did appeal to Jackson probably because of its bizarre comedy. It was at his suggestion that Bernard Hepton directed *One Way Pendulum* by N.F. Simpson in 1960.

But it was not enough. The Royal Shakespeare Company, based in Stratford-upon-Avon, and within easy reach of Birmingham, would develop a dynamic approach to Shakespeare nourished by a parallel focus on radical new drama staged in the company's London venues. No matter that Barry Jackson had laid the foundations for the RSC during his tenure at the Shakespeare Memorial Theatre; or that former Rep players like Eric Porter and Ian Richardson were among the first to sign the RSC's groundbreaking three-year contracts, the Rep was stagnating. Also the substantial state funding which started to flow into both national companies meant better resources, more ample rehearsal time and more sophisticated production values which then created a major imbalance in perceptions of excellence. Even as regional theatre began to regenerate, there was a growing suspicion that further marginalisation lay in the future.

A New Beginning

Not long before Bernard Hepton left the Rep, he and Peter Hall took part in an extended newspaper debate about the desirability of the proposed National Theatre building in London. Hepton warned that it should not be built at the expense of regional theatres. The country needed, he claimed, not one National Theatre 'but six up and down the country—all with equal status and grants' (*SH*, 28.7.61) The Rep had entered the age of subsidy in 1951 when Birmingham City Council approved an annual grant of £3000. Nancy Burman who had been Jackson's assistant since his Stratford days, had set about educating city dignitaries on the needs of the theatre. In 1954 she persuaded Jackson, always uncomfortable discussing money, to apply for the Rep's first Arts Council grant of £500. From 1957 onwards the City Council intermittently addressed the issue of a new theatre, but in the event it would be more than a decade of uncertainty before the new building materialised. The more urgent task was to build new audiences for a modernised artistic policy.

Nancy Burman was appointed Administrator shortly after Jackson's death. Refusing to wallow in Rep nostalgia, she was characteristically vigorous in her approach to the future challenge. Lloyd Evans quoted her in his 1963 article 'Our task is the raising of the status of provincial theatre. This is beginning to happen, but we have a long way to go. We want to avoid using the words Repertory Theatre, which leaves a nasty taste in the mouth'. Almost immediately after her appointment she invited John Harrison to take over as Director of Productions. Hepton, who had been part of the acting company since 1953, was, and remains a very fine actor. But following on from Douglas Seale's dynamic theatricality he had been less successful as a director.

Even so by the time Hepton left the Rep at the end of December 1961, the programme had already started to look more up-to-date. Not only did Hepton himself play Sir Thomas More in Robert Bolt's *A Man for All Seasons*, but he also played brilliantly the title role in *Krapp's Last Tape* which was the Rep's first production of Beckett. This was in a double bill with *Traveller Without Luggage* by Jean Anouilh who Jackson had helped to introduce to the British stage in the early 1950s. In September Rep audiences encountered their first Pinter. Bernard Hepton directed Derek Jacobi as Mick in *The Caretaker*. Direction was shared with David Buxton who had collaborated with Hepton on *A Man for All Seasons* and then directed Arnold Wesker's *Roots* with Rosemary Leach as Beattie Bryant.

Buxton was Production Manager with stage management and directorial experience at both the Nottingham and Oxford Playhouses. It was by no means uncommon at that time for the senior stage manager to act as relief director in a rep company. Effectively head-hunted by Nancy Burman in 1960, he had only agreed to come if he could direct the occasional play—an arrangement he had enjoyed with Frank Hauser in Oxford.

Buxton's memories of Sir Barry Jackson, recalled over thirty years later[5], reflect both the homely atmosphere of the Rep at that time and the founding father's solemn view of his theatre's mission:

> **Sir Barry was a very cultured gentleman (Edwardian to the end). And he was a great man of the theatre. He said to me, when we met soon after my appointment (he always dropped in for a cup of tea with the cast in the foyer when he saw the show; usually by now after a matinée. He was immensely approachable). "You and I, David, must always remember that we are servant facilitators to an Art".**

1 For a general account of the growth of the repertory movement see A. Jackson and G.Rowell, *The Repertory Movement: A History of Regional Theatre in Britain* (Cambridge University Press, 1984)

2 Claire Cochrane, *Shakespeare and the Birmingham Repertory Theatre, 1913-1929* (Society for Theatre Research, 1993)

3 Ibid, p.30

4 Sir Barry Jackson, 'The Repertory Movement' (unpublished paper, 1932)

5 All David Buxton's memories of the Rep were recalled in a letter to the author dated 12 April 1996.

3. After Jackson: John Harrison

The Family

What comes across overwhelmingly in conversation with those who worked in Station Street at the start of their careers in the 1960s is a warmth of feeling for what was effectively a family environment. The intimacy of the building combined with the intensity of creative effort, where everyone worked in close proximity, gave the Rep an extraordinary atmosphere. There was a strong sense of continuity with the past. The old Jackson-family dinner-gong continued to sound before each performance, while the theatre's elderly retainers carried on as part of the fabric of the household. The ticket-collector, Martha Jordan (Jordie) had been employed since 1914. She had scrubbed floors and sold coffee and made tea for the company's afternoon break. Doris Watkins (Auntie D) had provided pre-show and interval music on the piano stationed in front of the stage for seventeen years, and before that had sung in the small-scale operas which were a feature of the Rep's programme in the 1920s. When she retired in 1964 she had been Musical Director for twenty-one years. Kath Freeman, the stage door keeper, had first been employed as an usherette for 1s 6d a play in 1927. Since 1936, the theatre's accounts had been managed on a part-time basis by Harold Adkins, who worked for a local firm of accountants. For roughly a week out of every month he sat calculating the Rep's financial fluctuations in a murky little room with a view of a rusty iron staircase.

Others had gone away and come back again. Humphrey Stanbury, who returned to the theatre as manager in 1960, had been a student at the

14

Birmingham Theatre School run initially at the Rep by Mary Richards during the 1940s. In 1949 he joined the staff acting variously as electrician, ASM and walk on. From 1956 until 1959 he was box-office manager and public relations officer. Diana Dewes became resident designer in the autumn of 1962 when Finlay James decided to go free-lance. In the 1950s she had been a student with both James and the legendary Paul Shelving who designed Rep productions for over forty years. She has vivid memories of Jackson depositing vegetables from his Malvern garden in the theatre foyer for the company to take their pick. Dewes' subsequent professional experience included the rigours of weekly rep in Guildford and an eighteen-month stint at the Belgrade where she encountered the radical new ideas of designers like Sean Kenny and Jocelyn Herbert. But when James asked her to return to Station Street in 1960 to scene-paint she came back to what were still excellent resources.

The Working Environment

The Rep was self-sufficient in set-building. The workshop area was attached to the back of the theatre on the corner of Hinckley Street. A cast-iron spiral staircase led from the carpenter's shop up to the scene-painting room which was some twenty feet high and fitted with two enormous paint frames which could be winched up through slits along the walls. Furniture and props were stored in the cellar. The characteristic smell of hot size and dry powder paint mixed in buckets was much the same as it had been fifty years before.

The stage was not only very small but also raked and there was very little wing space. At the time that David Buxton arrived the grid was in a poor state and there was no counterweight system which made flying scenery a very strenuous exercise. Buxton commented 'the stage was appallingly lop-sided. The funny little circular staircase upstage left was actually frighteningly near to stage centre. There was not a right angle in the place. I must have worked there for fully eighteen months, before I was forced to realise…that if the set was exactly right and never fitted, then the Ground Plan must be wrong'.

Overall production conditions had changed relatively little. The work was hard and the financial rewards slight. Even though the Rep's four (usually) week runs were relatively luxurious, productions had to be designed, rehearsed and mounted within a month. The turnaround between shows was less than three days. Sets would be dismantled following the final performance on a Saturday night; Sunday and Monday would be devoted to erecting the new set and technical rehearsals. A dress rehearsal on Tuesday afternoon would be followed immediately by the first night. A few days' break for shopping, laundry, visits to the dentist etc. and the whole cycle would begin again. There was no rehearsal room as such. Bernard Hepton rehearsed in a room over a nearby pub. John Harrison insisted on rehearsing on the stage.

Jennifer Hilary, nineteen years old in 1962, winner of the Bancroft medal at RADA and with a short season at the Liverpool Playhouse behind her, came to the Rep to work a thirteen-hour day for £15 a week. Her first role was Miranda in John Harrison's production of *The Tempest*. Lucky to be home in her local bed-sitter by 11pm, she was then expected to be back in the theatre by 10am the next day to rehearse the next production until 6pm when it was time to prepare for the evening's performance. She remained in the company for more than a year often cast opposite Derek Jacobi. His three years at the Rep gave him experience in an astonishing range of roles in plays which spanned four centuries. He finished in May 1963 with an heroic Shakespearean triple: Troilus, Aaron the Moor, and Henry VIII—an opportunity afforded by Harrison's decision to complete the canon of Shakespeare's plays staged at the Rep. When Jacobi then went to the Chichester Festival Theatre to join Sir Laurence Olivier's company, he was going with much the same grounding as Olivier himself had received in the Rep company more than thirty years before.

But inevitably the presence of a group of ambitous, thrusting young actors rather gave the lie to the notion that the atmosphere at the Rep was always cosy and friendly. In fact the rivalries were intense. Buxton recalled:

> **Every four weeks on the Friday before change-over weekend, the cast list went up on the notice board for the play that was to rehearse the following week. And every four weeks several hearts were broken. Quite seriously so! The company contracts: 'play as cast' led to a great deal of bitterness and frustration.**

John Harrison and the new regime

Harrison's links with the Rep went back as far as the Second World War. As a young actor in 1944 he had been directed by H.K. Ayliff, the formidable creator of many of the productions which had made the Rep famous in the 1920s: the man who had terrified Olivier and nurtured the skills of Ralph Richardson and Cedric Hardwicke. In 1945 Harrison played in the three Peter Brook productions and then moved on to Stratford for two seasons and married Daphne Slater, Brook's choice as Juliet. Harrison then turned his attention to directing and from 1952 until 1957 was Director of the Nottingham Playhouse which had only been established in 1948. Battling with fortnightly changes of bill, he presented balanced programmes which combined new plays by Ustinov, Fry and Eliot, with classical rarities like *'Tis Pity She's A Whore* performed by actors of the calibre of Joan Plowright and Derek

Godfrey. After a period directing in television—now an increasingly potent force—Harrison came back to Birmingham confident that he could build on the values of the past. 'Barry Jackson's kind of theatre', he declared, for the benefit of the *Walsall Observer* (12.1.62), 'is my kind of theatre'.

Buxton, however, was less than thrilled to be reunited with his former boss from the Nottingham Playhouse. Harrison had wasted few friendly words on him during an unhappy year and disliked Buxton's directorial efforts. Buxton described Harrison as 'a cool and very reserved man. His gentle aesthetic exterior masks a very great deal of determination, ruthlessness and obstinacy. This is true, probably, of all good theatre directors'.

Harrison immediately made it clear that there would be little chance of a main stage production, but could Buxton get some lunch-time theatre going? Buxton rehearsed in the theatre wardrobe and presented Ionesco's *The Lesson* for two performances. Harrison was impressed and from then on his support never wavered.

With Jackson gone, more and more would now focus on the responsibilities of the Artistic Director (Harrison claims to have invented the title), and the powers of the Board of Management which inevitably underwent some restructuring. The new Chairman of the Board would have been much to Sir Barry's taste. Sir Robert Aitken, an eminent physician and Vice Chancellor of Birmingham University, was somewhat taken aback to be approached by the Rep directorate to become their principal figurehead. Although he and his wife were seen regularly at Rep first nights, he claimed to know relatively little about theatre. But Jackson had always cultivated links with the academic world and Aitken was assured that Nancy Burman and her colleagues would provide practical support. When his appointment was announced in January 1962, the Board he was to lead was for the most part made up of eminent and distinctly elderly men mostly drawn from various important spheres of Birmingham life who had long-standing connections with the Rep.

Jack Mayers who became Secretary when Sir Barry Jackson's former press officer and close associate,Tom English, resigned in September 1961, was trained as a civil engineer and was the managing director of a local firm. Eric Vincent was not only the managing director of the family firm (Blue Bird Toffees), but had formed the Eric W.Vincent Charitable Trust and was co-author with Asa Briggs of a history of Birmingham University. Sir Wilfred Martineau, a solicitor by profession, had a distinguished record in the post-war cultural regeneration of the city. S.T. (Bob) Walker was an important Birmingham architect. There were two former Lord Mayors: Alderman Sir Alfred Bradbeer, originally an accountant, had been Leader of the Labour Group on the Council, while Alderman J. Lewis, a director of Beaumont Fuels Ltd., was a leading Conservative. The only non-Brummie, and indeed the only member with direct theatrical experience was Charles Landstone, the General Manager of Bristol Old Vic and former Deputy Drama Director of the Arts Council.

The First Year

The future looked bright. Audience figures in 1961 had been up on the previous year with overall attendance in the region of 115,000. It was also noticeable, however, that audience patterns were changing. There was a decline in the number of regular loyalists and distinctly different constituencies of interest were attracted to specific productions. Hepton had worked hard to attract young audiences, giving lectures outside the theatre and bringing groups into the building for Saturday morning workshops.

It was never going to be easy to fulfil the expectations provoked by the arrival of a newcomer who inevitably had to perform a precarious balancing act: avoid frightening away the established audiences who had formed the backbone of the Rep's support—and this of course also included his own Board—and find ways of building new audiences. Harrison's company had a nucleus of eight actors. Jennifer Hilary was joined by other recent RADA graduates: American-born Paul Carson who had also worked in Liverpool and Desmond Gill who had a season in Frinton behind him. Ralph Nossek and Lesley Nunnerly were both well-known from television and Georgine Anderson's background included a repertory season at the Alexandra Theatre as well as work at the Shakespeare Memorial Theatre. Derek Jacobi and Arthur Pentelow were retained from the previous company.

Harrison's personal directorial interests lay, as had Jackson's with classical or modern literary drama and the programme for the first twelve months looked very much like Jackson's kind of theatre. There were the staples of Shakespeare (*The Tempest*), Sheridan (*The Rivals*) and Shaw (*Getting Married*). Harrison also continued the Jackson tradition of presenting his own adaptations. J.M. Barrie's early farce *Walker, London* was reworked as a musical and for Christmas 1962 audiences were treated to Harrison's own version of *Alice in Wonderland*.

His productions of John Whiting's *Saint's Day* and Christopher Fry's adaptation of Giraudoux's *Duel of Angels* clearly invited comparisons with the RSC's productions of both dramatists' work at the Aldwych Theatre in 1961 when Whiting's *The Devils* was premièred and Peter Hall directed Giraudoux's *Ondine*. But early Whiting and the witty, literary elegance of Giraudoux equally clearly attempted to cater for the intellectual appetites of audiences accustomed to Jackson's beloved 'fantasy and profundity'. Significantly the two comparatively safe forays into Royal Court-style realism were both entrusted to Buxton. He scored a success with Gwyn Thomas's ebullient South Walelian comedy *The Keep* premièred at the Court only the previous year, and at long last staged *Look Back in Anger* the following autumn with Jacobi letting rip as Jimmy Porter opposite Jennifer Hilary as the long-suffering Alison.

Harrison's inaugural production of *The Tempest*, however, was something of a critical disaster, hampered by a visually evocative, but rock-and-rostra-obstacle-course set by Finlay James which only the critic J.C. Trewin (always a Harrison devotee) had kind words for. The actors were generally slated with the exception of Jacobi's emotionally and vocally passionate Ferdinand. What was meant to be a flexible,colloquial delivery of Prospero's speeches by Ralph Nossek was condemned as inaudible, television-style understatement. Lesley Nunnerley played Ariel covered entirely in green makeup and wearing a sort of bathing costume with fishnet tights and a pearl decorated cap.

Saint's Day which followed did not draw audiences. Premièred in 1951 at the Arts Theatre Club where it received a Festival of Britain Award, Whiting's bleak exploration of the darkness of human existence, had not been revived for eleven years and was presented in Birmingham as effectively a new play. Knowing that audiences had already responded to Pinter's deployment of elliptical menace in *The Caretaker*, it must have seemed like a justifiable gamble. Diana Dewes designed the set of a great, barren house standing in a limbo of lost hopes. Arthur Pentelow played the octogenerian poet, Paul Southman, who has lived for over twenty years in self-inflicted exile from a world he despises and fears. Georgine Anderson brought a hypo-sensitive realism to his faded and ultimately doomed grand daughter Stella while Jacobi played Christian Melrose, the leader of a trio of escaped army prisoners who bring death to the household.

The next big risk was taken in the autumn. In directing *The Double Deceit* by William Popple, an obscure eighteenth-century dramatist, Harrison was operating entirely within the Jackson tradition of reviving literary rarities. The local press was encouraged to stress the fact that the solitary copy of the 1736 text had been microfilmed specially for the Rep by Liverpool University Library. Jacobi and William Ingram played Young Courtlove and Gaylife to Hilary and Nunnerley as the Richly sisters—Harriet and Fanny—in a romantic plot of two young gallants and their prospective heiress brides simultaneously disguised as servants. Eileen Beldon who had played Katharine in Ayliff's celebrated modern-dress production of *The Taming of the Shrew* in 1928, was now cast as Widow Lettwell much to the delight of Gareth Lloyd Evans. He described her sailing: 'like a monstrous Golgotha through a part which is a glorious mixture of Mrs Malaprop and Lady Catherine de Burgh'. She wore 'makeup like animated putty and a costume like a flagday' (G, 2.11.62). Finlay James created a stage décor of softly-coloured and illuminated pivoting screens. Audiences came and enjoyed.

A Shakespeare Event

13 February 1963 was the Rep's fiftieth birthday. The very first production of *Twelfth Night* in 1913 had launched a distinguished record in the production of Shakespeare, but unlike the Old Vic or the Shakespeare Memorial Theatre, the

whole canon had never been staged. It was even suggested that Jackson had a superstitious fear that completion would herald his own death. The omission was remedied when a ten-week Shakespeare Festival opened on 12 February 1963 with *The Famous History of the Life of Henry the Eighth*, directed by David Buxton. Harrison's production of *Troilus and Cressida* followed on 19 February, while *The Most Lamentable Tragedy of Titus Andronicus* had its first night on 12 March directed by Ronald Eyre. In its ambitious scope, the Festival was a feat to equal the enterprise at Stratford where *The Wars of the Roses*, the Hall/ John Barton adaptation of the three parts of *Henry VI* and *Richard III* was due to open in April. However while the Stratford venture was widely publicised, the Rep's work received little attention outside the Midlands. Bernard Levin, then the influential drama critic of the *Daily Mail*, helped to redress the balance:

> **At the Birmingham Rep, the matinée ladies**
> **in their matinée hats look much as their London**
> **counterparts. But they were watching a matinée**
> **of Henry VIII and there's the difference. What**
> **is more they were watching a production of**
> **Henry VIII that is amongst the finest productions**
> **of any of Shakespeare's histories I have seen. (3.4.63)**

Buxton borrowed Robert Bolt's Common Man device from *A Man for All Seasons* to assemble a chorus of Tudor citizens played by Ingram, Gill and Roy Patrick. Often stationed behind the proscenium on what remained of the old apron stage, and armed with hand-props which included cushions, flags and packed lunches, they provided a stream of comment and humour at the moments when the text calls for extra gentlemen to discuss the fate of Buckingham or the coronation of Anne Bullen. Lloyd Evans, while waspish about the value of the play itself and some aspects of the production, praised Georgine Anderson's Katherine of Aragon with 'a voice of tempered steel and an evocative accent' (*G*, 3.4.63). Jacobi was universally applauded as Henry. Bernard Levin's comment emphasised the continuing special nature of the Rep's artistic policy and the expectations of its audience. In box office terms, the Festival was an unqualified success.

Staging the plays in repertoire was not easy because of the lack of set storage space. Finlay James, who designed the sets for *Henry* and *Titus*, had to achieve maximum impact for two very different plays with minimum resources. For *Henry* he erected a gilded colonnade which curved round the back of the stage meeting, on either side, a built section of wall gleaming bronze gold in the light. For *Titus* a rough-hewn, barbaric effect was achieved with little more than a painted wooden platform raised up from the main stage and reached by two short ladders. Voytek, a refugee from post-war Poland and a long-time collaborator with Harrison, adopted a simple expressionist approach in designing *Troilus and Cressida*. The Greek and Roman camps were distinguished by two massive alternating yellow and black animal emblems: an eagle for Greece and a lion for Troy which were framed by a sort of wooden goal post wrapped in barbed wire. A back-cloth depicted the dark-blue outline of a huge female figure emerging from a swirling mass of blood red.

Ronald Eyre came at Harrison's invitation after a schools' television production of *Julius Caesar* to make his Rep directorial debut with the gothic horrors of *Titus Andronicus*. Peter Brook had demonstrated in his celebrated 1955 Stratford production that atrocity could be successfully staged as ritual and there were signs of Brook's influence in Eyre's use of formalised movement and musique concrète. No-one fainted in the Rep audience as they had in Stratford, and even the laughter that greeted the sound of severing bone when Titus cuts off his own hand seemed acceptable as absurdist black humour. However the constraints of repertory casting—young white actors blacking up and aging up—created bigger problems. As Aaron, the devilish Moor, Jacobi looked positively risible in black golly-wog wig and makeup. Following in the shadow of Laurence Olivier as Brook's Titus, Desmond Gill struggled to be convincing as the ancient, gnarled Titus.

Harrison was determined to demonstrate that *Troilus and Cressida* spoke directly to the 1960s with what he called 'its disillusion with romantic idealism, with traditional inherited attitudes and values'. The costumes, ranging from Homeric to modern were eclectic. Lesley Nunnerley's Cassandra led a group of rucksacked peace-protesters, while Paul Carson as Hector looked like a Victorian vision of Sir Galahad. Jennifer Hilary did not play Cressida as a lubricious tart betraying Jacobi's passionately eloquent Troilus, but was encouraged to attempt a humane exploration of how 'we are devils to ourselves'.

New Ventures, New faces

As a centuries' old play was revisioned to address a rapidly-changing cultural climate, a swinging sixties icon arrived at the Rep in the shape of Julie Christie. When Harrison staged the Restoration comedy *The Country Wife* in June 1963, he cast his future second wife Linda Gardner as the wayward Marjorie Pinchwife, while Christie played her militantly-virtuous sister-in-law Althea. In August when Christie had to have time off from rehearsals for *The Good Woman of Setzuan* to attend the showing of *Billy Liar* at the Venice Film Festival, the theatre basked in the reflected glory. She delighted the press with her bare-footed charm but was also adamant that she valued the Rep experience even if it was for only sixteen pounds a week.

Despite the fact that *The Country Wife* was written in 1675, William Wycherley's raunchy tale of the lecherous Horner feigning castration to avail himself of yet more willing women was, in its way, a departure appropriate to the time. *The Good Woman of Setzuan* was theatrically a good deal more significant. This was the first Brecht on the Rep stage. The impact of Brechtian theory on British theatre, especially after the visit of the Berliner Ensemble to London in 1956, not only reinforced the desire to make theatre more politically relevant, but challenged naturalistic acting and production values. Carefully-masked representational scenery, hidden lights and even such time-honoured conventions as the use of velvet front curtains were gradually abandoned.

In Birmingham, *The Good Woman* was publicised as a 'charming fairy tale' which may have made more knowledgable Brechtians blink, but the production was received with interest. Linda Gardner was cast as the warm-hearted prostitute Shen who can only be cruel when assuming the role of her tight-fisted male cousin Shui Ta. A review in the *Stratford Herald* commented on the audience's involvement ' Here was earthy reality clothed in living actuality—and the house was spellbound' (6.9.63).

Immediately afterwards, Ronald Eyre applied Brechtian principles to the Absurdist comedy *Next Time I'll Sing to You*, a revised version of a play by James Saunders which had been produced at the Arts Theatre in London the previous January. The existential musing of five actors, brought together to rehearse the real-life story of a long-time recluse, was performed on what was little more than a bare wooden platform, harshly lit and dominated by the abstract figure of a man wrapped round with barbed wire. A year later when Eyre introduced Brendan Behan's *The Quare Fellow* to Rep audiences, he encouraged Diana Dewes to expose the fifty-year old bricks at the back of the stage which then became the wall of the Dublin prison where the Irish rebel is condemned to die. There were new young actors in the all-male cast. John Shrapnel doubled as the Boy from the Island and the Warder without a Landing, while Simon Ward played Mickster and Warden Grimmin. Derek Smith relished the Guinness-laden dialogue playing Himself, the Lancashire hangman, and Dunlavin, the meths-addicted old lag.

Derek Smith, yet another RADA gold medallist moved to the Rep from the RSC in January 1964 to play Bottom in Harrison's production of *A Midsummer Night's Dream* and enjoy considerable critical acclaim. His argument for staying on in Birmingham, despite more lucrative offers of work elsewhere, echoed Julie Christie's. The range of experience on offer seemed to offer unrivalled artistic opportunity. Even the pre-Christmas romp in December 1963 had promised a fashionable innovation. David Lodge and Malcolm Bradbury, both lecturers at Birmingham University who would find fame in another literary medium, joined with a student Jim Duckett to devise a revue *Between These Four Walls*. Shying away from the sharper satire typical of the cult TV show *That Was The Week That Was*, the humour was based on rather self-conscious theatrical parody. Christie, Gardner, Ingram and co. skipped through sketches which included 'Birth of a

Salesman', 'A Brechtian Pantomine', 'Room at the Bottom' and 'Theatre in the Round and Round'. It was fun but hardly *Beyond the Fringe.*

Upsetting Aunt Edna

It is difficult to grasp now the extent to which theatre throughout most of the sixties was constrained by the censoring power of the Lord Chamberlain, despite the veritable explosion of new writing. Experienced theatre directors grew wearily accustomed to arguments about language or stage action which was deemed to offend against public taste or indeed offend against leading politicians or members of the Royal Family. Inevitably the campaign against the censor was waged primarily in London because only the national companies and the Royal Court had the resources to mount substantial new work. In 1964 John Harrison publically supported RSC directors in the row which erupted over the Theatre of Cruelty season staged at LAMDA. Ironically the charge of indecency levelled at the RSC was made by one of its own board members, Emile Littler, the former Rep manager in the 1930s. One of the most cogent arguments put forward by the commercial theatre managers like Littler, who were the principal defenders of the Lord Chamberlain, was that the official licence awarded to a play protected it against the infinitely more troublesome outrage which could be encountered in regional audiences and watch committees. There were far more Aunt Ednas, as Terence Rattigan dubbed the archetypal conservative theatre-goer in the benighted provinces, than in London it was reasoned.

But if new audiences were to be attracted to the Rep, then a challenge to Aunt Edna was both an artistic and economic necessity. A sequence of plays staged in the summer of 1964: the world première of Evan Hunter's *The Easter Man*, Bill Naughton's *All in Good Time* and Anne Jellicoe's *The Knack*, directly addressed the experience of the young amidst rapidly-changing sexual mores. When the curtain went up on 2 June for the first performance of *The Easter Man* to reveal a dingy garret with peeling brown wall paper, cast iron stove, plastic sink unit and overstuffed upholstery leaking at the edges all created by Diana Dewes, it looked like a setting for a standard piece of fifties social realism. In fact the American author of *The Blackboard Jungle* had written a frank, well-made play about two college boys anticipating a sexually pleasurable weekend with two girls. Harrison brought in Ian McShane and Robin Hawden, both well-known from television, to play opposite Karin Fernald and Suzan Farmer in a slick, exciting production which subsequently transferred to the Globe Theatre in London. Hawdon played Nick who is finally reborn, like the Easter Man of ancient ritual, to a mature relationship with Kathy who wants more than superficial sex. McShane was brilliantly convincing as the unregenerate Ralph while Derek Smith was a hairy, sax-playing beatnik who practises in the communal lavatory and is afraid of mice. Aunt Edna manifested herself most prominently in Alderman Lewis who staged a widely-publicised walk-out which almost certainly contributed to the play's success with less prudish Brummies. The London transfer was the first in six years.

All in Good Time, which Buxton directed in August, is a warm-hearted, humane play about the sexual problems of a newly-married couple beginning their married life in the cramped, working-class parental home. Derek Smith played Ezra Fitton, a gas works labourer with Eileen Beldon as his wife Lucy. John Golightly was cast as his cinema-projectionist son, Arthur opposite Celestine Randall as his new wife Violet. Simon Ward and John Shrapnel made their first Rep appearances as Arthur's assistant and younger brother. Even those who objected to the subject matter could not claim that it was broached insensitively. *The Knack* which Harrison directed, was a different matter. The play is a bawdy, experimental excursion into the theme of seduction and the balance of sexual power. Derek Smith played Tolen, a strutting know-all in sunglasses, leather jacket and beatle boots who claims the knack of pulling girls conspicuously lacking in the nervous, withdrawn Colin who was played by Simon Ward.

Problems

But Harrison was already beginning to look rather beleagured. In April 1964 Nancy Burman announced her resignation. Her explanation was that she wished to retire to her home and garden to make room for someone younger to guide the Rep into the new building which was by then at an advanced planning stage. Rather unexpectedly she was not asked to join the Board. There had been changes there too. Between May 1963 when Albert Bradbeer died, and September 1964 when Charles Landstone resigned, four long-standing Board members disappeared. Both Vincent and Martineau died. Alderman Harry Watton, the leader of the dominant Labour group in the City Council replaced Bradbeer while in October 1964, Oscar Hahn and Richard Hoggart became new members. Hoggart, the author of *The Uses of Literacy* had become Professor of English at Birmingham University in 1962, and by 1964 had established the Birmingham Centre for Contemporary Cultural Studies. The academic debate about the growing economic power of popular culture and issues of elitism surrounding the provision of high art conducted at the Centre, was a matter of no small practical concern at the theatre a few miles down the road.

The departure of Nancy Burman 'a woman of large mind', as Harrison described her, was a major blow. She had invested a good deal of personal and professional capital in her support for the director. The emotional upheaval caused by his relationship with Linda Gardner, coupled with increasing press criticism of his artistic policy may have contributed to a feeling of disenchantment. It was equally clear that raising the Rep's profile was not going to be plain sailing.

Harrison had promised in 1962 that the experimental and the new would be balanced by the established and traditional. 1964 began with Harrison's production of *A Midsummer Night's Dream*, which gave Angela Pleasance her first professional role as Titania, and ended with *The Seagull, The Beggar's Opera*, and at Christmas, the perennial favourite, *Charlie's Aunt*. But along the way there was some damaging criticism. Despite Derek Smith's success, *The Dream* had proved an eccentric disaster. Gareth Lloyd Evans, reviewing in April *The City Madam*, a seventeenth-century play by Massinger, complained about 'the awful dead acting weight that, recently, the Birmingham Rep seems to have landed itself with'(G, 9.4.64). *Spring,1600*, a play focusing on the first performance of *Twelfth Night* and Richard Burbage, by Emlyn Williams, which followed played to poor houses. Although *The Easter Man* did well, *The Knack*, despite full houses towards the end of the run, averaged only 46% of capacity. In general the audience figures dipped in the autumn.

Part of the problem lay in the changing perception of repertory theatre of which Nancy Burman had been all too well aware. As feared, the two national companies—especially the RSC—with their growing subsidies and extended rehearsal periods, were beginning to create a dangerous imbalance in the capacity for innovation and excellence. The regions were losing out. It was becoming more and more difficult to hold onto young actors to maintain the traditional repertory companies. Television not only offered greater financial rewards but set standards in naturalistic acting which, as we've already seen, meant that old-style repertory casting was beginning to be less acceptable. Harrison continued the policy of maintaining a more or less permanent core of young actors but increasingly he began to bring in well-known guest actors. It was remarked that the standard of acting in *The Easter Man* was better than usual.

This could of course backfire. For *The Seagull*, Dulcie Grey came to play Madame Arkadina with Simon Ward as her doomed son Konstantin. The critical consensus was that her performance was altogether too mannered and melodramatic. However when Harrison directed Wendy Hiller and Jeremy Brett in the British première of Steve Passeur's *A Measure of Cruelty* in February 1965, there was praise for both performances. Wendy Hiller, was in fact a distinguished graduate of the Rep. In 1936 she played both St Joan and Eliza Doolittle at the Malvern Festival much to Shaw's satisfaction. When Ronald Eyre directed what Lloyd Evans described as a magnificent production of *Heartbreak House* in April, Edgar Wreford, who had acted in the legendary *Henry VI* productions in the early 1950s, returned to play Captain Shotover. Lloyd Evans wrote that Wreford: 'sensitively uncovers the spiritual flaw in the great hulk that is Shotover—a man at odds with his conscience and limping to perdition with all his sins, imaginary and real, on his head' (G, 15.4.65). The production, along with *Candida* which Harrison directed, was taken on tour to Europe.

In October Harrison explained his policy in an interview with J.C.Trewin in the *Birmingham Post*. Because of television, he argued, actors could only be tempted into the theatre for short periods 'But we *need* the best actors'. The days when provincial theatres were simply perceived as training grounds should be over: 'There must be greater dignity than this. So one's company tends to be composed of a group of young people—more or less permanent—at a fairly probationary stage and of other players who come and go' (2.10.65). The statement sounded confident enough, but in a pattern that will repeat itself several times in the course of this history, the artistic director had to carry the can for the problems which the theatre was experiencing. Burman's departure made tensions between Harrison and Humphrey Stanbury, now General Manager, more acute. Harrison's relationship with the Board was undermined as Stanbury attempted to groom Buxton for the job of Artistic Director. 'My head', wrote Buxton, 'was under water a lot of the time. I couldn't see beyond the next rehearsal, let alone the next programme of plays'.

Trying to Change

In general 1965 saw a vigorous attempt to upgrade the Rep's image. A smart, new magazine programme, *Proscenium*, was introduced and edited by Stanbury and Brian Spiby. There were now cast photographs and biographies, introductions to the plays, editorials on a wide range of subjects from the role of the Arts Council to the joys of school audiences. Graham Winteringham, the designated architect of the new theatre began a series of articles outlining his vision for the building which was about to begin.

Despite the fact that the Rep staff had made it clear that the exhausting experience of staging plays in repertoire could not possibly be endured again, Harrison repeated the experiment with a six-week Comedy of Manners season which began in May. Harrison directed Vanbrugh's *The Provoked Wife* and Wilde's *An Ideal Husband,* while Buxton tackled Coward's *Design For Living*. John Turner, an Old Vic player and well-known from television who played Leontes in Braham Murray's production of *The Winter's Tale* early in the year, now pulled off the acclaimed triple feat of playing Sir John Brute, Viscount Goring and Leo in the Coward. Lloyd Evans praised both him and Linda Gardner who was cast as Mademoiselle in the Vanbrugh and Mabel Chiltern in the Wilde: 'The theatre has in these two…players to whom comedy of manners seem brilliantly natural—they do not mistake posture for gesture or eccentric elocution for necessary affectation of speech (*G*, 27.5.65).

Audiences responded well to the classic strategies of the spring and summer and overall percentages improved although it must have been galling to be accused of conservatism by some critics. Barry Jackson's translation of Molière *The Doctor's Delight* was well reviewed and there was another University revue *Slap in the Middle* which targeted Birmingham itself. One of the jokes consisted of a Council proposal to organise a tour of Birmingham's night-life one lunch hour.

In between came a production which seemed to strike the right balance between artistic innovation and audience interest. Alan Vaughan Watkins directed *The Representative*, Rolf Hochhuth's dramatic indictment of Pope Pius XII''s failure to condemn the holocaust. Inevitably the subject matter was controversial and that brought in audiences. Another attraction was the casting of the comic actor Lance Percival as S.S. Colonel Gerstein whose Christian conscience leads to a doomed attempt to oppose Hitler. Brian Tully gave a coldly-precise performance as Pius, while another new young actor, Henry Knowles, played a Jesuit idealist.

The overall production values also provoked discussion. Dacre Punt, who took over from Diana Dewes as resident designer, projected huge blown up photographs of Hitler juxtaposed with images of Jews being led away to extermination camps. The images formed the background to the stark simplicity of the set which used thirty-three rolls of ex-War Department barbed wire. Between each episode, two spotlit figures told the audience the facts about the Holocaust. The front curtains remained up while stage hands changed the set in full view of the audience and all the actors apart from the Pope, walked off-stage carrying their hand props. Exposure to the mechanics of theatre was too much for at least one audience member who wrote to the press to complain. But controversy about the play itself created thoughtful debate.

Resignation

Harrison's time was rapidly running out. He asked the Board for a five year contract which would enable him to lead the company into the new theatre which he'd helped design. The Board, now with increased Council presence because of the projected new building, refused. Harrison resigned. There are different versions of what precisely went wrong. Humphrey Stanbury could use indifferent audience figures against him. In November a damaging letter was published in the *Birmingham Post* (22.11.65) claiming that the Rep had lost its pioneering spirit and that production and acting standards and play choice was barely adequate. The critical response to Harrison's work at this time, however, was actually rather good. His resignation was made public on 21 January 1966 while the Christmas production of *Treasure Island* was still running. Through his review column in the *Post* (5.2.66), Trewin expressed his alarm. But a writer in the university paper *Redbrick*, claiming to base his opinion on experience of fourteen out of seventeen productions in the previous year and half, damned Harrison as 'neither a good manager, nor a good artistic director' (9.2.66). Certainly the young appeared to have abandoned the Rep.

The final season brought in Renée Asherson as a guest player for *Twelfth Night*, Osborne's *Inadmissable Evidence* and Coward's *Private Lives*. Harrison's very last production was of Shaw's *Simpleton of the Unexpected Isles* which Jackson had first staged in 1935, and which now cast Benjamin Whitrow as the

Reverend Phosphor Hammingtap. In March, however, there was one last defiantly brilliant production by the outgoing director. The plays of Shakespeare's turbulent contemporary Christopher Marlowe had never been staged at the Rep. Harrison's production of *Edward II* compounded the challenge of an overtly homosexual king with the Brechtian techniques of alienation. The curtain was up when the audience came in. The set, designed by Finlay James was little more than a round platform with a huge symbolic crown suspended over it. The seventeen actors in basic, black costumes sat in a circle, moved onto the platform to perform their roles and then returned to watch from their seats. Some doubled and trebled parts, putting on richly-coloured costumes in full view of the audience. Henry Knowles played Edward moving from a forceful impression of Edward's obsessional sexuality trembling with rage and anxiety to mental collapse in the final scene. Gary Watson played the king's minion Gaveston as a blond sensualist. When on stage, the actors stood or sat side by side and openly embraced and kissed. Gabrielle Drake played Queen Isabella with Patrick Mower as her lover, Young Mortimer.

The theatre which Barry Jackson founded was not easy to run. In later years Sir Robert Aitken apologised to Harrison for what had happened. Ronald Eyre was offered the job but turned it down. Before his departure, Harrison discussed the problems awaiting his successor in an article published in the *Evening Mail and Despatch* on 22 June:

> **Will he–or anyone–dispel the determinedly**
> **unfashionable aura which hangs–has hung for**
> **the 20 years I remember it–over this attractive**
> **little theatre…There are many backwoodsmen**
> **to be encountered. He will need a strong heart**
> **and a ruthless hand with the axe.**

4. Breaking with the Past: Peter Dews

Peter Dews

The man who followed on was very tough and more than a little ruthless. For all his modernising efforts Harrison had been keen to honour the traditions of the past. Thirty years after Peter Dews' appointment as Artistic Director there were still Rep stalwarts who resented his defiant refusal to worship at Sir Barry's shrine. In December 1967, after a year in the job, Dews outlined the problems in an article published in *Plays and Players*:

> **Becoming Director of Birmingham Rep is rather**
> **like taking over Westminster Abbey...on the roof**
> **there are actually two great Olympic flame bowls.**
> **Whether they ever flamed, or await Promethean**
> **fire from some quarter or other I don't know.**
> **But they seem to symbolise all that was right and is**
> **now wrong with the Rep. For the loftiness that**
> **builds neo-Greek temples can turn to snootiness.**
> **The desire to give people only what is best for them**
> **characterises not only the Knight but also the Nanny.**

Born in Wakefield and with a degree in Modern History from Oxford, Dews' early acting and directorial experience had been with the Bradford Civic Playhouse —a background he shared with Bernard Hepton and Arthur Pentelow. He loved the theatre and for all his axeman's stance, he loved Birmingham Rep. His first sight of the Rep company in action had been Douglas Seale's production of *Henry VI Part Three* when it was staged at the Old Vic in 1952. This defining moment, he later claimed, transformed a vague ambition to be an actor into a determination to direct a company of his own ' Within the space of the next seven years I saw 67 of the Rep's productions, so I reckon I must be the only Director this Company has had who was promoted from the ranks of the audience'.[1]

Dews was also the first Rep director whose professional artistic experience had been largely shaped by radio and television. In 1954 after a period as a school master in Barnsley, he came to Birmingham to work with BBC Midland Region on some 130 radio productions. He moved gradually into television and after directing a televised *Henry V* left Birmingham to mount *The Age of Kings*, the whole cycle of Shakespeare's history plays which was broadcast on BBC Television in 1960 and won the Screen Writers' Guild Award. This ground-breaking project used several former Rep actors as well as a design based very substantially on that created by Finlay James for Seale's *Henry VI* Trilogy. *The Spread of the Eagle*, an equally ambitious cycle of Shakespeare's Roman plays, was shown in 1963 but was less successful. In 1964 after going free-lance, he formed his own theatre company which he took to the Ravinia Festival in Chicago with productions of *Twelfth Night, Hamlet* and *Richard II*.

His media background made him both more relaxed about the artistic influence of television and realistic about its power. On actor training, for example, he refused to accept that television experience was an inferior substitute for the traditional routes of drama school and regional rep 'Good acting is good acting the world over, whatever the medium'. The fact that television had made the domestic environment a place where well-presented, well-acted, good drama could be seen on a regular basis cheaply, and in comfort, was something which theatre directors now had to recognise. Moreover while most actors found live theatre more satisfying artistically, financially they were better off in television 'There is a lot of talk these days about subsidies, but the people who really subsidise theatres are the actors' (*EM*, 19.7.66). He might also have said the same about directors.

When appointed (the other candidates included Toby Robertson and Frank Dunlop as well as a young director called Clive Perry), Dews' brief from Richard Hoggart was to 'get the old hulk off the sandbank'. It was vital to rejuvenate the Rep and its audience. Strong-minded, vigorous, a self-confessed professional Yorkshireman and, on occasion, bully, he controlled and led the company through an increasingly complex pattern of work which laid the foundation for the transfer into the new theatre. John Harrison had been heavily engaged in the plans and design process for the new building. As the detailed discussion in the next chapter will show, the whole of Dews' directorate in the old building was undertaken against a background of constant political manoeuvring to get the new theatre built as promised. Putting the Rep back on the theatrical map was no easy task given the local environment and the legacy of the past. Dews' artistic acumen combined with a shrewd, popularising instinct, would make a sturdy fist of maintaining the Rep's status, and along the way earn him considerable personal kudos. In 1970, during the run of the British première of *The Sorrows of Frederick*, an ebullient historical romance about Frederick the Great by the American dramatist Romulus Linney, Dews was unrepentant about what some saw as vulgarian theatricality 'I am not your great bright penetrating intellectual. I am a getter-on and getter-off in good order. I have a grammar school-masterly approach. I want them to understand what they're saying, not stand round looking pretty and moo-ing' (G, 13.2.70)

Dews was being somewhat disingenuous about his intellectual credentials, but his was an approach which yet again made the Rep the nursery of future stars. Brian Cox was in the first company in 1966. Michael Gambon, sent to learn his craft at Birmingham Rep by Laurence Olivier, arrived in 1967. Cox played Iago to Gambon's Othello the following year. The director, however, also liked to act. While by no means an actor-manager in the tradition of John Neville in Nottingham, Dews regularly cast himself in plays and functioned as the company understudy. During the run of his first Christmas show *1066 and All That* he took on some thirteen roles because of various cast illnesses.

Change

Dews' two-year contract carried with it the assumption that work on the new building was about to start. By the time Dews settled into Jackson's former office in July 1966 it was obvious that a long wait lay ahead. Despite the uncertainty, however, change was in the air. As time went on fresh artistic, technical and managerial expertise was introduced in the shape of new permanent staff, several of whom would eventually go on to work in the new theatre. David Buxton, however, stayed only long enough to see the new regime well-settled before departing for a new career as a free-lance director. Dews at that time had wanted a Production Manager; not an Associate Director.

Other important newcomers were in place before Harrison left. The arrival of June Callear revitalised a problematic wardrobe department. The theatre had never really recovered from the wartime bombing which destroyed the priceless costume store in 1941. The low salaries paid by the theatre made it hard to find costume makers of sufficiently high calibre and there had been a tendency to hire more than make which was both economically and artistically wasteful. In Bernard Hepton's time, the cutting-out table had doubled as a table-tennis table for company relaxation. Callear's interest in theatre had been stimulated by childhood trips to the Rep but in the absence of specific theatre costume course she went to the Handsworth School of Dress Design where she was trained in cutting and making to couturier standard. Further experience as a costume maker for Emile Littler which enhanced her skills in tailoring and period design proved invaluable. As her department developed she was joined by Margaret Gillham and then by other young costumiers, in particular Sue Nightingale known to everyone as Tottie.

They worked in the very top of the building in what had once been Sir Barry's flat. Clambering up the stairs meant passing the dressing rooms so there was immediate contact with the actors and their costumes. The tiny kitchen with a fitfully-functional gas ring which was attached to the two wardrobe rooms was also used for laundering costumes. There are vivid memories of sitting drinking tea surrounded by dripping tights. By late 1967 the store of costumes had grown large enough to open a hire department initially located under the carpenter's shop and managed by Beth Gamble.

Alex Hamilton came as the first fully-trained Head of Properties in April 1966 after four years at a prop-making studio in St Albans. Up until then there had been a steady turn-over of property masters and the responsibility for prop-finding and making had been shared with the stage management team. Hamilton, aged 20 and spikily assertive about his hard-won craft-skills was scathing about make-shift methods. The basement where he worked was cluttered with piles of carpenters' litter and accumulated dumped properties, all of which had to be sorted out. But he, like so many others is emphatic about the extraordinary vitality within the building and the energy of the staff as they set about fulfilling Dews' artistic strategy. Not only was the true repertory policy continued but by mid-October 1966 there were four plays on offer each week. Everyone helped in the changeover between plays especially for the Wednesday and Saturday matinées when the transformation had to be achieved in an hour. In the summer of 1967 company members spent all-night sessions repainting the auditorium in various shades of brown. The collective spirit was still strong.

First Moves

Dews assembled the largest company since 1961 for an autumn season which consisted of Brecht's *The Life of Galileo*, Ronald Eyre's *A Crack in the Ice*—the stage première of Eyre's own television adaptation of a Russian story by Nikolai Lescov—David Halliwell's *Little Malcolm and His Struggle with the Eunuchs*, Albee's *Who's Afraid of Virginia Woolf* and the Feydeau farce, *The Birdwatcher*. Nothing except Eyre's play was new but there was an air of robust modernity. Dews explained 'you can't know about audience reaction, so the thing to do was to follow what was closest to your heart' (*WES*, 10.8.66)

Little Malcolm featuring disaffected art student and tin-pot Caesar Malcolm Scrawdyke who forms his three-man 'party of dynamic insurrection' to revenge himself on his art school principle, was put in to attract the young and did rather better than expected. *Virginia Woolf*, Buxton's valedictory production, which brought a recent, controversial London success to Birmingham also did well. At the start of the season, audiences would have noticed another significant, symbolic absence. The old family dinner-gong sounded before each performance was abandoned. But Dews also made a graceful gesture to the past in casting Edward Chapman as Galileo. After the first performance Chapman stepped forward to reminisce with the audience about the Rep in the 1920s when he was in a company which included Ralph Richardson and Peggy Ashcroft. The old favourite, *1066 and All That*, which played for a straight ten-week run over the Christmas period, was every bit as popular as it had been at its première in 1934.

In general, the emphasis was on youth in the thirty-strong company. Some actors like Henry Knowles, Benjamin Whitrow, Frank Moorey and Eric Woofe were retained from Harrison's company. Whitrow co-directed *Little Malcolm* with Dews, and played Brecht's Cardinal Barberini, and the elderly effeminant Lt. Kirov in *A Crack*. Knowles played Malcolm—sustaining a broken nose during a performance. Two of the newcomers attracted particular attention. Colin Farrell, RADA-trained and with experience at the Royal Court, which included Wesker's *Chips With Everything* and the musical *Half a Sixpence*, not only acted but played the guitar in *Galileo*. Dundee-born Brian Cox was twenty one and had been in the Edinburgh Royal Lyceum production of *Galileo* which Dews had directed with Tom Fleming in the title role. When Cox played Private Postnikov, the hapless young soldier who leaves his sentry post to rescue a drowning drunk who has fallen through the ice in Eyre's play, J. Trewin, praising the actor, quipped that he was the only Scottish sentry in nineteenth-century St. Petersburg. Gareth Lloyd Evans liked the production, Cox and the directorial style: ' suddenly discipline has entered the company and a relaxation which suggests an ease of companionship and an understanding of what repertory theatre is for' (G, 15.9.66)

It was a hectic time. In November when *The Birdwatcher* came into the repertoire, the Albee and the Feydeau alternated while the *Little Malcolm* company toured to other venues in the Midlands. Performances were given at Keele and Loughborough universities and at the Theatre-on-the Steps in Bridgnorth. The following March, *The Birdwatcher*, which played to only thin audiences in Birmingham, was staged at the Nuffield Theatre at Southampton University. There was also an experiment with Sunday night theatre. Directed by Whitrow, Brian Cox played Robert Burns for a single performance of Tom Wright's *There Was A Man*…on 29 January. Because of the prevailing Sunday Observance laws, it was illegal to stage a public performance of a play to a paying audience. And so the large audience were effectively 'invited' to the Rep for free. Unpaid actors turned usherettes and coffee sellers for an evening which despite another production of the play on television, was a great success. Clearly all this extra activity was aimed at spreading the Rep's local and regional profile. What happened next probably exceeded even Dews' wildest dreams.

With Shakespeare to Carnaby Street

Rather unexpectedly he had not launched immediately into Shakespeare but waited until the following March to present *Richard II* in tandem with *As You Like It*. The comedy was meant to be an enjoyable romp for the actors to offset the serious business of the history play. In the event, although *Richard II* was clearly familiar territory for Dews, the reviews were mixed—especially of Henry Knowles as the deposed king. Trevor Pitt's multi-levelled set cramped the actors and Lloyd Evans remarked rudely that the back-cloth meant to evoke pestilential decay made it look as though the production was taking place under water. Brian Cox, however, was singled out as a thoughtful, withdrawn Bolinbroke. Two actors made their professional debut in an assortment of parts. Oliver Ford-Davies (acting at that time as Oliver Ford), an ex-Edinburgh academic made a strong impression as John of Gaunt. Timothy Dalton played the young Hotspur.

There was an important spatial innovation designed as the programme noted, to heighten the play's impact by narrowing the gap between actor and audience. For both productions the front row of audience seats was removed to permit an apron stage to be built out over the pit area very like the one used in the earliest years of the theatre. The programme note for *As You Like It* reminded the audience of the Rep's pioneering productions of modern-dress Shakespeare in the 1920s. This was the theatre which 'gave the world a *Macbeth* in kilts and a Parolles in co-respondent shoes'. Now Dews, with his designer Pamela Howard, gave the world a Carnaby Street *As You Like It*.

Part of the visual inspiration came from the Polish Folk Theatre which accounted for the peasant capes and jerkins worn in the Forest of Arden and the lace and ribbons for the wedding clothes. But the overall high-coloured eccentricity of the costuming: the jokey military uniforms, the embroidered waistcoats and the orange corduroy trouser suit worn by the disguised Rosalind were completely in tune with the late sixties. *Sergeant Pepper's Lonely Hearts Club Band* brought to life on the stage and in Shakespeare.

Audiences and critics alike loved the vocal and visual wit, the stylised nursery-naïve set with its cut-out trees, flowers and sheep—there was lots of off-stage baaing in the forest. Not only did the production play at the Rep for eight weeks, but there was a West Country tour before the impresario Peter Saunders brought it to the Vaudeville Theatre in London for a ten week season. Brian Cox as a distinctly virile Orlando looked like a hero worker in boots and a John Lennon-style cap. Timothy Dalton played his wicked brother Oliver in vivid hunting pink and extravagant lace ruffles. Oliver Ford-Davies played the good Duke Senior as a walrus-moustached headmasterly figure lecturing his freezing courtiers in the wintry forest. Colin Farrell, who also composed the music, turned Touchstone into a cheeky personal valet in a striped waistcoat and cuban-heeled boots. Paul Chapman as Jacques looked like a seedy undertaker. In all there were three

Rosalinds. Andree Melly played her in Birmingham until an emergency appendectomy caused the first cancellation of a performance since the Second World War. Jane Sandbrook, a student from the Birmingham School of Speech and Drama stepped in and then played the part on tour before Deborah Stanford took over in London.

And with the Pope to Broadway

As You Like It put the Rep back on the metropolitan map. No one, however, could have anticipated the international success of the world première production of Peter Luke's *Hadrian VII*. Admittedly the success took its time. The play had been rejected by several managements before Dews agreed to take it on in association with commercial producers Bill Freedman and Charles Kasher. When it was staged in May 1967 Birmingham audiences were largely indifferent to this quirky, oddly celebral piece. Based on a book by Frederick William Rolfe (Baron Corvo) the play is about an embittered would-be priest who, in the teeth of constant rejection, dreams of becoming Pope. Alec McCowan played Rolfe (Luke transposes the central protagonist's name) as a nicotine-addicted, waspish, witty and vindictive little man at odds with authority and the contradictions within himself. The play itself divided critical opinion. Lloyd Evans praised McCowan but condemned the supporting narrative as a 'past-board charade' (*G*, 11.5.67) with no dramatic logic. The major London critics like Irving Wardle and Eric Shorter who trecked to Birmingham were more intrigued.

Dews, with Tim Goodchild as his designer, capitalised on the visual possibilities of ecclesiastical ceremony. The first half was played in the gloom of Rolfe's dingy London lodgings. When the dream shifted to the papal election in Rome, two chanting processions of clergy moved down the steep aisles of the theatre to form a brilliant purple and vermillion semi-circle round Rolfe. The stage was stripped bare to the back wall except for two great ceremonial candlesticks. Years later June Callear still identified the *Hadrian* costumes as her most exciting project—filling her sewing room with huge swathes of fabric. In a largely male cast, Oliver Ford-Davies and Paul Chapman were singled out as the bailiffs who reappear as the Bishop of Caerlon and the Archbishop of Pimlico. Brian Cox played the Belfast bigot Jeremiah Sant who ultimately shoots the new Pope. Gabrielle Laye was Rolfe's interfering landlady while Peggy Aitchison was the simple housekeeper Agnes who brings the Pope some home-made pickle.

A year and a lot of negotiations later, the play transferred to the Mermaid Theatre in London in April 1968 with McCowan again in the title role and several of the original cast. With inevitable cast changes the London run lasted two and a half years. On 7 January 1969 it opened on Broadway where it won Dews a Tony award for Best Director and suddenly a whole new career opportunity.

A Triple Strategy

Broadway however, lay some distance in the future. Once the initial excitement of the new regime had worn off, the core problems were lying in wait as always. A year after *Hadrian VII*'s Rep première, and while it was packing audiences in at the Mermaid, Peter Dews told a sub-committee of the Parliamentary Estimates Committee that Birmingham audiences did not take kindly to new plays. (*BP*, 14.5.68). *Hadrian* which played in Station Street to audiences of some 43% of capacity, was programmed in as part of a clutch of challenging drama presented through the late spring and summer. Roger Milner's serio-comic Absurdist play *How's The World Treating You*, Eugene O'Neill's gruelling autobiographical tragedy *Long Day's Journey Into Night* and the introduction of the work of two very different dramatists. John McGrath's attack on British post-imperial military policy, *Events While Guarding the Bofors Gun* had been presented the previous year at the Hampstead Theatre Club, while Joe Orton's *Entertaining Mr Sloane* was first seen in London in 1964. Clearly for a company of hungry actors this was a rich diet. Michael Gambon's first role was in *Events*, and two actors who would settle down for a long stay in Birmingham, Jane Freeman and locally-born John Baddeley, manoeuvred expertly between black farce and tragedy in *Sloane* as Kath and Kemp.

The challenge was to make Birmingham audiences equally hungry for theatrical diversity. The policy of guest players continued. Bernard Hepton's wife Nancie Jackson, returned to play the morphine-addicted Mary Tyrone in *Long Day's Journey* and Nicky Henson came to play Mr Sloane. A local critic W.H. Wagstaff was amused by the response to Joe Orton directed by Maurice Stewart in July 'As for the *double entendres* it is no small achievement in Mr Orton to produce from the sophisticated audience of the Repertory theatre the sniggers that any competent blue-nose comedian can extract in the less exalted atmosphere of the music-hall or the working man's club on ladies' night' (*BP*, 21.6.67). But did this audience have such a clearly-identifiable character? It was certainly not young but it did like an enjoyable night out. As Dews ruefully acknowledged in his *Plays and Players*' article, *1066 and All That*, which played for a 101 performances at capacity, could have carried on running for ever.

With the Board's support a triple strategy was launched. True repertory programming was retained, but now generally based on a more manageable two plays a week instead of three or four. Dews continued the policy of presenting classic plays and recent London successes, but the more radical work aimed at young adults was now to be shown in late night performances once or twice a month. The other new departure, a Saturday morning young people's theatre club, Theatre '67, had been established in the summer of 1967. The management already offered 'Teach Ins' on individual productions, backstage tours and talks in local schools. This venture was more ambitious. With the incentive of a modest

Arts Council grant aimed at cultivating new, young audiences, the club was the brain child of the assistant manager Michael Starke. The first meeting attracted thirty young people who were immediately formed into one large committee. Before the year was out, the membership numbered nearly one thousand for a programme of Saturday morning talks and workshops. By Christmas, an enthusiastic group was even helping to redecorate the theatre.

So from mid-1967 through to the end of 1968 the backbone audience was offered what was a relatively safe diet. There were three productions of Shakespeare. A good dollop of Shaw in *The Doctor's Dilemma* and *St Joan* was served up with Coward's *Blithe Spirit* and *The Circle*, a play by Somerset Maugham first staged in 1921. Anna Calder-Marshall was cast as a very young Jennifer Dubedat before tackling St Joan a few months later. Dews indulged himself with the plum roles of Shaw's medical buffoon Bloomfield Bonington and Lord Porteous, a crusty, but sentimental old buffer in *The Circle*. J. B Priestley's dramatisation of Iris Murdoch's novel *A Severed Head* offered some 1960s' ethical subversion albeit via a very familiar playwright. Michael Gambon moved from one of Shaw's inept doctors, Sir Patrick Cullen, to Murdoch's sexually free-wheeling psychiatrist Palmer Anderson. Alison Key played his samurai sword-wielding half-sister Dr Honor Klein. In November 1967 Dews directed an ambitious production of Ibsen's rarely-staged *Peer Gynt* with designs by Pamela Howard. Brian Cox played Peer and Calder-Marshall Solveig with a company of actors which had gradually built up to full strength during the autumn. Dews had learnt to his cost that launching a season with a large ensemble created an embarrassing number of under-employed actors. He was equally cautious about brand new plays waiting until August 1968 to première Leslie Sands' *Investigation* which was a *Z Cars*-style detective saga set in a Northern police station. Dews himself played Det. Supt. Wade.

The late-night strategy was a spectacular success especially with students. Between November 1967 and February 1968 single performances of plays by Jean Genet, Olwen Wymark, Fernando Arrabal and Beckett were given to young, enthusiastic audiences. Genet's *Deathwatch* was a British professional première as was Arrabal's *Fando and Lis*. For Beckett's *Endgame* long queues formed outside the theatre and many were turned away. Beckett, of course, was ideal for late-night, small-scale performance. A year later Jane Freeman had the opportunity to play Winnie in *Happy Days* which was subsequently taken to the Theatre-on-the-Steps in Bridgnorth. It was a time of experiment for everyone concerned. In March 1968, the programme for *Anticlockwise,* a new play commissioned from company actor Jeremy Mason, claimed that its homosexual content would not have survived the scrutiny of the Lord Chamberlain a mere two years earlier. By the end of September, however, the Lord Chamberlain no longer mattered. In London on 27 September, two days after the 1968 Theatres Act which abolished direct censorship came into force, rows of cheerfully-naked actors were displayed in the rock musical *Hair*. After decades of improbably constrained stage dialogue, the language of common experience could be heard at last. At the Rep what was coyly termed a banned 'b' word previously deemed unacceptable on a public stage was reinstated in the script of *Investigation* for the final performances. Peter Shaffer's *White Liars* and *Black Comedy* could be spoken exactly as the author intended.

Unlike the Birmingham Arts Lab, which was also launched in September 1968, the Rep could never fully engage with the counter-culture which began to flourish on the margins of mainstream theatre in the late 1960s. But as the late-night experiments continued through to 1971 the directorate was putting in place the policy which would ultimately inform the programming of the new theatre's studio space. Some plays like Strindberg's *Miss Julie* and Genet's *The Maids* still carried with them the faint echoes of the Lord Chamberlain's disapproval. When, in November 1969, a compilation of verbal experiments was staged by Philip Draycott under the title *Words,Words/Come and Go*, it included *Tests*, sketches written by Paul Ableman which were used by Peter Brook in his notorious 'Theatre of Cruelty' season. That night the audience also saw the first professional production of Beckett's *Come and Go*. Draycott who was appointed assistant director in 1969, after leaving Cambridge, and given responsibility for the late night programme, also directed Frank Marcus's *The Window* consciously trying to introduce the kind of new, short plays unlikely to be seen elsewhere in the region. During the final season in Station Street there were productions of Howard Brenton's radically-violent *Heads* and *The Education of Skinny Spew* and Stoppard's *After Magritte*. All of this demanding activity was made possible by the enlargement of the theatre's artistic and managerial staff.

Broadening the Base

Humphrey Stanbury resigned in April 1968 after what was termed 'a disagreement with the Board'. When John Greenwood, who had acted at the Rep in the early 1950s, started work in the summer he found few formal business records. The Artistic Director carried the greatest weight of production administration and there was no sustained marketing policy. On a very basic level there was even a dire shortage of telephones in the building. This was remedied and David Isaacs, the drama critic of the *Birmingham Post* was installed as publicity manager. Later in the year Roger Popplestone, formerly General Manager of the Hampstead Theatre Club, was appointed as the new House Manager. Dews and Greenwood knew each other well. Greenwood had fight-directed on *The Age of Kings* and acted as the Company Manager for Dews' Chicago venture. They now worked together costing proposed seasons, casting from outside the semi-resident acting company and engaging guest directors and designers.

Dews had effectively held a gun to the Board's collective head in May 1968. He was exhausted. The continuing delays over the new building and frustration over the generalised managerial and technical difficulties were exacerbated by the outdated resources of the theatre which could no longer cope with the increasingly sophisticated demands of new design and lighting practice. Despite some respite offered by guest directors, Dews declared himself fed up with bearing the burden of directing eight productions a year, often working a thirteen-hour day. 'I directed *Othello* in my sleep', he complained (*SM*, 26.4.68) He would now only agree to a further one-year contract and moves were made towards finding an Associate Director. As Dews revealed under rather different circumstances some years later, he also extracted an agreement from Robert Aitken to have more freedom to work outside Birmingham in return for a considerable reduction in his basic salary.

A succession of young men, funded by externally-promoted director training schemes, provided the human resources for the artistic expansion. When the late night experiments were first launched Martin Kinch, who came to Birmingham on a Canadian government scheme, and Peter Jefferies, an ABC TV trainee, devoted part of their time to going into the student communities to publicise their productions and build the audiences through personal contact. Subsequently Gilles Provost also came from Canada while Israeli Oded Be'eri benefited from a scheme promoted by RADA. Strategies put in place by the independent television companies since 1958 was recognised as an important means of feeding back into the theatre some of commercial profits from television which of course depended on a steady supply of good actors and directors. Established in 1960, the ABC scheme, which offered trainee directors to prominent theatres such as the Belgrade or the Derby Playhouse for a twelve month period, had already produced Trevor Nunn and Ken Loach as well as Clive Perry. Dustin Hughes who directed the Brenton plays in October 1970 came as an ABC trainee and completed his work at the Rep directing Shaw on the big stage of the new theatre.

The new Associate Director, Michael Simpson, was in post by September 1968. As an Oxford graduate and a television director with nine years' experience with the BBC there were clear parallels with Dews. However a record of work on the hard-hitting realism of the *Z Cars* series and some of the celebrated 'Wednesday Plays' offered the possibility of a useful artistic counterbalance. Appropriately enough, Simpson's first production was a single performance of Charles Wood's play about racial prejudice in the army, *Prisoners and Escorts*, but immediately afterwards he was plunged into a great vat of Christmas cheer. This director was going to have to turn his hand to anything.

The festive Old Time Music Hall included 'Your very Own' Philip Garston-Jones, 'Titters and Glitters' Jane Freeman, and 'Holding his Own' Desmond McNamara. The Christmas play, John Dalby's adaptation of Thackray's *The Rose and the Ring* was designed by David Cockayne who could draw on the grotesque appeal of Tenniel's original illustrations. The characters of the kingdoms of Paflagonia and Crim Tartary wore a collection of grotesque noses: some like pointed icicles; others like bulbous tomatoes. Of the actors, David Kincaid played the cantankerous, usurping King Valoroso with Jane Freeman as his garrulous, gluttonous Queen. A locally-born and trained actor, Paul Henry, who had been part of the company throughout the year, scored a popular hit as Prince Bulbo singing his 'Collywobblues'.

A Shakespeare Bonanza

Christmas cheer was an economic necessity. Shakespeare brought in school parties. But Rep Shakespeare had always meant more than audience fodder and, pragmatism aside, it was appropriate that the final phase of the company's work in the old building should include no less than six plays. In February 1968 with productions of *Othello* and *Romeo and Juliet*, Dews repeated the strategy of presenting two plays in tandem. Anna Calder-Marshall played Juliet opposite Anthony Corlan as Romeo. Although they played in Elizabethan costume, Dews was determined to reject romantic lyricism in favour of an emphasis on youth and physicality. The production's rough-edged quality was both deliberate and accidental. Suffering from a mixture of throat-infection and nerves, Corlan virtually lost his voice on the first night while Calder-Marshall, passionate and attractively gawky, disconcerted critics with an oddly-clipped enunciation of the verse. Brian Cox was an energetically-butch and distinctly un-poetic Mercutio. The basic set designed by Gordon Melhuish challenged the limitations of the stage. Three sixteen-foot, birdcage-like towers shifted in flexible arrangements for each location, proved a nightmare to winch along the stage despite a temporary level floor intended to combat the permanent rake.

Othello was given a low-key Crimean-war setting. Desdemona (Alison Key) was murdered on a brass bedstead which upset some of the critics, while Cox played Iago as a podgy, unkempt NCO in a frogged jacket and pillbox cap. Laurence Olivier's virtuoso negroid impersonation, first seen in 1963, cast a long shadow and the Rep troupe were incredulous when Gambon received a telegram from Olivier on the first night. Lloyd Evans decided that the young actor relied too much on Olivier's intonations but noted, as did other reviews, a powerful, individual stage presence. It was indicative, however, of a shifting cultural climate that Dews felt obliged to justify a white actor blacking up for the role. This, Dews claimed in the programme, was written by Shakespeare as 'a white man's burden'. The following autumn, however, for *The Merchant of Venice*, he invited the Pakistani actor, Zia Moyheddin to play Shylock adding a disturbing contemporary relevance to Shakespeare's exploration of racism and cultural alienation. Icily-controlled, this Shylock was the only plainly-dressed character amongst the satin and brocades worn in Melhuish's eighteenth-century Venetian design.

When Barry Jackson and H.K. Ayliff came up with the idea of modern-dress Shakespeare the 1925 'plus-fours' *Hamlet* was arguably the most influential production of its time. Dews' invitation to the American television hearthrob, Richard Chamberlain, to play Hamlet in early 1969 was probably his most outrageous artistic gamble. The Station Street box office positively exploded with audience excitement. Obviously it was an astute commercial move, but it also said a lot about the Rep's continuing status that Chamberlain was both flattered and prepared to take a considerable personal risk. Dews started to prepare the actor while in New York basking in the success of *Hadrian VII*. So nervous was the star that individual rehearsals continued back in England at Dews' Whitstable home, and even in a locked and otherwise empty Rep on Sunday afternoons. As Chamberlain was only too willing to concede, this Hamlet was very much the director's creation. The play was given an early twentieth-century setting analogous to a collapsing, decadent pre-revolutionary Russia. Finlay James devised a filigree bronze Art Nouveau set with a central platform and stairs which gleamed dull gold in the light. Chamberlain's romantic good looks were emphasised by the elegant, close-fitting costumes. In one white and gold-frogged uniform he looked like a hero from an Ivor Novello musical. An unusually large number of national critics came to Birmingham for the opening night on 12 March and, on the whole, to report back sympathetically. There was a strong supporting cast. Gemma Jones as Ophelia, palely exquisite in a white dress ornamented by a single rose, was praised for her carefully-developed portrait of psychological and sexual repression. David King's Claudius looked like a drunken-gangster version of Edward VII, while Linda Polan played a faded worldly Gertrude.

The advance publicity for *Hamlet* benefited Simpson's companion production of Ben Jonson's *Volpone* which deployed most of the same actors. But punters who came to a much less familiar play in the hopes of seeing Chamberlain tackle another Renaissance role were to be disappointed. David King dominated the stage as a physically-bulky, strong-voiced Volpone with Keith Drinkel coolly intelligent as his parasite Mosca. *Hamlet* was revived in February 1970 but with Alec McCowan, back from Broadway, in the title role and Anna Massey as Ophelia. Inevitably McCowan's reading was totally different. Chamberlain was the dashing, handsome prince faced, as if for the first time, with a difficult moral problem. McCowan's Hamlet was intellectually rigorous and emotionally chilly. The critic John Peters, writing in the *Sunday Times* decided the production was more than a revival 'the action is sharper, crisper, and the play moves from mood to mood with a sense of controlled rhythm and tense unobtrusive style: the hallmarks of a master director' (15.2.70).

Two Directors

The master director was flying very high indeed—so high Dews was pretty much out of sight of Birmingham for a lot of the time. Simpson, taking on the lion's share of the directorial load for the final phase in Station Street, had to display the time-honoured repertory theatre versatility. He directed the last two Shakespeares: *Henry IV Part One* and *A Midsummer Night's Dream*. He directed *The Government Inspector*, *Waiting for Godot*, *The Italian Straw Hat* (in his own translation). He directed *Saved*, arguably the most controversial play of the late sixties, using designer Robert MacQueen's projected grainy black and white images of slum-nurtured despair and violence. The two plays which followed on from his production of Chekhov's *Three Sisters* in March 1970, *Pygmalion* and Noel Coward's *Tonight at 8.30*, were taken in August, with a tour-only production of *The Caretaker*, for a five-week season at the Ravinia Festival in Chicago.

Dews, meantime, was enjoying making money. Some of it was for himself along with the growing prestige. But a lot of it also benefited the theatre. The royalities from *Hadrian* paid for new equipment like washing machines and airing cupboards for wardrobe. A new bar had been installed which further increased theatre revenue. A building opposite the theatre had been bought to operate as a wardrobe store. As a guest director at the Chichester Festival Theatre in the summer of 1969 Dews directed John Clements and Margaret Leighton in a production of *Antony and Cleopatra*. In 1970 his Chichester première of Robert Bolt's *Vivat, Vivat, Regina!* with Eileen Atkins and Vanessa Redgrave quickly transferred to London. Clearly Dews was excited by the prospect of entrepreneurial success, but how far external critical acclaim, London transfers and even big-name actors influenced the local core audience is debatable. At the Rep, following on from Alec McCowan's Hamlet, John Wood, another guest, gave a prodigious performance as Frederick the Great in *The Sorrows of Frederick* leading his troops into battle on a huge wooden horse. The production did not achieve the success of the *Hadrian* phenomenon, but Lloyd Evans commented on Dews' 'talent for dignifying the trivial with superb theatrical know-how' (G, 12.3.70).

David Turner's satirical musical *Quick, Quick, Slow*, which Dews premièred at the Rep in August 1969, might have been dismissed as trivial but for the fact that it was the first substantive attempt to present a new work which not only derived from, but was also set in, Birmingham. Jackson's preference for what he termed 'great masterpieces', his dislike of social realism and 'microscopic themes—peering into the back parlours of Manchester' as he once put it[2], had meant there had never been an active policy to cultivate local writers. With music and lyrics by Monty Norman and Julian More, Turner's book targeted the world of competitive ballroom dancing. His programme note made it clear that he was protesting against the ever-increasing emphasis on commercial progress to the detriment of older, more creative traditional values. Turner described his Birmingham childhood and the disappearance of much of the city he had known in the past. 'Emotional remnants' still remained, he claimed, along with the 'competitive energy of the old

Brummie' in the kind of activity which *Quick, Quick, Slow* explored.

There were some fears that it might be construed as patronising to Birmingham and there was certainly no rush to transfer it to London as was hoped. John Baddeley 'with hideous Brummagem vowels' (*DT*, 21.8.69), played Arthur Bradshaw who owns a chain of hairdressing salons and attempts to buy success for his none-too-bright daughter Linda by subsidising an inarticulate, but ballroom-nimble, factory worker as her dancing partner. Jane Freeman played his wife with Tina Martin as his daughter and Jeffrey Shankley as Norman the working-class 'waltz wizard' with whom she inconveniently falls in love. Despite songs which were jokey rather than tuneful, the production was both swift and effective with striking numbers like the first 'A Tiny Silver Pot' set in a dance-hall toilet and a sequence in a dance school where stuffed dummies were used as partners. There was also some mild controversy over the more sexually explicit 'Gang Bang'. In the event the Rep did not assist at the birth of a great musical.

Looking Forward and Looking Back

While the company looked forward to the new theatre and trainee director Dustin Hughes compiled his programme of late-night macabre and surrealist drama, audiences could still indulge in nostalgia. Even the relatively new play Alan Bennett's *Forty Years On*, a school-play story of twentieth century England through two world wars, was an appropriate choice to launch the final season in August 1970. The Rep auditorium became the school hall draped in union jacks. Brian Oulton and Peggy Thorpe-Bates returned to the theatre where they had worked as a young married couple in the 1940s to play the retiring headmaster and the school matron. David Glover played Franklin, the author of the school play and the headmaster's successor who intends to sweep away outmoded ideas and attitudes. It had been hoped that Alan Bennett himself would come to Birmingham to play Tempest, the junior housemaster. But Bennett withdrew and Paul Chapman got the opportunity of the multi-role playing star turn.

But there were also reminders of past glories. *The Barretts of Wimpole Street*, Rudolf Besier's play about the courtship of Robert Browning and Elizabeth Barrett which Jackson premièred at the Malvern Festival in 1931 was directed by Philip Dudley. Elizabeth Bell and David Glover took on the lovers first played by Scott Sunderland and Gwen Frangçon-Davies. Ronald Adams played Edward Moulton Barrett, the role which Cedric Hardwicke had so memorably created. Simpson and Dews joined forces for a final *1066 and All That* at Christmas when the whole company could let their hair down. There was one more production. Dews directed what was designated a 'Studio production' of John Bowen's *Fall and Redemption of Man*, a modernisation of selected medieval mystery plays. But the final impression was of *1066 and All That*.

The theatre closed with a gala performance on Saturday 3 April. Many past luminaries were there including Felix Aylmer who spoke the very first lines as Orsino on the stage; his wife Cicely Byrne who was Jackson's niece, and Brenda Bruce and Alfred Burke. Before the fun began actors took part in a verse and prose compilation called *The Mighty Line* which Dews had devised. The bust of Sir Barry Jackson was spotlit on the stage. Elizabeth Spriggs who played Cleopatra in the last production he saw, spoke the Egyptian queen's dying words. She said afterwards (*BP*, 5.4.70)

> **I feel tremendously sad, but for the right reasons.**
> **I don't think the Rep is dying. I think it will go**
> **on and be better than it has ever been.**

1 Peter Dews in Roger Southern (ed), *The Birmingham Repertory Theatre 1913-1971* (Birmingham Repertory Theatre, 1971) p. 11

2 Barry Jackson, ' Literature and the Drama' (unpublished paper, 1920)

5. The New Building

A Dead Centre and Old Dreams

The joke in *Slap in the Middle* about the lunch-hour tour of Birmingham's nightlife was in reality no laughing matter. The centre was dead at night and despite the Rep's international status and the city's strong music-making tradition, post-war Birmingham seemed like a cultural desert. Most of the grander arts-oriented amenities were concentrated round or near Joseph Hansom's Town Hall which had served as the focus for Birmingham's music since the 1830s. All later nineteenth-century building in the vicinity: the Council House, the Art Gallery, the Central Library and the Midland Institute had to take account of its sheer scale. After the First World War, city planners dreamed of extending what came to be thought of as the civic centre right up Broad Street with yet more grandiose buildings.

Despite money spent on acquiring the land, the economic pressures of the 1920s and 30s meant that the dream had to be modified. In 1925 the Hall of Memory (designed by the Old Rep's architect S.N. Cooke) and its companion arcade were dedicated to the war dead but the monumental scale was reduced. A 1926 competition produced a Beaux Arts-style scheme which never got further than the award-winning design. In 1933 a team which included Cooke came up with yet another plan of neo-classical symmetry which was only partially implemented. By the outbreak of the Second World War, a Masonic Hall, the Municipal Bank and Baskerville House were built in splendid isolation on either side of Broad Street. There were further plans for a huge skyscraper Council House but that was abandoned. Hopes for a new library and concert hall were also shelved.

What all this emphasis on civic pride seemed to ignore were the more basic needs of the citizenry. Apart from pubs there were few sources of reasonable food and drink at night. There was a vague dream that a so-called 'theatre land' could be created around John Bright Street where the Alexandra Theatre was sited which was close to Station Street. But with the Hippodrome on Hurst Street and not much chance of a replacement for the Theatre Royal which closed in 1956, a Birmingham equivalent of London's West End seemed highly unlikely. In the late fifties both the Alex and the Hippodrome were facing uncertain futures, while at the Rep the size of the building and the limited audience capacity were seen as more and more problematic. Double the number of seats, it was considered, would mean that revenue from popular productions would finance more experimental work. Jackson himself had suggested a possible 1,200. At a meeting held in February 1960 between Jackson and his co-directors with representatives of the City Council and the Arts Council, the financial security of the Rep was guaranteed. It was also confirmed that the old building would need to be demolished in order to make way for the development of the Inner Ring Road.

Changing the face of the city

The new road scheme which had been first mooted in 1917 and revived in plans drawn up in 1943, made an explosive start with demolition on Smallbrook Street in 1957. The first phase was opened in 1961 and the circle was finally completed in 1971, the year the new Rep building opened. The road scheme was part of a massive reconstruction of the city centre, made necessary to be sure after the depredations of war—but it also meant that the old redbrick heart of the city was torn out turning Birmingham into a shrine for the car. Birmingham with its Hill Street subway was the first city in the country to force its pedestrians to cross a road underground. Equally controversially, much needed new housing and offices were provided in tower blocks which began to dominate the skyline. The boundless 'never had it so good' optimism of the time which saw no hidden dangers in these dynamic changes lay behind the commitment to a new theatre double the size of the old. The Rep Directors recommended a seating capacity of not less than 900.

The Location Debate

Where should the new theatre be built? Should it be built within the hypothetical 'theatre land' or in the 'civic centre' off Broad Street? Jackson had been dead for scarcely three weeks in April 1961 when doubts began to be raised that the retention of the Rep's separateness might imply a degree of cultural discrimination. An article in the Birmingham Mail on 21 April worried about potentially disastrous segregation with 'implications of chalk and cheese, sheep and goat, highbrow and lowbrow'. At a meeting in the Council House on 25 April the opposing cases were presented. The Chairman of the Public Works Committee,

Councillor Dennis Thomas argued that the Rep should be built on John Bright Street. It would be near the Alex and in close proximity to a proposed new multi-storey hotel as well as shops and restaurants. All of which would make the whole area more attractive as a leisure facility and provide potential increased income for the theatre. The Council minutes record his opinion that it would be a tragedy to move the theatre to the Civic Centre where patrons might be limited to the more serious theatre-goer. It was a powerful argument.

The directors of the Rep Board, however, including Bob Walker and Councillor Margaret Cooke, were as determined as Nancy Burman on the civic centre site. What emerges from their argument is the perception that the Rep was indeed different from the other theatres. It had a world-wide reputation and was therefore special. The new Rep should be autonomous with its own self-contained facilities including exhibition spaces and a restaurant. Another Rep director, Ald. Harry Watton was in the Chair and he seemed to clinch the matter: 'the new theatre must be built with ideals in mind about the future, and he did not want to see it surrounded by coffee stalls and sweet shops which might detract from it'.

Even though the meeting ended with a resolution in favour of the civic centre site, the debate continued in the press. In a letter published in the *Birmingham Post* on 1 May Sam Cooke recalled the decisions of fifty years before:

> I did propose that the finest position for the Repertory Theatre
> would be on the old canal building site in Easy Row which
> was to be demolished and a new road constructed across the
> canal basins, on the site where Broad Street Chambers now
> stands. Unfortunately this had to be abandoned. We now
> appear to have another opportunity—do not let us miss it
> this time. Incidentally, the theatre I studied in Munich and
> from which I gained much inspiration was situated in a park
> in beautiful surroundings.

On 16 August Jackson spoke as it were from the grave through a letter written to the *Birmingham Post* by Tom English. The tone was unmistakable; the challenge as uncompromisingly patrician as ever. Jackson had always regretted the Station Street site which had been chosen in contradiction of his father's opinion that cities tend to develop westwards. The founder of the Rep was 'absolutely in favour' of the civic centre site:

> not only because of its westness, but because he envisaged a noble
> building in fine surroundings, that would be a credit to the working
> theatrical profession and to the city itself. " It is an insult to put up
> such places with their entrances wedged between cigarette kiosks

and what are generally shops of the cheaper and vulgar variety", he said. "A theatre should be a place of beauty inside and out. Apart from its essential work people should want to be seen there and take a pride in going".

In November it was announced that the new Rep would be built in the civic centre 'fronting on to lawns and a water feature and will adjoin a multi-storey car park' (*BP*, 13.11. 61)

The Vision

The architect was to be Graham Winteringham who was a partner in the firm of S.T. Walker. In 1951, while a student at the Birmingham School of Architecture, Winteringham had collaborated with two other students in an alternative plan to redevelop the civic centre which was published in the *Architectural Review*. Some ninety acres were to be cleared to create a visionary townscape, Cobusier's 'La Ville Radieuse' in the middle of Birmingham. New modernist buildings, including a theatre and a concert hall, designed to harmonise with the best of the old would line not only a paved square, but a great green 'plant square' and a large 'water square' which would exploit the resources of the canal basin.[1] Ten years on the canal system remained in its dank obscurity and the chances of clearing the dilapidated environs of Broad Street seemed remote. The Birmingham Rep commission was a chance to fulfil a little of the youthful dream.

Early the following year Winteringham presented a report to the Chairman and Directors of the theatre which incorporated an earlier document 'The Birmingham Repertory Theatre, its Present and Future' compiled in November 1960 by Nancy Burman.[2] This laid down the artistic philosophy underpinning the project and gave broad details of building specifications. It was recognised that patterns of entertainment had changed radically from the days when Jackson had opened his austere little playhouse. Now what was needed was more than simply the opportunity to see a good play. It was necessary to create 'a sense of occasion' with the provision of ample public spaces with bars and good restaurant facilities. Furthermore it was important that the resources of the building should be exploited as fully as possible. Not only should the technical and managerial parts of the building be in use for about eighty hours in the week, but the public areas should be adaptable for daytime lectures, films, conferences and recitals. The extensive archives of the theatre would be stored and made available for research purposes in a specially-designated room. A number of self-contained flats were to be provided for staff and artists.

Perhaps most importantly it was stressed that the old economic and inevitably social divisions which prevailed in most theatres should be abandoned. The old

48

Rep, despite the democratic sweep of the stalls still had a separate entrance up steep, gas-lit stairs to the balcony. The Belgrade Theatre for all its glass and steel modernity, retained stalls, a circle and even boxes. At the new Rep while a 'one-price' auditorium was deemed impractical, it was to be without obvious physical divisions. All patrons 'should be welcomed in one central foyer' and 'have access to all the amenities offered the public'. The proposed 900-seater auditorium would aim for a feeling of intimacy and unity in the audience experience.

Audiences and Auditoria: Contexts

The Rep document acknowledged the wider contemporary debate about stage configuration and the relationship of the performance space to the audience. The Belgrade had opted for a traditional proscenium stage, but the actor-manager Bernard Miles' experiments in Elizabethan-style staging during the 1950s had culminated in 1959 in the completely open stage of the Mermaid Theatre. Stephen Joseph's theory and practice in theatre-in-the-round underpinned the design of the New Victoria Theatre, a refurbished cinema opened in 1962. In the same year, inspired by Tyrone Guthrie's Festival Theatre in Stratford, Ontario, the Chichester Festival Theatre was built with a full thrust stage which created a good deal of controversy. At the Nottingham Playhouse where the curved circle created a Victorian-style ambience, there was an attempt to provide maximum flexibility with an open stage which also had the focus of a proscenium arrangement.

The argument in Nottingham that regional theatres had to offer a very broad range of classic and modern drama was taken up in Birmingham. The report states very firmly that 'the conventional picture-frame stage cannot be beaten as an all-purpose platform from which an author is to speak through the actors' but then goes on to stress its obvious limitations for pre-naturalistic drama. While flexibility was to be the aim it was also obvious that expensive technology for a radically-adaptable stage in such a large auditorium was impractical. This was an important point. Graham Winteringham was already under commission to build the new Crescent Theatre which was to be resited off Broad Street. This amateur Little Theatre which seated just under 300 opened in 1964 with a completely adaptable stage which could revolve to form a traverse. This radical option, however, was rejected because of the potential maintenance costs. The report settled for a compromise:

> **Rather than attempting the true 'arena' stage plan form where the audience encircles the stage, the stage is opened up to the full width of the auditorium, thus removing the visual barrier of a proscenium arch between the two elements. Just as the cinema has the wide screen so the theatre will have the wide stage.**

The suggested minimum width of the proscenium opening was to be 30 feet for a stage 50 feet deep.

Certainly the belief that a clear demarcation between audience and actors was necessary was held by John Harrison and apparently confirmed by the controversy which raged round the auditorium structure of the Chichester Festival Theatre. Just like Sam Cooke fifty years before, he and Graham Winteringham (albeit separately) went off to West Germany to look at new theatre buildings. On 25 July 1963 John Harrison described in the *Guardian* the trip which included visits to Mannheim and Gelsenkirchen where large glass-walled theatres resolutely linked the play-going experience to the outside world. Massive state subsidy and enormous staffing resources often enabled two auditoria. The larger might seat nearly 1000 with a second 300 seat auditorium. Advanced technology enabled all kinds of adaptability. But Harrison wanted simpler means to preserve 'the magic of the acting area' :

> **There is an acting place and an enjoying-the-acting-place.**
> **All efforts to cross the gap are doomed to gimmickry.**
> **There should be the possibility of close soliloquising.**
> **Intimacy without the embarrassment of charades…**
> **[the audience] come to see and hear, to be shown and**
> **told. Their physical participation in the evening is**
> **confined to the social activities of bar and foyer.**

That reference to 'the embarrassment of charades' has an echo of Barry Jackson's taste. In 1955 he had expressed a dislike of arena theatre stating that he found the all too visible presence of other members of the audience a distraction. The Rep's cinema-screen-like opening was to be wide. How wide it ultimately became was, Harrison later claimed, down to the issue of audience sightlines. The steeply-raked Jackson/Cooke auditorium in Station Street was basically a rectangular box. In 1912 the fan-shaped auditorium was rejected to ensure good sightlines on to the small stage. The single democratic sweep envisaged for the new building had to provide double the number of seats without the help of circles or balcony. Once the decision had been made to go for a modified proscenium albeit with a removable apron stage over an orchestra pit, the opening, Harrison decided, had to be exceptionally wide to ensure good visibility. The consequences of that decision for all future directors and designers in the new theatre were to be momentous.

The other priority which was stressed in 1962 was the desire to make the external appearance of the theatre an exciting statement. Theatres, it was claimed, 'are very seldom really *seen*'. Interestingly the Shakespeare Memorial Theatre which of course both Jackson and Burman had helped to develop, was given as a famous exception. What was envisaged, and became part of Graham Winteringham's brief, was a site which allowed 'free access from some distance'. In other words a building set apart. Winteringham later expressed his vision of modernist concrete, glass and light as a 'jewelled brooch glittering on a plain gown' (*BP*, 26.3.66)

Preliminary Calculations

In 1962 Winteringham proposed a two and half years' preparation and consultation period leading to the start of building in August 1965 with a completion date in 1967. The estimated total cost was £493,000. In the event the building cost £1,016,000 and it opened in the autumn of 1971.

At first everything appeared to go well. There was none of the acrimony which had accompanied the planning phase of the Nottingham Playhouse for example. On 23 April 1964 the General Purposes Committee of Birmingham City Council gave unanimous approval in principle to a commitment to build the new theatre at a predicted cost of £500,000. In discussion however, there had been a much publicised dissenting voice. Councillor Charles Collett, a persistent thorn in the Rep's flesh, objected that the money would be better spent on the four to five thousand Brummies waiting to be housed 'Of course we need culture and refinement of mind, but how on earth can you ask a person living in a pig sty to live in the future and have a refined mind?' (*G*, 16.4.64) Accompanying the press report of the meeting was a letter from Collett (*G*, 24.4.64) explaining his decision to vote for the project derived from a reluctance to appear churlish. But he also raised more controversial issues. Why was the use of the new theatre to be confined to the Rep company?:

> **The only justification for such a building costing £500,000 and a minimum annual subsidy of £58,000 would be if other theatrical companies could use it, but this is not intended. In support of my statement, the proposed theatre will have twice the capacity of the present one, which the repertory company are quite unable to fill.**

This of course was a crucial issue. Would the new building be economically viable? The financial budget for the year 1961-2 allowed for a box office income of £31,819 based on forty eight performance weeks with an average attendance of 55% together with catering, bar and programme income of a further £1,500. Estimated expenditure was £49,637 leaving a trading deficit of £16,318. Grants from the City and the Arts Council of £5,000 and £10,000 were augmented by further grants from ATV and ABC Television of £500 each. The theatre in Station Street was thus very substantially dependent on grant aid in order to survive.

Calculations made by Nancy Burman and sent to N.V. Linklater at the Arts Council in early 1964 show that she estimated the annual running costs of the new theatre to be in the region of £145,300. With a medium seat price of 8s 9d audiences would have to reach 70% of capacity to avoid loss. In 1963 Linklater had expressed worries about the size both of the stage and the number of seats in the auditorium. In response Graham Winteringham acknowledged the niggling doubts over the nine hundred seats but a decision had been made to play the potential problem down. Linklater recognised that the large stage would make experimental work risky. Could, he wondered, the size of the rehearsal room next to the stage be increased to permit small-scale production? Thus the seed for the Studio Theatre was sown.[3]

Winteringham's Plan

When the Rep magazine *Proscenium* was launched in 1965, it carried short articles by Winteringham outlining the principle features of the new theatre. Retaining the steep rake of the old auditorium but for double the number of patrons meant that he was effectively designing a 36-storey building. The whole public experience was to be radically different. The great foyer staircases rising gently to a series of landings would permit ease and speed of movement. The main entrance doors on the east and west of the building leading into the common foyer would be complemented by several doors into the auditorium itself. The street level foyer was seen as a continuation of the pavement outside rather like a city arcade. The centrally-placed box office would be in a comparatively 'neutral zone' so that tickets could be booked or collected without disturbing free public movement. Not only would there be a promenade between the theatre and the lake with its fountains, but patrons would be able to look out over and beyond the water from 'viewing decks' which would extend from the restaurant and upper foyer bars. The exterior of the building was to be faced with light-weight grey serrated concrete. The fact that the proposed theatre fitted into the overall civic centre plan was much emphasised. The new Rep was to be part of a larger, grander design for the city of the future.

Disruption and Delay

Suddenly the aesthetic principles of the past intervened. It was objected in Council meetings that the modern concrete exterior would be out of keeping with the portland stone which had been used for the neighbouring civic buildings. The delay caused by this minor dispute proved disastrous. In March 1966 the Government imposed restrictions on local government spending. In July 1966 the Minister of Housing and Local Government rejected the City's application to begin building.

There were times during the next three years when it looked as though the theatre would never be built. Hopes were dashed yet again in 1967. As the scheme to develop the Station Street site did not materialise, theoretically the Rep Company was doomed to struggle on in the old building. Alternative suggestions included proposals to amalgamate the Rep with the Alex—an idea that was greeted with little enthusiasm—and more seriously a scheme to refurbish the Hippodrome as a new home. A detailed feasibility study of ATV's offer to sell their freehold interest on the Hurst Street building to the City revealed that overall purchase and conversion costs would be too high. By the summer of 1968 Sir Robert Aitken was warning that the Rep could not survive much longer in the existing conditions and Peter Dews was threatening to resign. Finally the City agreed to give the Rep what Aitken called 'a healthy creative theatre of its own'.

Building began at the beginning of March 1969. On 25 October Jennie Lee, Britain's first Minister for the Arts, laid the foundation stone. Ironically the very foundations created more problems both financially and structurally. New building regulations meant that they had to be dug deeper and the drainage system revamped. Deposits of neat acid from the remains of a tin-plate factory had to be dealt with. The positioning of the theatre over the tunnel which runs from New Street Station also threatened the noise of trains during performance. The answer here was to isolate the auditorium from the main structure by mounting the walls and floor on a sound absorbent synthetic material and similarly 'floating' the seats. A very thick plaster ceiling which moves fractionally with vibration again absorbed sound. The whole auditorium was envisaged rather like an egg in a box.

By 1969 estimated costs had risen to £900,000. The City contribution was limited to £640,000; the Arts Council would provide £150,000 while the theatre itself was committed to raising £96,000 by public appeal. In January 1970 however, the City agreed to find an additional £36,000 for stage lighting. By late November the General Purposes Committee was told of additional costs and professional charges amounting to £30,000. The furnishing costs were up by £21,000 and the cost of equipping what was now designated a Studio Theatre had increased by £14,700. The press gleefully trumpeted the news of 'an extra bill shock', but few could have been genuinely surprised. The Calouste Gulbenkian Foundation contributed £50,000 which provided the additional funds needed for the Studio, stage lighting and equipment.

There was one last battle over the theatre's name. A decision to name the theatre after Sir Barry Jackson was overturned. This was a civic theatre built with civic money and the Birmingham Repertory Theatre it was to remain.

The New Theatre

Up until that time no other new theatre in the country had been given such an architecturally-dominant site. In some respects the sheer drama of Winteringham's original vision for the theatre's external appearance was not unlike that proposed for Denys Lasdun's defiantly modernist National Theatre on London's South Bank which would open in 1976. Lasdun's building overlooks the Thames. Winteringham's dream of a glittering vista of water vanished never to return. The great curved frontage of the new Rep created a wrap-around effect where the full height windows of the public foyers were framed by a pre-fabricated panel system which looked not unlike giant tuning forks. The controversy over the external facing had been resolved by using hopton wood stone aggregate with vertical ribbing which encourages efficient water drainage. Winteringham himself supervised the casting of the moulds which were patterned like tree bark. An extended description of the theatre in *Building Design* (29.10.71) commented that the web of tracery looked almost too delicate to support the weight of the massive fly tower.

Inside was all light and space enhanced by the soaring staircases. The ground-floor foyer which led to the bar, coffee bar and restaurant had a shining brick floor—a more economic alternative to the rubber floor originally planned. The cloakroom and ample provision of lavatories insisted on by Nancy Burman a decade before were tucked under the curve of the auditorium. The box office on the opposite wall was actually rather easy to miss—something which had to be remedied later. *Building Design* detailed the overall effect 'purple painted walls, red-walled stairs…furnished low, wide and handsomely with ochre upholstered and white melamine table-topped, black tubular steel-legged furniture'. The design was repeated, but more narrowly, on the first floor with a curved bar and salad restaurant, and then on the second floor with a bar. Those hectic 1970s colours were augmented by the brewers Ansells who proclaimed their catering franchise with 'acres of blue Babycham type satin' back-draped over the bars.

The fan-shaped auditorium sat 901 in colour areas which decreased inwards from perimeter brown to mid-purple to centre red. The idea was to allow the outer seating to merge with the walls so that at thinly-attended performances the actors could concentrate on the central red areas. There was unusually good leg room and as originally promised no one was more than 65 feet from the stage. Frederick Bentham in *Tabs* (12.12.71) described 'twenty-one steeply-stepped rows of Rank Strand luxury, cinema-type seats which evoke in me the feel of the enormous circle at the old Empire Cinema, Leicester Square'.

The walls of the auditorium form a natural proscenium frame giving a front opening 50 feet wide and 27 feet high with a total width of 80 feet. It was bigger than the stage at the Royal Opera House. The depth from front to back was 56 feet and the height to the grid 75 feet. The central area of the stage measuring 46 feet by 39 feet was modular floored on removable pillars so that any part could be moved, removed, raised or lowered to take a revolve or a trucking mechanism. An apron stage could extend over the orchestra pit. Bentham exclaimed at the 'niggling economy' of not providing forestage/orchestra lifts for quick conversion'. The proposed Studio Theatre, not yet ready for use, measured 50 by 30 feet with an anticipated audience capacity at that time of 160. Some economy, niggling or otherwise, was essential.

The design intended direct access onto the stage from the scene dock and from the scene dock onto the street. It was boasted that a pantechnicon could be driven straight onto the stage. The lighting system was controlled by a Thorn Electric Q-File computer with 140 circuits and 100 memories . A complete lighting plot could be programmed and stored. Plans to have an internal television for latecomers to watch performances had to be abandoned because of the cost. Backstage the dressing rooms were on the same level as the auditorium while stairs led to the administrative offices up a further two floors. There was no backstage lift, however, another necessary economy. To get to the top of the building then, as now, two flights of concrete stairs had to be climbed. The unusual addition of four flats (rather than twelve as originally planned) attracted the attention of commentators. Dual-level bedsits complete with kitchen and bathroom were to provide accommodation for visiting artists.

The critique in *Building Design* noted the exposed plumbing and ducting. Not, the writer decided, because of conscious 'new brutalism', but more crudely because of lack of finance. Winteringham's vision of a gleaming expanse of water reflecting back light from the great glass windows which would in turn entice the public to come inside, would never be fulfilled. He had to be content with a grassed area where newly married couples from the Registry Office across Broad Street could have their photographs taken. Bentham pointed out, however, that the visual impact was ' largely bestowed on circumnavigating motor cars puzzling their way through Birmingham's traffic engineering'. The other problem, exacerbated of course by the ceaseless and rapidly expanding traffic, was that the windows got dirty very quickly and were very expensive to clean.

Early Problems

All large enterprises carry with them inevitable flawed thinking and downright mistakes. This theatre was very much the product of an earlier, more optimistic era. The financial implications of this heroically-proportioned plant would rapidly become frightening. There were immediate practical problems. In the workshops the relationship between the area of manufacture and the area of assembly was designed much as it was at the Old Rep. Constructed scenery was to be winched up from the carpenters' shop to the paint shop above. But the fact that the machine tools now used for carpentry created considerably more noise and dust than in a more manually-oriented era meant that the dust-free conditions necessary for scene-painting were impossible. David Williams, who came new to the theatre as Head of the Scenic Department, described the paintshop as a hell-hole with dust rising like smoke to damage the intricate scene-painting required by designers like Finlay James. The solution was to drill away the concrete stairs leading up to the paintshop and fill in the void over the carpenters' shop which was designed to provide the height for large scenic pieces. For the next twenty years scenery had to be taken up a ramp outside the theatre and manually carted three hundred yards down to the external doors through to the scene dock and the paintshop.

The scenic pieces were huge of course because the stage was so large. A strategy for narrowing down the width of the stage opening had been provided in two movable proscenium towers which were to have lights fixed to them. While the off-stage floors were concrete, the stage floor was wooden and threatened to collapse under the weight of the fully-laden towers. They had to be abandoned. Another consequence of cost-cutting was that the sound-proofing between the scene dock and paintshop and the stage, and eventually the main stage and the Studio, was inadequate. Michael Simpson also recalled the amusing consequence of the red central seats in the auditorium. These were naturally the best and most expensive. On a thin night they would also be the least populated so the actors were very conscious of a red glow from the middle of a half-empty theatre.

Much more serious however, was the effect of the structure of the auditorium and the relationship of the audience to the stage. As Iain Mackintosh has pointed out in his book *Architecture, Actor and Audience*, the grand democratic sweep of the seating was a product of social theories of the 1960s. This in turn had derived from the similar radical thinking at the beginning of the century which produced the Old Rep. Recent revisionist thinking now claims that the despised structure of Victorian theatres with their circles and boxes means that even a half-empty theatre can seem fuller and more actor/audience friendly. Also the much-vaunted principle of no seat being further than 65 feet from the stage was what Mackintosh described as 'the functionalist fallacy' which tended to prevail over auditorium design theory. [4] The new Rep's fan-shaped auditorium meant that the back row stretched for more than 100 feet and thus the largest single unit of patrons was furthest away from the stage. As successive actors and directors at the Rep continue to point out, the experience of the audience is quite different depending on whether they sit near the front or the back.

Controversy over the size of the stage erupted almost immediately and indeed has continued. At the time of the opening Graham Winteringham appeared unperturbed. As far as he was concerned designers had to find new solutions to a new challenge. As we shall see much of the success or failure of successive directors have depended on how they tackled the challenge.

The most negative critique of the building came from Colin Amery writing in the December edition of *Architects Journal*. After a perfunctory visit to Birmingham, he likened the theatre to 'a confident paddle-steamer—large and already rather out of date'. He made no secret of his preference for the Crucible Theatre which opened in Sheffield the same year. He decided that the exterior of the Rep was an architectural mess 'a melée of misunderstood stylistic gimmicks' and that the theatre looked like two separate buildings: … 'a solid rectangular stage block and an ovoid–shaped auditorium block'. The junction where the audience and the players met, he claimed, could never create the magic which would be possible with the Crucible open thrust stage.

In 1972 however, the Royal Institute of British Architects gave Winteringham an award for the best new building in the West Midlands. They too were concerned that externally the building 'was somewhat uncontrolled' but overall the theatre epitomised 'the optimism, energy and liveliness of post-war Britain'. Winteringham had created his 'jewelled brooch glittering on a plain gown' to lure the people of Birmingham into the building and then into the auditorium. Would they come?

1 Gordon Cullen, 'A Scheme for the Centre of Birmingham', *Architectural Review,* 109 (February 1951), pp.90-7

2 Held in the Barry Jackson Archive, Birmingham Central Library, MS 978/72/1-59

3 City Council minutes and other correspondence held in Barry Jackson Archive, MS 978/1/6/101

4 Iain Mackintosh, *Architecture, Actor and Audience* (Routledge, 1993), p.106

6. A City's Theatre: Peter Dews and Michael Simpson

The Task Ahead

With hindsight it is obvious that it was going to be no easy task to make the new theatre work both artistically and financially. Michael Simpson acknowledged the anxiety before the move was made: the uneasy feeling that potentially disastrous decisions could not be revoked. The hard facts were that the Old Rep had played to houses averaging 59.5% in 1968-9, 55.4% in 1969-70 and 60% in 1970-71. It looked as if Dews' strategy was working but even in a glamorous new theatre could all those extra seats be filled? Peter Dews was characteristically bullish about the move, but he was faced artistically with a totally altered spatial and technical challenge. His initial response understandably was to think big and popular. On 5 October 1971 he described his policy in an article in the *Daily Telegraph* 'We will continue to do a repertory based on classical plays with a permanent company as in the old theatre. But we must widen our doors with bigger productions and more musicals, make it a big night out in the city'.

The first three shows of Dews' inaugural season were not only new but also demonstrated the sheer amplitude of the stage and the dynamic aspirations of the design team. The first production was an American musical based on Jane Austen's *Pride and Prejudice* aptly called *First Impressions*. Patricia Routledge came as a guest star to play Mrs Bennett. Finlay James' décor, framed with his beloved filigree screens, treated the audience to a smooth-flowing succession of elegant sets: a parkland vista with curved bridges leading to a bijou decorative pavilion; the domestic comfort of the Bennett drawing room and a huge ballroom with whirling dancers. Three hundred yards of fabric went into the costumes. Alex Hamilton built a period carriage which was drawn by a real live Welsh mare called Ada. The next production, *Roll Me Over*, a new Joan Littlewood-style East End farce by Bill Canaway set in a car-tyre yard was a very different kind of play but still the emphasis was on bold visual statements. A panorama of over 300 used tyres plus three eight-foot polystyrene replica tyres stretched the full extent of the stage. There were full-size factory gates, roller-shutter doors and a tap which gushed water into a pool. It was commented that the overall effect was like watching a play in the street. The Christmas show was *Good Time Johnny*, an updated musical version of *The Merry Wives of Windsor*. The main attraction of Dews' production lay in the casting of Joan Sims as Queenie, the proprietress of the Garter Inn, and Ronnie Barker as Sir John—or it did until Barker was forced to pull out because of a throat ailment.

Inevitably audiences came to *First Impressions*. Box office takings averaged 96% but the critical response was less than enthusiastic as it was to *Roll Me Over* when the audience average slipped to 60%. Gareth Lloyd Evans, in a vicious review of Canaway's play, noted that the audience applauded David Cockayne's set 'Why should an audience clap 500 tyres I asked myself and got no answer' (*G*, 12.11.71). After *Good Time Johnny* Judith Cook described herself as 'stunned…by the third production through which I had sat in which the script was poor and the show unimaginative to a degree…A rather tedious dirty joke was spread over two hours and 40 minutes' (*BP*, 29.12.71).

If the critics were hostile, there were also other negative factors. The Royal Gala performance of *First Impressions* when Princess Margaret formally opened the theatre was covered extensively by the local newspapers and indeed by a generously-illustrated account in the *Stage*. But some of the media publicity seemed less than whole-hearted. The opening was scheduled to coincide with *Curtain Up*, a special television programme put out by ATV. But the attention devoted to the Rep was perfunctory. All that was shown was the arrival of the royal guest and the unveiling of the commemorative plaque. Then the programme moved swiftly on to survey other regional theatres. There were some immediate letters of protest from local people. Why had not the theatre been shown in detail with a scene from the opening production perhaps? Why had all the work and effort which had gone into the creation of the new theatre been celebrated more fully? From the beginning the new Rep had to adopt a defensive stance.

Another problem lay in the perceptions of Old Rep devotees who clung to their golden if perhaps mythical memories of the past and now felt themselves disappointed. If nothing else the physical shock of the massive scale and altered ambience of the theatre was acute. The intense intimacy of the old theatre had gone. These feelings also affected members of staff who tended to forget the former cramped conditions and limited resources. Again the size of the building was a major problem. The wardrobe staff felt it very keenly. The cutting and sewing rooms were light and spacious, and June Callear had insisted on a pink décor to impart a feeling of warmth. But housed in the basement, the team felt very isolated from other departments. June Callear would go home and telephone colleagues rather than trudge up the concrete stairs to find a distant office. The senior management offices were down a long corridor on the second floor.

Peter Dews consciously set out to retain something of the intimacy generated so effortlessly in the old building. Whenever he was in the theatre he visited each department to make them feel part of a team. David Williams recalled that when he worked late on a set, Dews would appear to invite him for a drink in his flat. The problem was, however, that Dews was not so regularly in the theatre as the Board of Management might wish. It was left, for example, to Michael Simpson to field Judith Cook's criticism in the press. Dews was in America.

He was increasingly in demand as a director outside Birmingham. The London success of *Vivat! Vivat Regina!* had led to another Broadway opening. He was in New York in January 1972 savouring a critical triumph when he received a letter from the Rep Board refusing his offer to spend forty weeks and direct three plays a year in Birmingham. They wanted total commitment. Dews' resignation was announced in February to take effect the following July. In an interview published on 4 February he talked to the *Birmingham Evening Mail* critic Fred Norris about the background to his extra-curricular activities and the dilemma which continues to face artists working in the subsidised regional theatre. Dews spoke of the personal artistic and financial crisis in 1968 when the remuneration of about £60 a week for virtually single-handed directorial responsibility forced him to ask for leave to work elsewhere—not just for enhanced earnings but also for additional creative stimulus. He decided, it was revealed to drop his salary to a weekly £10 a week plus expenses in return for opportunities to place his skills on the open market.

Four years on he insisted that even with expenses the weekly cost to the Rep was a maximum of £35. The offer from the Board had been for a salary of £100 for each of 44 weeks spent in the theatre plus £50 for weeks spent away. For his current success on Broadway he was receiving £300 a week, but money, he insisted, was not the primary motivation. He had a deep-seated need, he claimed, for what he called 'artistic bigamy' but nonetheless he felt part of the fabric of the Rep 'Let me say I love this place. I don't think there is anywhere else I would have worked on such terms for the honour of directing here'. He commented wryly on the commitment of the Board members once a month to dictate the fate of full-time theatre workers. He had reminded them that his contract was due for renewal. Ironically in March Dews became the recipient of the Midlands Man of the Year Press, Radio and Television Award made annually to the man or woman who had done most to increase the prestige of the Midlands. Certainly the resignation generated controversy in the press.

What If…

Ironically there were signs in the early months of 1972 that the programming was beginning to take on a more familiar look. Dustin Hughes' production of *Man and Superman* with designs by Hugh Durrant struck the right balance. Jennifer Hilary returned to the Rep company a decade after her debut to play Anne Whitefield opposite Patrick Mower's Jack Tanner. There was near unanimous praise for the way the dimensions of the stage were exploited. Actors made their entrances quite deliberately through open space towards a defined acting area which was built over the orchestra pit and permitted Shaw's polemic to ring clearly round the auditorium. B.A. Young, noting the director's youth, recalled Peter Brook's 1945 production when Paul Scofield played Tanner (*FT*, 22.2.72). A student critic in *Grapevine*, the university newspaper, excited by Mower's be-whiskered resemblance to Che Guevara, decided that Hughes had achieved a serious, young, bang-up-to-date production which deserved a young serious audience: 'If this is an intimation of what *could* happen at the Rep, then we must support it' (March, 72).

The policy of playing in repertoire had continued into the new theatre and so up until July audiences could choose from two mainstage shows. *Man and Superman* played alongside Dews' production of *Vivat*. Michael Simpson's production of *The Recruiting Officer* opened in April and then in May could be seen alongside the double bill of *The Critic* and *Oedipus the King* which brought Derek Jacobi triumphantly back to play Mr Puff and Oedipus. Another double bill of Stoppard's *The Real Inspector Hound* and *After Magritte* accompanied Pinero's *Dandy Dick* in July. By that time the average audience attendance was 584, 64.8% of capacity.

In 1977, Peter Brigg, a Canadian academic, published a marketing case study of the new theatre's early years comparing the Old with the New Rep and making a further comparison with other regional theatres. Although the management in Birmingham could not claim spectacular success, audiences were substantially larger than at the old theatre. Brigg's survey revealed that the Belgrade averaged 42.1%, the Liverpool Playhouse 57.6% and the Crucible 56.1%.[1]

Relatively speaking the Rep was doing rather well and with a substantial, diverse programme of mainstage plays. What might have happened if a compromise had been reached; if Dews had stayed? Back in February (*EM*, 23.2.72) Fred Norris had warned:

> **The Rep does seem to have developed a habit of**
> **creating its own crises—often when they don't**

exist…The Rep will be hard put to find a man of
the same stature of Peter Dews as its new Director.
for many people in theatre Peter Dews Is the
Birmingham Rep.

First Among Equals

Despite a large number of external applicants, Michael Simpson's appointment
as Artistic Director was announced in May. Three years later, defeated and
frustrated by artistic and financial constraints, he resigned to resume his career in
television. Interviewed not long before his death the nonagenarian Sir Robert
Aitken, frail and with a flickering memory, confessed that he had known little
about the world of professional theatre at the time of these momentous decisions.
Michael Simpson, he suggested, was not 'big enough' for the Rep and it also
seems that he had problems maintaining authority amongst staff resentful at the
loss of Dews. But at the time of his appointment Simpson was very clear about the
change of directorial style which he intended to introduce:

I want to create here a total working unit of people
committed to the theatre…I believe in a team: it's
part idealism, part practical. I want to de-centralise
the Birmingham Rep and share out the work…But
I must have the last word. I have to be first among
equals (*Warwickshire and Worcestershire Life*, October,72).

Twenty years on Simpson maintained that the principal problem facing the Rep
was the constant sniping from those for whom criticism of the theatre could serve
to fulfil local personal or political agendas. Indeed he even stated that conflict
about the theatre could be deployed as a useful distraction from other more
sensitive issues in the Council House.

Clearly the situation was rather more complex than this rather sinister theory
suggests but the issues of civic responsibility and prestige were significant. There
was always the worry that this new civic showcase could be subjected to civic
interference. At its most alarming before the theatre opened serious proposals
were made to include a clause in the new lease which would give the Council
powers to force the theatre to withdraw and replace productions felt likely to 'lead
to a breach of the peace', or cause offence on moral or political grounds. Chairman
of the General Purposes Committee Ald. Eric Mole attempted to assuage worries
with assurances that all that was intended were the normal licensing safeguards.
At the meeting on 2 August 1971 Councillor Mrs Nora Hinks warned darkly about

the control of the theatre drifting into other irresponsible hands in the future 'We could have nudity on the stage and all sorts of theatrical rubbish' (*EM*, 2.8.71). Fortunately the clause was dropped. But there were to be other, apparently more trivial matters which ultimately had serious implications.

The tussle over the external appearance of the theatre had of course helped create the circumstances for building delays. Now this gleaming palace of culture was in place nothing vulgar like promotional material should deface its appearance. Up until October 1974, posters, billboards and neon lights advertising the theatre were banned by City planners. Even relatively modest strategies like illuminated pavement advertisement stands took months to negotiate. For casual passers-by the theatre was not unlike a huge austere modern cathedral set 300 yards away from the road with inevitably, given its proximity to the roaring traffic, tired-looking grass in between. Matters were not helped when the small Manzoni Memorial pool was constructed in 1976. It rapidly filled up with rubbish.

The other issue which became subject to local interests was catering. The dream of making the Rep a civilised night out with good food and drink very rapidly turned into an ongoing nightmare. Birmingham in 1971 was not noted for its haute cuisine. Instead of seeking advice and service from an imaginative and experienced restaurateur, the catering franchise went to the local brewery Ansells. The service in the bars, especially during intervals was inefficient; the top floor bar usually closed and coffee unobtainable on the first floor. The food in the restaurant was uninspired, even unpleasant, and relatively expensive.

But in May 1972 Simpson was irrepressibly optimistic. He wanted, he declared, to keep 'open house' at the Rep:

> **What I'm really saying to the theatrical profession**
> **and to the public is that this is not a closed shop…**
> **I want them to come in and try things other than**
> **plays, to come and experience the building and**
> **have fun in it (*EM*,11.5.72)**

The Brum

The Brum, as the Studio Theatre was jauntily dubbed when it opened in October 1972, was perhaps the most important aspect of Simpson's dream of creating a feeling of local ownership of the Rep. This was to be an autonomous unit with its own director, administrator and resident company. 'Our little laboratory of interesting new writing from inside the theatre and out and about in Birmingham' as Simpson put it (*EM*, 11.4.72). The first director, Christopher Honer, was 24, an Oxford graduate with experience of some thirty productions as Studio Director at the Belgrade Theatre where he had launched a rent-a-play scheme for local schools and pubs. With him, also from the Belgrade, came Roger Lancaster as Studio administrator. Five actors (three from the Belgrade) Mike Hadley, Robert O'Mahoney, Colin Starkey, Pauline Kelly and Ruth Tansey made up the company producing work which aimed mainly at the 16-25 age group.

When the audience arrived for the first performance on 17 October 1972 they encountered actors trying to entice them into playing fairground games. There was no stage; indeed the space resembled a television studio rather than a conventional theatre. To avoid being dragged into the games it was necessary to negotiate a way through assorted, scattered props to reach a haven on one of the banks of raked, portable seating which for this inaugural production were arranged on three sides of the action. The play called *Grab*, scripted from company improvisations by Albert Lyons, was a light-hearted satire on greed in society very loosely based on Aristophanes' *Plutus*. It was rough-edged, highly variable in quality and acting expertise and occasionally tedious with clumsy, noisy scene-shifting. A high point was Pauline Kelly's demonstration of her ability to balance a pint of beer on her head while bending down to pick up a handkerchief with her teeth.

Whatever the artistic limitations, the message was clear that here was a place to be young, relaxed and distinctly anti-establishment. Round the corner in the main house there were still patrons who turned up in evening dress. In December, a still younger audience was targeted with Reg Stewart's *Nick and the Dragon* the first of a series of Christmas shows written specially for the under-eights. The story proper only began after the interval. The first part of the show was taken up with the actors introducing themselves to the children and encouraging them to take part in the action. A review in the *Sunday Mercury* (28.12.72) described what happened:

> **We shouted and we kept ever so silent.**
> **We made noises like aeroplanes and cows**
> **And everything we wanted to make noises**
> **Like. We played games, we sang songs and**
> **We passed imaginary ice cubes and even a**
> **Car along the rows.**

In between came the Brum's first staging of a play by David Edgar who had worked with Honer at the Belgrade. *Death Story*, written following a week of company improvisations on *Romeo and Juliet*, was a play about doomed love in the context of a warring community which inevitably set up resonances of Northern Ireland. This time when the audience arrived they were greeted by the sight of a corpse on the floor: a young man killed by a stone in a street riot. Tough, violent and sexually explicit—the Romeo character was completely naked in one scene; the Juliet character forced under interrogation to re-enact her lovemaking—

the verbal polemic rammed the political commitment deeper home.

Years later Edgar described the Studio as 'a funny old space'—not pretty and slightly too regular, but with a height which lends it 'a certain grandeur'. That quality of 'grandeur' could, as future users of the space were to discover, also alienate when audiences were thin, but its total flexibility offered ample opportunity for innovation. The primary emphasis was always on the new even if that meant a reworking of a classic text like Shakespeare's *Measure for Measure* which Honer staged with six actors in June 1973. When financial constraints began to bite deeply in the second year of the Brum's operation which necessitated the abandonment of the principle of a separate Studio company, the input of more mature actors from the main company allowed another kind of flexibility. The programming became more eclectic with plays by Ibsen, Shaw and Brecht as well as a David Rudkin premiere *No Title*, David Mercer's *After Haggerty* and Bond's *The Pope's Wedding*.

The Brum also became a microcosm of innovative theatre nationwide. Ken Campbell's anarchic Road Show, and The General Will, the Bradford-based company David Edgar was associated with, came as part of a programme called Ad Hocs which brought in outside companies with alternative plays, revues, jazz and poetry evenings. Roger Lancaster also organised weekly folk evenings which became hugely popular. During the autumn and winter of 1973-4 Paradise Foundry performed another Edgar piece *Operation Iskia*. Prospect Theatre Workshop gave a late night performance of Jean Genet's *Deathwatch*. Athol Fugard came with the Royal Court's Theatre Upstairs Company to present his *Sizwe Bansi is Dead*. The newly-formed Joint Stock Company came with *Speakers*, a company-devised piece derived from Heathcote Williams which turned the Brum into Hyde Park Corner for the night. The performance art pioneers, Welfare State, gave four simultaneous performances in sand craters repeated as different sections of the audience arrived. In August 1974, Lancaster collaborated with the Birmingham Arts Lab to mount the first ever International Performance Art Festival. A highlight was Welfare State's giant fire sculptures in the yard of St Philip's Cathedral.

Some homegrown productions were toured. Honer's production of Beckett's *Endgame*, first staged in January 1973, toured after achieving a modest success at home. There was a packed, animated audience for a one-night stand in Bridgnorth for example, and sufficient enthusiasm for it to brought back to the Brum in April. The level of activity at this time was so complex that it is now hard to reconstruct. Touring meant exposure for the company's work in locations as diverse as Keele, Malvern and Kingswinford. It also meant a long-suffering—but for all that enthusiastic—stage crew bundling into an ancient Bedford van with the production manager Jeff Kitto to work long hours collecting and transporting sets and technical equipment. Just before Christmas 1972 there was an end of term lark, a

'Have a Go' opportunity where members of the main company moved into the Brum with three shows: an evening devoted to Dylan Thomas, as well as Charles Wood's *Dingo* directed by Tony Craven, the Company Manager, and *White Wire With Wheels*, a brand-new Australian play directed by the Stage Director Hugh Rule.

Using the theatre

What happened in the Brum was of a piece with Simpson's overall policy of opening the building up. A series of Sunday concerts was introduced into the main house; there were exhibitions of work by local artists. Playdays linked to productions in the repertoire brought young people into the theatre for talks and workshops followed by special matinée performances. The Young Rep, a series of professionally-led theatre skills workshops were held on Saturday mornings again to encourage young people. Simpson invited the newly-formed Birmingham Youth Theatre to use the Brum as its performance base—a relationship which continued until the mid-1980s.

There was a strong sense of continuity with the core company which included familiar faces like Paul Henry, John Baddeley, Frank Moorey and Jane Freeman, who by then was Simpson's wife. David Edgar remembers the open and accessible atmosphere in the theatre and meetings which took place in the bar. Sebastian Barnes who was first taken on as a casual member of the stage crew and eventually became Technical Manager, has happy memories of the company atmosphere, the camaraderie of the touring van, and an approachable Artistic Director in Michael Simpson.

In the main theatre the repertoire system was extended to three plays in any one week rather than two. Indeed during one week at the beginning of 1973 there were twenty seven public performances with a choice of four plays and two concerts. Small-scale new and experimental work in the Brum was combined with a mainstage programme of solid classic fare: Shaw and Coward (*Caesar and Cleopatra*) and (*Present Laughter*) and for the more adventurous Pinter and Behan in *The Homecoming* and *The Hostage*. Simpson also commissioned a new translation of Molière's *The Miser* from David Turner. There were two productions of Shakespeare. Derek Goldby directed *Macbeth* in October 1972 while the following June Peter Dews returned to direct the Rep's sixtieth anniversary production of *Twelfth Night*. Turner also contributed to the one major experiment aimed specifically at the local audience and using writers with local connections. *Up Spaghetti Junction* was a drama documentary-cum-revue devised by Malcolm Totten with input from David Edgar, Turner, and John Clarke with music by Jon Raven.

As directors and designers continued to grapple with the challenge of the main stage, Simpson refused to be daunted. 'My attitude', he declared in 1973, 'has always been, don't let's carp, let's *use* the theatre' (*BP*, 10.1.73). Some of the props for his production of *Caesar and Cleopatra* were 14 feet high. John Napier's design for *Macbeth* used a black cyclorama behind a circular sandpit. After the spectacularly brutal fights orchestrated by John Greenwood, the bits of Macbeth's disembowelled body were left in the sand for the witches to scavenge. The audience were enveloped in the action not only with the witches' voices reverberating around the auditorium but with the apparitions emerging from the steep height of the back rows like a phantasmagoria of tall masked and cowled figures. The following spring the resident designer, Hugh Durrant, indulged himself with the set of *The Miser* which Turner had updated to nineteenth-century London in an irreverent, colloquial translation. The stage was filled with the entire ground floor of a double-fronted suburban house with a carriage on the road outside, and a back garden complete with bee hives where the miser Harpagon was seen hiding his hoard of gold. The director, Donald Sartain, orchestrated a constant stream of extra-textual activity with servants bustling about, shopping, cooking and dusting furniture

Guest actors came to play leading roles. Bernard Gallagher gave a virtuoso farceur performance as the miser Harpagon which some critics found self-conscious and overblown. Not so Robert Ray in the *Guardian* who described Gallagher's 'physical contortions of misery at the mere mention of spending money reach the superb absurdity of Jacques Tati' (30.4.73). In *Macbeth* Keith Baxter and Sara Kestelman played the murderous central couple. Again critics were divided on the production overall and the central performances. But Harold Hobson responded powerfully to what he called Baxter's 'rich and resonant' performance (*ST*, 15.10.72). Kestelman was more than a match for her partner establishing a strong sensual control and equally strongly signalling her collapse.

For Rep regulars, however, they could in time-honoured fashion watch the company's established actors move from play to play. Jane Freeman suffered rather in her husband's production of *Caesar and Cleopatra* when her Ftatateeta was described as looking like Harry Secombe in drag. But otherwise her roles included Mrs Dangle in *The Critic*, a member of the Chorus in *Oedipus*, and the wife of Macduff when John Greenwood saw to it that her killing was particularly nasty. She also played a corruptly-maternal Mrs Thrips in David Turner's Anglicised version of the matchmaker Frosine, in *The Miser*.

Giving a bit of Birmingham back to itself

In the old theatre David Turner's *Quick, Quick, Slow* had been the first whole-hearted attempt to stage drama inspired by life in Birmingham. In the new theatre it seemed crucially important to inculcate a sense of local ownership. In February 1973 the home production team of Simpson, Honer and Durrant worked on *Up Spaghetti Junction*. Visually and conceptually *Spaghetti* was an affectionate send-up of Birmingham's seemingly endless desire to remake itself. One of Jon Raven's songs had the refrain 'Tear it down and build another one in its place'. The permanent set was a framework of scaffolding around a new concrete building linked to the remains of a now rejected red-brick house. Ladders and staircases gave the impression of flyovers and subways.

One sketch had Varna Road prostitutes lamenting the demolition of their favourite stamping ground. Naturally as this was a show about the workshop of Britain there was no attempt to resist yet more real technology. An antique Austin 7 was brought on as well as a whole fleet of bicycles including a penny farthing. The local references were made clearer by the use of Paul Hill's back-projections and actors playing Brummie workmen with John Baddeley as principal native dogsbody and warmer-upper. There was formal history, including the Royalist attempt to burn out the parliamentarian Brummies during the Civil War, and the eighteenth-century luminaries Watt, Bolton and Murdoch. But there were also excursions into popular history like the auctioning for one shilling of a woman called Mary Whitehouse by her husband in 1773. Queen Victoria played by David King came to life from her pedestal in Victoria Square. Blacker and politically sharper, an extended sketch by David Edgar on the Chamberlain dynasty culminated in four crates forming the plane in which Neville Chamberlain flew to Munich.

On the whole the four writers avoided sentiment. In the midst of the ebullient singing and dancing by the twenty-strong company there were harsher notes of industrial unrest, narrow-mindedness and racism. There were however, complaints about a rather ill-informed account of the local Asian communities. The appearance of the black actor, the Nigerian Olu Jacobs, in a Rep company as a token gesture towards Brum's burgeoning racial diversity marked only the second appearance (Zia Mohyeddin was the first) of a non-white actor in a Rep company. Cast later in the season as a black character in *The Hostage*, his casting as the servant Hake in *The Miser* adaptation was a miniscule step towards the much more significant racial strategies adopted in later years.

The Brum followed on with a similar experiment in May. Malcolm Totten and Jon Raven joined forces again on *The Nail Makers*, a folk-musical documentary based on the exploitation endured by mid-nineteenth-century manual nail makers in the Black Country. Much of its success derived from the substantial audiences built up for Roger Lancaster's late-night folk concerts. Authentic urban folk songs from the period made up about half the twenty songs in the show while Raven 'reconstructed' the others. Diana Greenwood's set not only included a nail-making forge, but the Brum was turned into a saloon bar where wine and beer could be bought. Staging the production club-style encouraged the audience to sit at tables, relax, smoke and drink. Older playgoers came in to watch actors recreate the harsh working conditions as well as the background of beer-swilling, cock-fighting, badger-baiting and bare-fist fighting. Terry Molloy played the Tipton Slasher based on a real-life prize fighter who lost all his possessions in his last fight. The plot focused on one nail-making family, the Blys and their subjugation to the unscrupulous 'fogger' or nail dealer played by Robert O'Mahoney. Jenny Cryst was praised for her performance as the crushed, coarsened mother Lucy Bly

Almost exactly a year later in May 1974 *The Canal Show* was an attempt to repeat the success of giving a bit of Birmingham back to itself, as Honer put it. Focusing on the waterways which had provided thousands with work in the late nineteenth century, Jon Raven again unearthed about twenty period folk songs as well as writing a select few himself. Malcolm Totten had been killed in a tragic accident and so *Crossroads* writer Mike Jackson was responsible for the script which delved into events and developments in Birmingham history to provide a context for the canal story. The critical response, however, was disappointing. Gareth Lloyd Evans was equivocal about a 'chummy amateur rapport' with the audience (*G*, 9.5.74) while David Isaacs damned a 'tepid script' and 'limp music' (*CT*, 15.5.74)

Worse was to come in the autumn when Honer moved onto the main stage to direct *The Thingummybob That's Going to Win the War*. Scripted by Stephen Fagan and based on recollections of Birmingham during the Second World War it was clearly not suited to the big stage and drew poor audiences. The pub bombings which brought the conflict in Northern Ireland right into the heart of the city on 21 November, half-way through the run, would have taken away any local appetite for memories of past wars, and kept citizens away from Broad Street. The larger lesson to be learnt was that the Brum tended to be viewed as a completely different organism to the main auditorium. Small-scale success could not necessarily be replicated as the same but bigger. Also as successive directorates were to discover, local appeal was very difficult to predict. *Up Spaghetti* had been sympathetically reviewed, but Birmingham audiences could hardly be described as wildly enthusiastic. In general audience loyalty was proving difficult to maintain. By the summer of 1973 the overall percentage of attendance had slipped to 41.1% of capacity.

In January 1973, the theatre critic of the *Birmingham Post*, Anthony Everitt interviewed Michael Simpson. Pressures were beginning to build and Simpson was now more guardedly optimistic. He admitted both to the size of the task facing him and to planning and communication problems in maintaining the bustling level of activity. Everitt (who eventually became Secretary General of the Arts Council) remarked on the uniform competence of what he called 'good, solid, respectable theatre', but 'I, for one, am waiting for something more than these unexceptional but unexciting virtues. The Rep has not yet swept us off our feet, and it is high time it did. With a bit of luck, it looks as if this time is approaching' (10.1.73) Unluckily, however, by the time *Up Spaghetti* finished its run at the end of March it was clear that the theatre was heading for a deficit of £50,000.

The City Intervenes

Faced with a request for an increase in grants from £88,000 to £135,000 from the Arts Council, and from the City Council of £44,000 to £65,000, the City Council Labour Leader, Councillor Stanley Yapp announced that no funds would be forthcoming unless the Board of Directors was restructured. In particular it was objected that five members out of ten, including Sir Robert Aitken and the Board secretary were all over 70 and thus too old. The system of apparent appointments for life was to be abandoned. Six directors: Aitken, Mayers, J.E. Bywater, the Council representatives Fred Hall, John Lewis and Harry Watton submitted their resignations immediately. Three other local politicians Marjorie Brown, Dick Knowles and Jim Sweeney joined Margaret Cooke to make up the four Council representatives. Richard O'Brien, a company director was also invited to join. When later in the year Bob Walker and Derek Salberg stepped down, David Rose, head of BBC Television regional drama, and John Bettinson, a local solicitor became new directors. Jack Mayers, however, continued as secretary until John Bettinson took over the role in July 1976 and even then Mayers remained on the Board until 1985. Aitken did not retire until April 1974 when Marjorie Brown succeeded him as Chairman.

Mrs Brown became Birmingham's first woman Lord Mayor in 1973. Physically slight and self-effacing, she was very different to the austere, patrician Aitken who was capable of making this ordinary-seeming woman feel socially insecure. But in her own way she was clearly quite formidable. Mark Everett, who a decade later became General Manager, described her as a tough, bright little woman. Beginning her working life as a copy typist, she became welfare manager at GKN in Smethwick. She had been a Labour Councillor since 1954; sat on numerous committees and ultimately created the Birmingham Convention and Visitor Bureau.

Inevitably there were worries about future political implications although Mrs Brown was expected, and indeed proved to be, both friendly and impartial. She was known to love the theatre. In late 1972 the Board had debated City requests for increased representation. The suggestion at that time was to even out the party political balance and raise the the number of councillors to six, a prospect which Aitken regarded with deep suspicion. Local government reorganisation in 1974 meant that the idea was never followed through but clearly the City felt the need to exercise more influence on this money-draining organism.

The realisation was beginning to dawn not just in Birmingham but across the country that the kind of prestige cultural project which civic theatres embodied, and which the Arts Council had encouraged, was going to require massive financial support. And the Rep was bigger than most. Furthermore in radical artistic quarters the pendulum was beginning to swing against the whole notion of building-based, mainstream theatre. This was the decade of alternative theatre, street theatre, community theatre, small-is-cheap-and-therefore-accessible theatre. The continuing success of the Brum Studio was part of this phenomenon. It played steadily to over 70% of capacity but that capacity was so small compared to the overall size of the plant that the revenue was negligible. To balance the books, the main auditorium had to be filled and the Birmingham audiences were unpredictable. There was no 'right to fail'. An unsatisfactory production could repel would-be patrons for months if not years. For Marjorie Brown it was important that she should be able to fight the Rep's corner in the very heart of civic power but given the prevailing economic climate it is hard to see how the problems of management could ever be satisfactorily controlled.

A Bleak Outlook

A review of *Man and Superman* in February 1972 describes driving through the cold, dark streets of Birmingham in the middle of a power cut. These were the years of generalised crisis: growing unemployment, soaring inflation and a constant succession of damaging strikes. Birmingham's car industry was badly affected. One of the jokes in *Up Spaghetti Junction* consisted of 'The daffodils are out…Will that affect us?' The cost of basic raw materials had begun a steady rise even before the 1973 oil crisis sent prices spiralling out of control towards the 1974 miners' strike and the three-day week. At the Rep it was virtually impossible to reduce the ongoing expense of the lavish front-of-house construction, and difficult to maintain standards of set building when timber and canvas had doubled in price. Wages for backstage labour had increased between 80 and 100% in two years.

Natural redundancies were not filled which meant increasing pressure and a feeling of exploitation for existing staff. Towards the end of Michael Simpson's tenure a Staff Association was set up, not in opposition to management, but to ensure fair practice. The family of Station Street was now into the industrial relations of the factory. By the time Simpson resigned, inflexible overheads amounted to two thirds of its budget. Brigg records that the estimates for March 1974 until March 1975 show that over £237,000 of the theatre's operating budget went on fixed expenditures. During 1974 Equity fought for, and ultimately achieved, a minimum weekly wage for actors of £30. Brigg worked out an average cost for each of twenty full productions (which included the Studio) of £5,945. This covered artists' salaries, costumes and sets over a three week or longer run and three weeks of rehearsal. Any attempt to enhance performance standards with longer rehearsals was completely impractical.

It is against this background that Simpson's strategies in his remaining two years must be viewed. At the end of June 1973 the theatre closed and remained dark for thirteen weeks apart from performances by the Birmingham Youth Theatre. During this time the catering contract with Ansells was ended by mutual agreement and Courages took over but with little more success. When the new season opened in mid-September with *Guys and Dolls*, repertoire playing had been dropped in favour of three to four week runs. Turn rounds which had taken an hour in the old theatre now took half a day and required separate crews for each show. The Studio and Main House companies amalgamated and touring was abandoned.

A Company With Guts

Simpson, however, continued to journey hopefully. Laurence Olivier, no less, had been thwarted in his cherished ambition to stage *Guys and Dolls* by the National Theatre Board and in 1986 when the National finally did get round to presenting the musical it was conveniently forgotten that the Rep led by Michael Simpson had pre-empted them. In the event the Rep production was a delight— a classic piece of music theatre on a stage more than equal to its scale. Durrant designed a set described by Lloyd Evans as a 'light-hearted pastel-coloured impression of Times Square which looks as if it is made of giant-sized adhesive price tags' (*G*, 28.3.73). Rosemary Leach as Miss Adelaide, the cold-prone, would-be bride of fourteen years was the hit of the production. Lloyd Evans purred with pleasure at her expressive face and dextrous combination of intuition and technique. David Isaacs decided that she was capable of playing King Lear (*CT*, 28.9.73).

Simpson followed Damon Runyon and Frank Loesser with Thomas Middleton and William Rowley's rarely performed Jacobean play *The Changeling*. Ballet star Wayne Sleep choreographed the formal movements of the central characters through sexual power games, madness and murder on Durrant's geometric black and white set harshly lit by the lighting designer David Hersey. Jo Maxwell-Muller and Ian Hogg played Beatrice-Joanna and De Flores, noblewoman and servant lethally bound by murder and sex. Anthony Everitt dubbed them 'a satanic Romeo and Juliet' (*BP*, 18.10.73). While *The Changeling* was in performance Hogg rehearsed another unlikely, but infinitely more sympathetic partnership playing Will Mossop to Jane Freeman's Maggie Hobson in the much-loved (and well attended) *Hobson's Choice*. Hogg stayed with the company to play the hero-king in *Henry V* which together with *The Changeling* was taken on tour to Hong Kong. While they were away Rosemary Leach fulfilled a long-held ambition to play Hedda Gabler in a production by Terence Lodge which embarrassingly was neither a success critically nor with audiences.

With growing deficit unease, plans for ambitious excursions into the European repertoire had to be modified. Roger Planchon's *Blues, Whites and Reds* was put off until the autumn and Shaw's *You Never Can Tell* moved back to replace it in

April. Brecht's *The Caucasian Chalk Circle* in a version by Steve Gooch and directed by Howard Davies, survived the re-programming, however. Updated with designs by Chris Dyer to a grim, futuristic urban environment, again an epic play suited an epic stage. Michael Coveney then critic of the *Financial Times* praised carefully-controlled performances where comedy became an analytic tool rather than an excuse for self-indulgence (20.5.74). Steven Moore played Azdak with Jenny Stoller as Grusha and Cheryl Campbell as the ruler's wife fighting over the contested baby.

When the Rep season ended with Colin Welland's *Say Goodnight to Grandma* the overall audience average was a modestly improved 53%. Ironically there was a full house in July for the opening performance of Wedekind's exploration of adolescent sexuality *Spring Awakening* which the National Theatre brought to the Rep. There were some Rep Board members who would have preferred a less controversial play for the National's first visit. There was a certain defiance about Simpson's decision to mount largely new work for what in the event proved to be his final year at the Rep. Even *How the Other Half Loves* which opened in mid-September was the Rep's first encounter with the rapidly-rising Alan Ayckbourn. *Thingummybob* was of course brand new. For Christmas Keith Dewhurst wrote *The Magic Island,* a reworking of the Arthurian legend. This was followed by *Trinity Tales*, a new version of Chaucer's *The Canterbury Tales* by Alan Plater updated to feature a coach-load of rugby supporters on their way to London. Peter Dews was scheduled to direct both parts of Shakespeare's *Henry IV,* two epic political plays to match the equally epic political sweep of *Destiny*, a new play by David Edgar.

Roger Planchon's *Blues Whites and Reds*, however, which received its British première in October 1974 was arguably Simpson's boldest initiative. Just as Britain had been formally committed to the European Common Market, so Simpson brought Europe into the heart of Birmingham with a play which was a product of the Theatre de la Cité which lay on the outskirts of Lyon, Birmingham's twin city in France. Indeed Simpson could be seen to be allying himself with Planchon's defiant stance as a regional director. The play is about the 1789 French Revolution, the defining moment in French history, but viewed from the perspective of a group of free-thinking provincial aristocrats. John Burgess, who co-directed, provided the translation. Carl Davis wrote the music. The cynical message conveyed in a series of short, vivid tableau is that Utopian ideals are always compromised. Michael Billington pointed out that 'in the present nerve-shattered condition of regional theatre, it is good to find a company with the guts to tackle something big, foreign and difficult' (*G*, 11.10.73)

For once it was agreed that the Rep had found a play big enough to fill the stage with thirty four scenes and a plot spanning eleven years up until 1880. There were 200 costume changes alone. Pamela Howard's designs were in sharp contrast to the Victorian-gothic box set and Laura Ashley prints she provided for Simpson's 1972 *Dandy Dick*. All summer the Rep's technical team worked on the stage floor made up of manually-cast concrete slabs which thrust out into the audience to ground-floor level at row D. For scenes which Planchon calls 'popular prints': interludes of carnival effigies of the People's Revolution, the workers, disillusioned 'sans-culottes', came surging up steps from the red-lined pit carrying massive twelve-foot high puppets made up from broom handles, sheets and string.

The whole enterprise received considerable pre-show publicity, but yet again the critical response was very mixed. Planchon's play lacked, it was suggested, the clarity and force of Ariane Mnouchkine's *1798*, and it was agreed that in the early performances at least, Simpson's production needed more pace. But actors Isla Blair, John Rollason and Cheryl Campbell were praised and Billington concluded 'Neither play nor production are perfect; but to anyone who believes as I do, that theatre and politics are finally indivisible, the evening will come as a great lift to the spirits'.

Edgar, the Rep and Destiny

Early in 1974 David Edgar was proposed as the Rep's resident playwright financed by Thames Television. Despite his impeccable family connections, the evidence thus far of a strongly-held prediliction for radical politics expressed through radical drama, meant that his appointment was not greeted with unreserved delight by the Board. Indeed the Rep's old friend Charles Collet had raised objections in the local press which generated an amusing public exchange of letters as Edgar found himself defending his professional credibility. The plan was for Edgar to produce two plays: one for the Brum and the other for the main stage. Honer staged the Studio play *Oh Fair Jerusalem* in May 1975. *Destiny* should have been staged at pretty much the same time on the big stage.

Through a double perspective on the fourteenth-century Black Death and the twentieth-century plague of war post-Hiroshima, *Oh Fair Jerusalem* explores the evil which always threatens human existence. The audience became a congregation lining a dimly-lit church nave as they sat on either side of Chris Dyer's set. Only in the second act is it revealed that the drama of medieval characters is in fact a play in rehearsal in 1948 not 1348. The old plague has been cured; the new plague awaits cure. Between them Edgar and Honer created a passionate, allusive textually rich experience which to this day Honer regards as a high point in his work in Birmingham. Some reviews suggested the need for judicious pruning, but Harold Hobson devoted several column inches of his *Sunday Times* review (25.5.75) to an account of the narrative. The discovery of the plague on a girl tumbler's legs in the play within the play and the confrontation between a stalwart, blazered modern actor (David Quilter) and his director/playwright (Terence Davies) were the episodes most singled out for praise. Robert O'Mahoney's delivery of a tirade against nuclear weapons made a powerful impact.

Destiny, however, had already fallen victim to the same crisis of confidence which ejected Simpson from the theatre. *Destiny* had in fact been commissioned and then rejected by the Nottingham Playhouse. Given that the play was about racial issues and the potential rise of fascism in the West Midlands and was critical of both sides of the political divide, Rep Board members were already unhappy about a commitment to stage it. The usual uneven pattern of audience figures served as an entirely reasonable justification for removing it from Simpson's programme. Apart from the debacle of *Thingummybob* the Ayckbourn had played to 55% while the Planchon saw audiences dipping to 45.2%. After Christmas the rumbustuous humour of *Trinity Tales,* with actors like Colin Farrell and Bill Maynard in the cast, suddenly hit the jackpot at over 71% and was brought back for a second run in April/May. But the success came too late for Simpson. Even as *The Magic Island* with Bob Peck as Merlin and music by the felicitously-named Hedgehog Pie was playing to substantial audiences, the Board decided not to renew his contract.

By the New Year it became imperative to lop £30,000 off an anticipated expenditure of £350,000. On 12 January 1975, the *Sunday Mercury* carried an interview with Simpson where he outlined the need to go back to 'a more primitive kind of theatre'. Economies ranged from the more austere set for *Magic Island*, 'bare walls and empty spaces' and a reduced acting strength to only turning on the theatre's heating system after the staff arrived for work . Dews would now only direct two small-cast plays *Equus* and *Arms and the Man* instead of *Henry IV*. Even at the Board meeting of 14 January when his resignation was confirmed, Simpson tried to hang on to *Destiny* but it was deemed 'not acceptable'. The following year the RSC staged the play and launched Edgar as a major dramatist. The Rep did *The Importance of Being Earnest* instead.

Edgar retaliated with an article in the May edition of *Plays and Players* which stoutly defended Simpson's idealism and interrogated the 'hard-headed' realism of the Board. He began with the extraordinary statement (in the teeth of the continuing relentless criticism of the Rep's main stage) that 'the Birmingham Repertory Theatre is one of the most exciting large theatre spaces in England'. The theatre's great strength, he argued, lay in its inflexibility: in 'what it cannot do'. The middle-class, middle-brow constituency could not fill the theatre; thrillers and domestic comedy were dwarfed and big musicals were too expensive. Thus the only option was to find 'new, large-scale forms for a new, non-middle-class audience'. He pointed out that the so-called safe plays brought in to replace the original season had done no better at the box office. Indeed *The Importance* played to 47.1%.

In Limbo

This Board was in no mood for radicalism. The siege mentality which prevailed can only have been exacerbated by a blackly funny account of the Carvery in the restaurant which the food critic Derek Cooper wrote for the *Catering Times* in February 1975. The restaurant was empty. The chef had gone home, the assistant manager was in charge of the bar and the carver, Cooper discovered, was untrained. 'Was he used to having his food rejected? Such indifference in the face of whole-dissatisfaction revealed either a monumental degree of resignation or total indifference'.

John Greenwood's contract was extended and, while a new Artistic Director was sought, planned policy in a caretaker capacity. The autumn programme was typical with *A Flea in Her Ear* and *Move Over Mrs Markham* programmed with *As You Like It*. As if to reinforce Edgar's argument, neither of the farces reached more than 44%. At this crucial point in the theatre's history there was no firm artistic leadership and for a year the Rep simply drifted. By May 1975 it was known that the new artistic director would be Clive Perry, then Director of Theatres in Edinburgh, but the formal announcement of the appointment was delayed until November and even then Perry did not begin work in Birmingham until July 1976.

Honer continued to direct the Brum until the spring of 1976 when he left to go to the Chester Gateway Theatre as artistic director. Plays performed by the Company included David Rudkin's *Ashes* and David Hare's *Knuckle*. There was also one more Honer/Lancaster collaboration on a Barney play *Barney Joins the Fire Brigade*. In February 1976 Honer and Edgar joined forces for the last time at the Rep. *Events Following the Closure of a Motor Cycle Factory* was a musical documentary, in Living Newspaper mode, about the catastrophic effects in human terms of subjecting the regional network of old-established motor-cycle factories to high-powered profit and expansion-hungry managerial practices. Edgar threaded his way through a complex history of mergers, closures and redundancies culminating in a workforce sit-in at a factory in Wolverhampton which was on-going as the play was being written. The show did well in the Brum with critics dividing on expected political lines, but there was relatively little interest in the tour. An embarrassing muddle over advanced publicity meant that a special performance for Meriden factory workers had to be cancelled.

There would be no more touring for eight years and when Honer left, much of that anarchic, agit-prop quality went with him. But the Studio was established ready for a new era. In November 1975 Perry's stated aim, just as it had been for his predecessors, was to maintain a core permanent company of actors augmented by guest artists who would serve both the Main House and the Studio. Again the prestige of the old theatre was invoked. A permanent company would 'create audience interest' and 'build new reputations—as happened with all the great names of the past at the Old Rep' (*BP*, 11.11.75). But in many respects

Perry would come to represent a complete break with the past and unlike his predecessors he survived leaving the theatre eleven years later on his own terms. In view of subsequent events, it was characteristic that he should both take six months to make up his mind to accept the job and that he should begin in his own good time.

1 Peter Brigg, 'The New Birmingham Repertory Theatre: A Case Study in Marketing', *Educational Theatre Journal*, 29, no. 1 (March 1977), pp.95-107

7. The Subsidised Impresario: Clive Perry

Clive Perry

The Wizard of Oz, the first show Clive Perry directed on the Rep stage, could be seen as emblematic of the changing cultural and economic climate which he felt the need to address. Describing himself as 'a subsidised impresario' he made it clear when he arrived that he was committed to American-style hard-sell techniques. 'It's time', he declared, 'we treated our business as a business and not as an artistic industry…the cry in the theatre is that we can never be vulgar. But I see no reason why we shouldn't be vulgar if we get bigger box office sales that way' (*SM*, 18.7.76)

It must have been music to the Board's collective ears. Perry had an impressive record in building-based theatre management. After National Service and Cambridge, he had gone to the old Derby Playhouse as an ATV trainee, worked in Farnham and then became director of the Phoenix Theatre in Leicester. He was shortlisted for the Rep directorship in 1965, but in the event became director of the Edinburgh Royal Lyceum in 1966. After a spell working for the Arts Council, he then returned to Edinburgh to administer both the two main theatres, the Lyceum and the King's and advise on the Churchill Theatre. He was 38 at the time of his Rep appointment and, educated at Wolverhampton Grammar School, he even had acceptable local connections. It seems that Jack Mayer effectively head-hunted him and arranged secure contractual terms.

Perry did not present himself as an artistically ambitious director in his own right. He was, as it were, the safe pair of hands whose strategy was to direct only a few productions himself while assembling a small group of directors—one or two on a more or less permanent basis. Both Peter Farago who quickly joined him as Associate Director in the autumn of 1976 and Bill Pryde, who became Director of the Rep Studio in September 1977, had worked with him in Edinburgh. Farago had left his native Hungary after the 1956 uprising and read Philosophy and Psychology at Edinburgh University. His first professional work was at the Lyceum followed by directorial experience in theatres like the Chester Gateway. He too had worked for the Arts Council spending two years as Assistant Drama Director. Pryde was born in Scotland and cut his directorial teeth in student productions at York University. The work which had impressed Clive Perry included productions at the radical Traverse Theatre in Edinburgh.

Mixed with his entrepreneurial instincts was a genuine capacity for encouraging creativity and radical experiment in others. Richard Eyre who worked with Perry at the Leicester Phoenix warmly acknowledged him as a patron:

> **He was a short, shy man, who hid his feelings behind**
> **a closely preserved cladding of diffidence and sometimes**
> **spiky defensiveness which concealed an essentially kindly,**
> **if solitary soul. His generosity to me was unstinting, and**
> **his support unfailing; without his faith in me I would never**
> **have become a director.**[1]

Perry promised, moreover, that the Rep's essentially literary artistic responsibility would not be compromised and in that respect his opening gambit was very promising. The first two shows of the 1976 autumn season, Shakespeare's *Measure for Measure* coupled with Ben Jonson's *The Devil is an Ass*, both directed by Stuart Burge, were presented initially at the Edinburgh Festival. before opening at the Rep in October. In November, Peter Farago directed a 1901 dramatisation of *Sherlock Holmes* by William Gillette which played in repertoire with Rhys McConnochie's production of Orton's *Loot*.

While there was evidently no permanent acting ensemble, several actors from the Festival productions stayed on in Birmingham for a while. Alan Rickman and David Suchet formed a potentially dynamic partnership as Holmes and Moriarty. Rickman had played Wittipol and Friar Peter in *The Devil* and *Measure*, while Suchet had the plum role of Lucio in *Measure*. In the Studio Farago premièred *Pythagoras*, a play by Dannie Abse which saw Roger Sloman (Pompey Bum and Lawyer Eitherside in *Measure* and *Devil*) cast as a former stage illusionist confined to a mental hospital. Also in the Studio John Dove directed Cheryl Campbell as Theckla in *Schippel*, a send-up of the pre-first world war German middle class by Carl Sternheim.

At Christmas the theatre was packed for *The Wizard of Oz* which was staged with designs by Finlay James and featured the comedian Norman Vaughan as the Scarecrow. Bill Pryde directed the fifth Honer/Lancaster children's Studio show *The Magical Legend*. Lancaster who was now Associate to John Greenwood continued to programme in the Sunday concerts. In the Brum in March Farago elicited a mesmerising solo performance from his long-time collaborator David Suchet in *Iniquity*, Farago's dramatisation of Tolstoy's novella *The Kreutzer Sonata*. As the murderer Pozdnyshev explaining on a train journey why he killed his wife, Suchet held his audience spell-bound for some 100 minutes seated in a red-plush Victorian chair and hardly moving. The only other furniture was a samovar bubbling at exactly the right moments for dramatic effect. Not only was the production a success in Birmingham, it then went on to have a three-year life playing in America and Israel, at the Royal Court in London and then as a radio adaptation where it won Suchet a Pye award for best actor in 1979.

No Confidence

That success, however, took place within a wider context of crisis. Hopes of a bright new dawn were dashed in early 1977 when it became clear that the theatre was heading for an accumulated deficit of £90,000. At the Board meeting on 17 January Clive Perry was ordered to supply a detailed explanation of the reasons for the crisis and a 'firm and realistic projection' of the theatre's revenue up until the end of the financial year. Budgetary control had gone completely haywire. In particular the Edinburgh budget had been far too vague for a project which had proved predictably costly. It emerged that the stage management team had made sometimes daily journeys between Birmingham and Edinburgh for supplies which should have been found in Edinburgh. In general petty cash for ad hoc expenses was distributed too freely.

Marjorie Brown and Ian King (the financial advisor to the Board) were despatched to London to seek rescue from the Arts Council, and pleas for help were made to the City. Steps were taken to reduce costs on the projected Ayckbourn trilogy *The Norman Conquests* which included buying sets from the Globe Theatre in London. Apart from a week's revival of the Edinburgh plays in mid-May there were to be no more in-house productions until mid-September. The Brum Studio was to close down, indefinitely, until additional finance could be found. Inevitably there were staff redundancies and a larger number were put on season-to season contracts. In April, Roger Lancaster was a casualty of the crisis.

As they were effectively bound to do, the Arts Council and the City Council came to the rescue to help clear the deficit. Perry's other strategy to avoid complete closure was to bring in outside productions. The first venture was in fact a prestigious swop. When the National Theatre Company came in early May with the premiere of Robert Bolt's *State of Revolution*, the Edinburgh plays went to the

South Bank: the first regional theatre company to perform at the National. What followed was more controversial as the Rep went into partnership with the commercial producer Duncan C. Weldon and Triumph Theatre Productions. In June the West End doyen Frith Banbury directed Kenneth More and Patricia Routledge in Frederick Lonsdale's *On Approval* which then transferred to the Vaudeville Theatre in London. Perry's productions of Rattigan's *The Deep Blue Sea* with Honor Blackman and *A Perfect Gentleman* by Herbert Appleman, which starred Wilfred Hyde White, were both rehearsed simultaneously in London. On 22 July, Anthony Everitt trumpeted in the *Birmingham Post* the sensational news that the Staff Association had passed a unanimous vote of no confidence in the Artistic Director. Perry was in London about to give a radio interview for *Woman's Hour* when the news was brought to him.

Interviewed nearly twenty years later in 1993, and by then the immensely successful director of the Pitlochry Festival Theatre, Clive Perry claimed not to know why the Rep staff should have made such an unprecedented move. Certainly the upheavals of the early months of 1977 had taken their toll. In addition to the generalised financial crisis, there were the personal difficulties of staff attempting to cope on relatively low salaries at a time when inflation was a continuing problem. Indeed in June during the run of *On Approval* there had been an overtime ban in pursuit of higher pay and threats to more formally unionise the theatre. But the dissatisfaction went far deeper and was to do with the more fundamental issue of what kind of theatre the Rep might become.

Some important staff members, especially those who had worked at the Old Rep left of their own accord. Alex Hamilton had in fact gone the previous autumn angered by what he saw as a waste of talent and facilities. 'The Rep has lost touch with its roots' (*BP*, 22.7.77), he declared. Eric Pressley, head of electrics for a decade, felt as though the place was running down and resigned. The publicity manager Gillian Ingham, also disillusioned, left for a job with the RSC. Roger Lancaster explained his worries that the loss of the folk and other music concerts and, more importantly, the demise of the work for young people, was serious evidence that the theatre's responsibility to serve the wider community in Birmingham was not being fulfilled.

The staff also needed reassurance that their director's metropolitan activities with star actors was not profiting him personally. It was at this point that the *Post* alleged that Perry had a ten-year contract. Perry later insisted that it had simply been decided to let the initial contract roll on for a further three years. However Jack Mayer's statement made it clear that Perry had been in a strong position when recruited. It had been necessary to offer him security.

What was obvious was the complete breakdown in communication. In the course of the Board meeting on 12 September, John Greenwood outlined problems which ranged from further complaints about inadequate financial predictions and controls, together with over-spending on repairs and renovations, to deep dissatisfaction with co-productions and the relationship with Triumph. There was now, he claimed, 'grave difficulty' in getting people to work with the Director. Peter Farago spoke of a feeling of decisions 'dropping down on the staff from on high' and that Perry was a rather shy man who found communication difficult. At the end of the meeting Perry and Greenwood agreed to work together for the good of the theatre.

It was also alleged in the press, however, that the lack of communication extended to the majority of the Board members for whom the *Post* article was their first knowledge of the crisis. Even more embarrassing was the newspaper claim in December that Board members had not been apprised of the contents of a report prepared and given in August to Marjorie Brown by Richard Coverley and John McClymont, two post-graduate students from City University. The students, who were in fact a chartered accountant and a Canadian theatre manager, had investigated Rep policies on the suggestion of the Arts Council. The report leaked to the press emphasised the overall communication problems in the Rep; criticised some accounting practices and strongly endorsed Lancaster's suggestion that responsibilities to the wider community and to young people had been abrogated. A lively marketing policy was needed to encourage new audiences, while it was essential that a new accounting system should provide up-to-date accurate and regular financial information and budget comparisons. It was further suggested that the membership of the Board itself needed to be better balanced in terms of artistic knowledge.

Some remedial action had already been taken. Dick King, who came from the local firm Neville Industrial Securities had been appointed as Financial Administrator, and specific issues of finance, artistic policy and general purposes were now to be addressed in three separate Board sub-committees. There had been attempts to increase the artistic credentials of the Board. In 1976 Judith McKay, an American graduate in theatre arts with experience as a professional actress, had joined, and indeed would remain on the Board for nearly twenty years. Derek Salberg, now retired from managing the Alexandra Theatre, rejoined in August 1977. J.T.B. Spenser, professor of English at Birmingham University, briefly served after March 1977, but died a year later.

How to Succeed in Business

While attempts to improve the company infrastructure continued, and this included (within the constraints of government wages policy) raising the salaries of staff, the fundamental problem of attracting audiences and maintaining artistic credibility became even more acute. Questions of economic viability homed in on very basic issues like narrowing the differentials between the top and bottom ticket prices in the theatre, thus risking the loss of the less affluent sector in the audience. Could Friday night seat prices be raised to Saturday night rates without encountering stiff resistance? It seemed not. Was it in fact cheaper, as Clive Perry warned the Board in November 1977, to keep the theatre dark between May and September 1978, than to stage a popular play like *Hay Fever* to entice audiences. For Perry at this juncture the solution seemed to lie in bringing in touring productions during the problematic summer months. This of course threatened both the theatre's reputation as a major producing house and alienation of the permanent staff.

If the money-draining, but artistically successful, Studio Theatre was closed, innovation would be sacrificed and the Arts Council would object. Indeed both Arts Council and City Council needed reassurance and it was difficult for the theatre to plan a programme of work when grant levels remained uncertain. When Perry came up with a 'safe' season of plays then the absence of new work was regretted even by members of the Board. In early 1978 Perry canvassed the idea of converting the big main stage to create a medium-sized theatre and even (when it was pointed out that this would mean a damaging period of closure) the ultimate irony of utilising the Old Rep for more adventurous medium-scale work. It was impossible, he stated, to fulfil the role of the Rep, without staging contemporary and new writing.

By dint of keeping their collective nerve, however, the company and its director were surviving. The Studio had reopened in September 1977 (the Brum sobriquet was dropped) with Bill Pryde presenting a strong programme of both home-grown and new work. His opening production was the première of *The Seed* by Derek Nicholls and Ray Speakman which was effectively the theatre's first attempt to address the issues of a multiracial community. Inevitably the main stage programme for the year following October 1977, prioritised audience-pulling plays: *Pygmalion*, more Ayckbourn in *Absurd Person Singular*, *A Christmas Carol* (which did very well with local comedian Bob Grant as Scrooge) and after Christmas *Othello* which also did exceptionally well, and, indeed, *Hayfever*. Arguably the most heavyweight play, Brecht's *Mother Courage* which Farago directed, had the attraction of Peggy Mount in the central role and in audience percentage terms did pretty much the same steady business as *Pygmalion*. In general the storm clouds began to lift. The average attendance for the Spring season was a healthy 76%. Assurances made in May that the City's grant would rise to £196,500 matching a similar increase from the Arts Council to £240,000 enabled two more shows on the main stage. May and June saw Pryde's production of Goldoni's rarely-staged *Servant of Two Masters* and *Rosencrantz and Guildenstern are Dead* which Farago directed.

The management was also advancing other financial strategies. In April the Rep announced its own lottery scheme, which replicated a larger City Council venture. The aim was to boost revenue by some £4,000 at each fortnightly draw in order to meet the expense of replacing worn-out equipment such as the computerised lighting board and the front curtain lifting machinery. The stage floor needed to be rebuilt and it was also hoped to install an orchestra lift, as well as much-needed sound-proofing between the Studio and the main auditorium. In June Perry and the Rep's marketing manager Geoff Parker presided over the launch of the first subscription scheme to be introduced by a professional producing theatre. It was a project which had been close to Perry's heart since his appointment. He and the Board had been advised by the American theatre marketing expert Danny Newman, and the Arts Council had contributed a kick-start grant of £10,000. A subscription for tickets for eight shows at £6.70 each (a saving of 40%) enabled patrons to reserve the same seat in the theatre; have priority booking for extra events and have the luxury of their own subscribers' bar. The benefit for the theatre of course was an immediate influx of money into the Box Office and, it was hoped, a sense of loyalty and commitment to the Rep.

The scheme was an instant success. By the end of July not only had over 3000 subscriptions been sold, but it was also revealed that overall the season had grossed £271,520—a rise of 35.5% on the previous year. The theatre was in the black with a surplus of £56,541. £19,000 could go towards renovation expenses; the Arts Council £20,000 guarantee against loss could be refused, and £12,606 could be carried forward into the next season. The autumn of 1978 saw two major coups: the British première of Arnold Wesker's *The Merchant* on the main stage, and the world première of David Edgar's *Mary Barnes* in the Studio both directed by Farago. In November Perry staged a major revival of *Kiss Me Kate* which starred Patricia Morison who had played Kate in the original Broadway production. The Christmas show was a rhyming couplet reworking by Alan Brown of an 1894 pantomime of *Babes in the Wood* which exploited the conventions of the golden age of panto. Geoffrey Scott who was by now resident designer created a charming series of sets coloured like a child's pop-up book. There was a Harlequinade, a Fairy Queen, a comic dog, a ballet for antique bicycles and a nursery dream in which toys came to life. A song-sheet appeared about every five minutes with a host of well-loved music-hall songs.

After a year in which the home directorial team worked solidly on the main stage shows, 1979 saw more links with the wider world. There were guest directors. Gareth Morgan directed *Saint Joan* while Frank Dunlop directed the classic Ben Travers farce *Rookery Nook*. Keith Hack brought Janet Suzman to the Rep for the first time to play the title role in his production of Webster's *The Duchess of Malfi*. Only then did the theatre renew the partnership with Triumph Theatre Productions. To celebrate the centenary of Barry Jackson's birth and revive the time-honoured relationship with the Malvern Festival which Jackson founded in 1929, Shaw's *Misalliance* directed by Perry and Eliot's *The Elder Statesman* directed by Pryde were presented at Malvern and the Rep before going on tour.

84

Paul Rogers who had played Shakespeare's Shylock earlier in the year returned to the role of the dying elder statesman Lord Claverdon which he had created in 1958. His wife Rosalind Boxall who had been a leading member of the Rep company in the early 1950s, played his former lover Maisie Carghill.

Perry's programming policy for the main stage was based on a conviction that it was vital to hold onto the middle-class conservative audience—Birmingham's 'worthy burghers' as he put it. They could be relied on to attend well-loved classics like *She Stoops to Conquer*, *The Beggar's Opera*, *School for Scandal*, and *The Importance of Being Earnest*. Shakespeare, who also brought in school parties of course, made an annual appearance. Pryde's production of *The Merchant of Venice* was staged a few months after *The Merchant* which gave an opportunity to compare the original with Wesker's reworking. *King Lear* in March 1980 which Pryde also directed featured a powerfully moving performance from David Ryall in the central role. Inevitably given the Rep's allegiance to the dramatist who had found a patron in Barry Jackson, there was a lot of Shaw: seven plays between 1977 and 1983. The regular productions of Ayckbourn did well. In March 1982 Peter Barkworth's production of *Sisterly Feelings* (another Triumph-linked venture) played to over 73% audiences even though it was poorly reviewed.

A Slice of Cake

To be comfortably, classically mainstream even with plays like Shaw's which were once deemed radical, was acceptable policy within the model of theatre which the subsidised theatre sector had always represented. Engaging very directly not just with commercial producers but the big popular repertoire could, if successful, pay huge dividends. As we have seen the Christmas production was crucial in providing revenue for the rest of the year. In December 1979 Perry brought the former Royal Ballet star turned popular entertainer Wayne Sleep to play Pinocchio. But the following year he hit the jackpot with *Worzel Gummidge*. Based on the 1930s stories of Barbara Euphan Todd, the adaptation by Keith Waterhouse and Willis Hall had been intended as a film, but after several rejections, was taken up by Southern Television. With Jon Pertwee and Una Stubbs who played the lovable scarecrow Worzel and his disdainful beloved Aunt Sally the stories were turned into a hugely popular children's television series. The Rep production had all the authenticity of a new stage version with strong colloquial dialogue by Waterhouse and Hall and jaunty songs by Denis King all delivered by the original stars.

The show had a spectacular opening with a series of thunder claps to herald the birth of Worzel 'long, long time ago' and then moved to the present and the two children who come to stay at Scatterbrook Farm and discover the scarecrow. Geoffrey Scott designed great wooden barn doors which rolled across the proscenium as the scenes changed from the farm to the village fete. There was a remarkable sequence after the interval set in the Crowman's workshop yard when the stage was filled with an assortment of straw-decked scarecrows coming to life to dance and sing 'It's a Scarecrow Day'. The audience loved the scarecrows with names like Scabby Tater Blight and Saggy Tater Jack. In Robin Thornber's *Guardian* review (15.12.80), he described Jon Pertwee with a 'squashed voice, cracked grin, jerky movement and straw sticking out everywhere'. Una Stubbs was a delightfully prissy Aunt Sally. Jane Freeman returned to play Mrs Blomsbury Barton. At the end the stage became a giant illuminated dance-through cake—Worzel's 'very own birth'ee cake'. Fred Norris lovingly recalled the entire company singing 'Slice of Cake' as hordes of multi-coloured balloons floated down 'to be booted, bagged and bust by the audience' (*EM*, 15.12.80).

Candide

Big and bold did not always mean populist. Box office success could pay for experiment. The Rep was basking in the aftermath of record audience figures when Peter Farago's production of *Candide* opened the autumn 1981 season following its debut at the Edinburgh Festival. The original Leonard Bernstein/Richard Wilbur musical of Voltaire's picaresque sex-and-violence-laced satire on the Enlightenment's 'best of all possible worlds' had failed in New York and London in the 1950s. Much to the envy of other British managements, the Rep secured the rights to the 1973 Hal Prince version which boasted a much-improved book by Hugh Wheeler and additional words by Stephen Sondheim and John Latouche. Without Hal Prince's option to move audiences round a gutted New York theatre, Farago and his designer Poppy Mitchell had to create a set which permitted a fluid evocation of the hapless Candide's incident-crowded journey to a series of improbable exotic locations. The result was a multi-levelled structure with lots of stairs and walkways parqueted in tones of old rose and pistachio.

Farago maintained that one reason why the show had failed in 1956 was that an over-mature cast had made the rumbustious sexuality appear unseemly. The actors needed to be young, bright and energetic. All the rushing around playing multiple roles had to look like fun. Pat Doyle, for example, played a coolie, an aristocrat, a blackamoor, a monk, Father Bernard, a sailor and second sheep—which was pink. The complex Bernstein score required, however, a semi-operatic approach and for the role of Cunegonde, Candide's much-ravished beloved, Farago cast Rosemary Ashe, a soprano from English National Opera North. She was universally praised not only for superb singing but also for her ability to maintain an air of wide-eyed innocence as she lurched from Westphalian virginity to top-class whoring and expertise as a Turkish concubine. Mark Wynter, well-known as a 1970s' pop star was cast as her brother Maximillian at one point battling in drag against assorted pirates to preserve his virginity. William Renton played Candide as appropriately vacuous. Nicholas Grace not only played jutting-jawed, white-wigged Voltaire, together with a heavily-accented Germanic Dr Pangloss, but also popped up as an assortment of other characters.

The response in Edinburgh from the national critics was the usual lack of critical consensus on both the musical itself and the director. But Robert Cushman in the *Observer* review (23.8.81) carefully noted that while Farago lacked Hal Prince's skill in sheer pace and inventiveness, he succeeded where Prince had 'faltered' in maintaining the audience's interest throughout. There was unanimity on Nichola McAuliffe's appearance as the mono-buttocked Old Woman wooing several monied Spaniards by singing 'I am Easily Assimilated'. In Birmingham she was the hit of the evening with what the local critic Richard Edmonds who hailed 'a rolling triumph for a rich talent... How good to be bowled over once more in this beloved theatre' (*BP*, 11.9.81).

A Wesker Trilogy

While opportunities for major experiment on the main stage were comparatively rare, Farago's work on what was effectively his own Wesker trilogy of plays represented a sustained achievement. *The Merchant* in 1978 was the British première of a play first staged in Stockholm in 1976. Following the out-of-town death of the leading actor, Zero Mostel, the New York production in 1977 had closed after only five performances. Wesker's reworking of Shakespeare explores in great detail the intellectual climate of Renaissance Venice stimulated by the burgeoning printing industry and the cultural richness of life in the Jewish ghetto. Not only is Wesker's Shylock a great book collector and overall patron of the arts, but a good friend to the gentile Antonio. The 'merry bond' based on the pound of flesh is only devised to emphasise the pettiness of a law which forbids any transaction between the Jew and Gentile unless bound by a contract. Antonio forces Shylock to go through with the trial because to flout one law might make the Jews even more vulnerable. The Portia who thus rescues them both (although Shylock is condemned to lose his books) is a cool independent woman who ultimately rejects the selfish Bassanio.

Christopher Morley gave the play a strong Renaissance feel with period costumes and what Antony Everitt called a 'low-walled piazzetta floating in darkness and off-angled to the audience'. Behind on two gigantic screens were projected stunning images of Venetian splendour and poverty. A première of a play by Wesker inevitably attracted extensive critical attention, more interested in the effectiveness of the play than individual performances, although both David Swift and Angela Down were praised as Shylock and Portia. Swift's own daughter Julia played Jessica while Frank Middlemass played Antonio. Presented with a typically uncompromising Wesker the response was ambivalent especially to the intellectually complex discussion. Everitt summed it up as 'audacious, hectoring, persuasive, moving and unashamedly boring. The play is a bewildering mixture of naivety and sophistication, theatrical magic and pedestrian blundering' (*BP*, 13.10.78).

Clearly encouraged however— Robin Thornber hailed this *The Merchant* as a 'stunningly lucid production'— Farago moved on to *The Wedding Feast* the following year. He directed David Suchet as Louis Litvanov, the affluent manager of a Norfolk shoe factory and Jew of Russian descent who invites himself to the wedding reception of two of his employees. By then Suchet was very familiar to Rep audiences both for his work in the Studio and the main stage. He gave an especially finely-detailed performance as Reg, the estate agent in *The Norman Conquests*. Now he played an ex-East End Marxist, hopelessly compromised in personal insecurity and social guilt: catching his sleeve in a plate of pink blancmange on his first unwelcome entry and finally collapsing in a drunken stupor on the bridal bed. As the booze flows so the bitterness of class divisions begin to emerge. Morley's two-tiered set moved the play from one of Litvanov's country houses with its oak-panelled bedrooms, tapestried chairs and mirrored bathroom, to the terraced workers' cottage.

Nicola McAuliffe was cast as the 'dreadful' bride while Susan Brown played Litvanov's clever secretary. The chorus figure which Wesker introduces in the totally self-assured journalist Stephen Bullock was played by Patrick Malahide 'prowling round the action like a jackal waiting for the pack to kill his prey for him' (*S*, 16.6.80). There were the usual calls for textual pruning but the total lack of sentimentality in Wesker's approach was admired. The *Sunday Times* review was especially gratifying 'Peter Farago's direction is a brilliant piece of engineering which mines Litvanov's reception by his hostile, servile or uncomprehending hosts for all its worth as if Breughel had descended on present-day Norfolk and depicted some balefully vigorous festivity' (15.6.80).

Farago's 1981 production of *Chips with Everything*, drawn from Wesker's youthful experience of National Service, was the first major revival of the play since its first production. Again this play is concerned with the class struggle as it charts the eight week training of a group of young RAF recruits all of whom are working class except one, Pip Thompson, who is a general's son. Despite Thompson's efforts to achieve solidarity with his peers and an attempt to get them to rebel against the system, his class status is ultimately reinforced by the officers and he reverts to type. Critics like Gareth Lloyd Evans were less convinced by the political debate than by Wesker's detailed naturalistic evocation of camp life. There was a lot of pre-show publicity about the all-male cast learning to square-bash. For once the size of the stage added extra authenticity. Geoffrey Scott's permanent set was a concrete-slabbed square in front of barracks surrounded by a wire-mesh fence. Simon Dutton played the upper-class fish out of water with, as Lloyd Evans put it, 'loud-mouthed contempt' (*G*, 6.4.81) naturally turning into an officer after a futile attempt bayonet-practice revolt. Reece Dinsdale played the pathetic hero-worshipping Wingate, while Dennis Haythorne played the Wing Commander. Denis Richard turned the bawling corporal into a study of primitive cruelty.

The Studio

Constrained stability in the main house meant much greater flexibility in the Studio. With Bill Pryde as overall director, the emphasis on the new and experimental continued and both he and Farago presented acclaimed new writing. The tradition of staging a specially written play for children at Christmas was also continued. As a receiving venue the space continued to give a welcome and indeed a launch pad to the leading radical touring companies. In September 1977 Shared Experience premièred the first two parts of their important dramatisation of *Bleak House*. In October Hull Truck brought *A Bed of Roses* devised and directed by Mike Bradwell. In March 1979 Monstrous Regiment came with *Teendreams* created by David Edgar and Susan Todd—the first time this women's ensemble had worked with a male writer. Gay Sweatshop brought *The Dear Love of Comrades* in April. In September Foco Novo came with the British premiere of *The Guise* by David Moffat.

Of course as Honer had found before, the intimacy of the space also meant that well-known texts could be reconsidered and experienced more intensely. Following on from the 1974 *Ghosts* when the audience had effectively sat in the Alving drawing room to watch the tragedy unfold there were more productions of Ibsen. *The Lady from the Sea*, which Pryde directed in 1977, is less purely domestic with the sea a symbolic presence throughout. Poppy Mitchell designed an arrangement of poles expressive of the claustrophobia of the forest overlooking a fjord. Michael Rowntree's light filtered from above casting shadows. In 1980 when Pryde directed David Ryall as Solness in *The Master Builder*, there were tall, narrow columns at the end of Geoffrey Scott's stripped-pine traverse set which suggested the tower from which Solness fell at the end of the play.

Reviews of the production focused on the physical as well as the intellectual experience of the play. Ann Fitzgerald writing in the *Stage* acknowledged that the Studio setting reduced the scale of the play but intensified the personal drama. 'We are drawn into the long searching conversations like participants in the drama, listening, considering and responding to the dialogue and being made acutely aware how modern in spirit are the ideas with which its characters are wrestling' (16.10.80). David Ryall played Solness as both a sad grand figure and a frightened middle-aged man 'terribly afraid of youth'. As the relentlessly young Hilde Wangel, Lynsey Baxter's slight physique and fey blonde prettiness made the strength of will that compelled Solness to climb the tower all the more formidable. A local critic Michael Rowberry, writing in the *Coventry Evening Telegraph*, described what for him was a magical climactic scene: 'one looks up involuntarily, half-expecting to see the master-builder actually climbing to his doom' (25.9.80).

In 1978 Pryde worked with Poppy Mitchell to update *All's Well That Ends Well* to the 1930s and transposed Shakespeare's background of the Renaissance Italian Wars to the Spanish Civil War. Mitchell designed a set of pink columns with pretty painted screens for the French scenes in the first half which became a rough-hewn exterior after the interval. Marilyn Taylerson and Paul Geoffrey played the mismatched central couple Helena and Bertram while Rosalind Boxall played the Countess of Rousillon. The following February Perry directed Boxall and Philip Madoc in Strindberg's *The Father*. Perry presented this intense study of how obsessive parenthood turns love into jealousy and madness without an interval and with the audience seated on both sides of a traverse playing space. At one point when Madoc's Captain threw a blazing oil lamp at his wife fragments appear to narrowly miss the onlookers. 'No pins were dropped', wrote Eric Shorter after seeing the production along with a largely young audience, 'we would have heard them' (*DT*, 2.2.79).

Getting to Grips with Birmingham

Bill Pryde admitted to a personal as well as an artistic agenda in promoting locally-based new writing. It was important for him as a native Scot to 'get to grips with Birmingham'; make the Midlands seem less alien and impersonal after Edinburgh where 'I knew everybody and they knew me' (*S*, 19.3.81) Derek Nicholls and Ray Speakman who wrote *The Seed*, Pryde's first Studio première, were accustomed to creating devised drama out of the local and personal experiences of their youth theatre members, many of whom over the years had been from minority ethnic communities. The play, set in Birmingham between 1952 and 1977, focuses on Alaf, the confused son of a marriage between a Moslem Pakistani man and his white British wife. Darien Angadi of Indian parentage played Alaf, while Renu Setna the Pakistani actor well-known from *Crossroads* played both the father Khalid, and Khalid's father Hashim, who of course suffered cultural trauma when Khalid married. Both actors were enthusiastic about the opportunities offered by the play, and happy to endorse the felt authenticity of the Asian community experience represented. The critics who reported back on the experience of the production certainly acknowledged the commitment of individual performances, especially from Setna and Sheila Kelley as his English wife. But artistic necessity tended to get overwhelmed by social concern.

In May 1978 when Pryde directed Vince Foxall's *Gestures*, set in a Birmingham comprehensive school, the designer David Fisher constructed a neat matrix of glass partitions dividing the staff room and classrooms all with their own distinctive characteristics and disconcertingly real props. There was a tiled floor, ceiling and wall lights, desks and cupboards. The audience were invited to pick a seat on any side of the set to listen, as the school bell rang, to the thoughts and experiences of four very different teachers. Lindsay Duncan played Ann, a limp, scarcely-motivated young English teacher, Desmond Adams played Kriple, a physically and mentally twisted geography teacher. The young dynamic, but sexually hung-up, drama teacher played by Peter Whitman, and Susan Brown as the cosy deputy-head 'heart of the school', completed the quartet. The pupils were invisible except one 'Kid', Peter Biddle, as a withdrawn aberrant product of a bleak home who wanders the corridors flailing about with violent language reinforced by an equally alarming axe.

Although the play was about the inadequacies of the school system itself, it was also fairly obviously a way of exorcising Foxall's own traumatic experiences as a teacher in Willenhall. Gareth Lloyd Evans was vituperative about drama which he claimed 'confuses diarrhoea with wit' and went on to criticise the Rep's 'growing recklessness in choice and judgement' in accepting work by budding young dramatists (*G*, 10.3.78). All new work is a gamble, however and appeals in different ways. In the *Birmingham Post* (9.3.78) D.J. Hart wrote that *Gestures* 'goes deep, as if a kind of love is waiting to break out'. Certainly the play grew in estimation to the point where it won the John Whiting Award.

Mary Barnes

David Edgar's *Destiny* went on an increasingly triumphant journey after it was rejected by the Rep. After the RSC's Other Place production in 1976, it transferred to the Aldwych Theatre and then, given a television production, won the John Whiting Award in 1977. *The Jail Diary of Albie Sachs,* his most recent play, had also been premièred by the RSC. *Mary Barnes* is about the healing of a diagnosed schizophrenic described in the book *Mary Barnes: Two Accounts of a Journey Through Madness* written by Barnes and her therapist Dr Joseph Berke. Interviewed for the *Birmingham Post* (12-18. 1.79) , Edgar explained a three-fold motivation behind the play:

> **I had wanted to do an adaptation of a book…**
> **and also wanted to do something about the**
> **late 1960s. I had written two or three plays**
> **dealing with psychologically deviant behaviour**
> **and I felt it would be good to deal with a real**
> **case. Madness is very difficult to write.**

He was introduced to the book by the actress Patti Love who was ultimately cast as Mary. Barnes herself came to the Rep to observe and assist in the rehearsal process. The shifting around of events and the fictionalised amalgam of certain characters created no problem: ' the vital thing is that the message—the truth comes across'. The message itself came from the ideas of the radical psychiatrist R.D. Laing who set up the Kingsley Hall experimental therapeutic community in the 1960s.

Edgar's play shows how Mary through a re-birthing process was helped to shed the destructive childhood and family experiences which had propelled her into madness and achieving healing without chemical or surgical intervention. The play pulls no punches about the questions raised by Laingian theory or the more distressing aspects of some schizophrenic behaviour. Indeed Edgar saw her story as a metaphor for the late 1960s when it became important to confront pain rather than hide behind a repressed façade of contentment. At one the Joseph Berke character Eddie, played by Simon Callow, accompanied a naked, faeces-covered Mary up to the bathroom and 'the protective womb of her bed'.

Even those who were unconvinced by the central thesis bore witness to the power of the play and individual performances controlled by Farago's unsentimental direction. Callow brought an ebullient humour to the American psychiatrist who commits himself to taking Mary from bottle-fed dependence of a wilful elderly child to someone capable of caring for others. Donald Sumpter played the Laing character Hugo as Coveney put it 'a laconic guru who takes a paradoxically authoritative back seat' (FT, 4.9.78). Timothy Spall and Roger Allam played a variety of supporting roles. Barnes' deep Catholic commitment was offered as a reason for the heavy religious symbolism and off-stage choral music. Andrea Montag's two-tier set created an upper level for the growing process while downstairs the problems of running the community were explored. Props like a battered chair with its escaped stuffing, a mattress on the floor and Barnes' vigorous paintings on the walls helped to evoke the reality of the original Kingsley Hall.

Women Speak for Themselves

Edgar's play put the story of a marginalised woman centre stage, and in so doing gave an opportunity for Patti Love to recreate her journey in a performance that formidably stretched her artistic skills. Gradually Studio policy began to foreground women's work and experience not just in subject matter (Farago regarded *Iniquity* as a feminist play) and performance but in writing and ultimately direction as well. The spring of 1979 saw three premières of plays by women: Fay Weldon's *Action Replay*, *Idle Rich*, a play devised and directed by Sheila Kelley, and Louise Page's *Hearing*. The Birmingham connection was also strong—even Fay Weldon was born on the outskirts of the city—and the dramatists offered wide-ranging diversity and theatrical experiment.

Weldon was the most prestigious writer although better known for her wickedly subversive novels. *Action Replay* (her third play) directed by Farago and with a multi-levelled tawny-carpet set by Poppy Mitchell is a kind of dramatic puzzle spread over twenty-five years from the mid-1950s to the 1970s. Sorcha Cusack, Mary Tamm and Arwen Holm played three women exploring (through re-running scenes) the various choices available to them during a period which saw radical changes in attitudes to women's expectations. over a twenty-five year period. *Hearing* enabled the audience to experience (for the first time it was claimed) a deaf actress working with a professional hearing company. Jean St.Clair played Gale, a born-deaf typist in a sugar factory who forms a relationship with Ian (played by Rod Culbertson) another employee of the factory developing deafness as a result of the working conditions. The underlying documentary nature of the piece exploring causes and attitudes to deafness polarised critics and compelled audiences to confront the jarring truthfulness of the deaf actress's voice.

Sheila Kelley's play utilised the character-creation techniques learnt at first hand from Mike Leigh. Through close observation and improvisation the company of four actors devised first their characters and then the narrative about a newly-redundant car-worker and his wife in South Yardley. Kelley herself was born in Birmingham and had already been praised for the striking authenticity of her mixed marriage wife in *The Seed*. The result of the company work was an evocation of the manners and behaviour of a certain kind of lower middle-class milieu which was both funny and bleak.

The Old Order and Harvest

At the heart of *Idle Rich* lay a recognition of the human costs of the crisis-ridden car industry which had brought sudden wealth and then encroaching recession to the Midlands. Stephen Bill, Sheila Kelley's husband premiered his play *The Old Order* in October 1979 just after Margaret Thatcher came to power. Set in a light engineering firm in a Birmingham back street, and drawn from Bill's own knowledge of his father's small business, the play tackles the core issues at the heart of the troubled industrial relations in the late 1970s: inflation and wage rates, working conditions and the demand for automation. But the play is also shot through with work place humour and given a concrete physical ambience. Once again the Studio audience was thrust into an environment as it sat on both sides of Poppy Mitchell's traverse setting where as Fred Norris put it 'you can taste the oil, the grime and metal, yesterday's sour milk and today's stewed tea' (*EM*, 5.10.79). Robin Thornber describing the scenic clutter of presses, polishers and bits of metal was reminded of 'real, living newspaper stuff' (*G*, 6.10.79), but distinguished it from the consciously two-dimensional theatre of agit-prop because of the depth of characterisation. Bill insisted that the nine actors should have West Midlands roots believing that non-natives find both accent and the dry style of humour difficult to assimilate: 'there's no point in writing a play about Birmingham if you get that awful cod Birmingham accent which is halfway to Liverpool' (*BP*, 29.3.79). Actors over forty prepared to admit to coming from Birmingham were difficult to find, he claimed, because they had to lose their accents in order to find work. It was yet another sign of an old order fading away that vocally-skilled actors in the younger age group were in plentiful supply.

For Thornber, despite the play's discussion of the different philosophies behind working practices: the old order of benevolent paternalism and Dickensian-style drudgery versus the ethos of modern management, the real clash arose from personalities with colliding views of the world. Stephen Macdonald played Ralph Jackson running his Dad's firm as he always has—relying on personal knowledge of his 'lads' rather than industrial-style arbitration methods. When a fight exacerbated by drunkenness, racism and threats of a lost order occurs, loyalties become stretched too far and Jackson's long-assumed authority is no longer adequate. Dennis Holmes played the creepy foreman Cook who has never forgiven the TUC for selling out in 1926 and vents his frustrations in unintelligible obscenities. Lloyd McGuire played the decent hard-working family man who brings in the union official to counter Cook's spite, while Roy Barraclough, well-known as a stand-up television comedian played the Welsh-accented, sheep-skin clad union man.

The following year which saw *The Old Order* win the John Whiting Award, Ellen Dryden also won the award for *Harvest* which again dealt, albeit in the rural setting of her native Warwickshire, with the weight of the past on a rapidly-changing present. There was a distinctly autobiographical, even Weskeresque, dimension to Dryden's story of a brisk and brainy daughter Marion, played by Elizabeth Bell, educated beyond her family's limited horizons and returning sardonic and disruptive to her grandfather's funeral. This time the Studio became a Methodist chapel with the Fenton family on pews set amongst the audience. Perched on a piano opposite the pulpit Marian sat commenting on the hypocrisy of a service for an unpopular, dead atheist. The funeral ambience was vividly evoked 'all ham sandwiches, little old ladies in black hats, and the parson praying for a man he's never met and no one ever liked' as Robin Thornber described it (G, 27.10.80), reminded as he was of his own lapsed Methodist past. Bernard Hill played Ted, Marion's plodding, selfless brother who much to his sister's chagrin has given up on an improving literature course and still loves his domineering wife.

Extending the Range

Studio policy was not only to produce work by and for the Midland community, but also to broaden audience horizons beyond the local and the comfortably familiar. Of the ambitious programme of four premières presented between February and June 1981 only one could be regarded as a safe night out. *Haworth*, Beverley Cross's dramatisation of the life of Charlotte Brontë with Polly James as Charlotte and Tim Brierley playing everyone else, was directed by Clive Perry and marked the Studio design debut of Finlay James. Images were projected onto tombstones which paved the floor and back wall of the set evoking the churchyard at Haworth.

In complete contrast, both *Midnite at the Starlite* by Michael Hastings and *Hosanna*, the British première of a play by Canadian playwright Michael Tremblay, focused on the vulnerabilities and confusions associated with gay sexuality. *Midnite* featured Peter Sallis as the MC in a seedy dance hall where a down-market ballroom dancing competition is taking place. Maria Charles played his wife insulated from reality by her nostalgia for ballroom dancing. The dances—all powder-puff skirts and patent shoes—performed by the company which also included Sheila Kelley provided a disturbing counterpoint to the revelation of the MC's homosexual past. For *Hosanna,* the closeted lives of gay lovers were played out in brutally bitchy dialogue by Jim Hooper and Ian Gelder. The designer Ultz created a cheap-scented boudoir draped with homosexual icons and luridly lit by Michael Rowntree in shades of orange, pink, purple and green. In the course of the play Hosanna (the hairdresser Claude Lemieux played by Hooper) has to come to terms with the nature of his masculinity after a very public humiliation at a transvestite ball. The Studio audience held its collective breath as Lemieux, finally admitting he is a man to his biker lover, divested himself of all his treasured female clothing.

In between, however, came David Rudkin's *The Triumph of Death* which had been conceived seven years before but not staged until the Rep directorate felt that audiences would accept Rudkin's radical exploration of the way the aspiring human spirit has been subjected to degradation through time. Farago warned the Board that the play, which moves from thirteenth century religious dogma and intolerance to aimless modern materialism, was likely to prove controversial. He was proved correct. Michael Billington described it as 'a half-cooked Irish stew of a play in which religion, death, defecation, copulation and capitalism were all thrown into the steaming pot' (G, 10.3.81). The narrative first focuses on the primitive descendents of the ill-fated Children's Crusade, which in 1212 launched thousands of children across Europe to their deaths en route to the Holy Land. The sheer abundance of ideas and images added up to an *embarras de richesses* which proved difficult to assimilate.

The reviews gleefully supplied details of sequences which included a female mental asylum inmate straining to defecate while declaring herself to be Martin Luther; a nun suddenly ripping apart her habit crying 'I am Jerusalem', to a simple lad who was exhorted to lick her breasts; the woodland orgy where Christ turned into Pan complete with massively expressive genitals. Some of the more sympathetic reviews came from unlikely sources. Nora Lewis in the *Birmingham Evening Mail* (10.3.81), for example, empathised with the idea of a rural community 'innocently preoccupied with basic bodily functions, coping in their own way with birth and death' until destroyed between the devil and the Catholic Church.

There was generalised praise for Veronica Roberts as the tormented, physically twisted Jehan who transmutes into Joan of Arc to be burnt and swept away as a pile of ashes, and Freda Dowie as the ancient mother-figure Heniot who becomes, at the end of the play, a white-coated psychiatrist. Sheila Gish, back in Birmingham after twenty years, played the death-bearing, bodice-ripping nun. Few denied the composure and commitment of the cast, or the sheer theatrical power of Farago's production. Christopher Morley designed a set of trodden earth which changed to flag stones in the second half as civilisation moved on. There were moments when floors and doors literally vibrated with passion. The opening image was stunning. Harold Innocent played Papatrix, a grotesque Pope figure squatting on high in a vast, billowing blue gown.

Exciting times then, in a performance space which Pryde and Farago had made exemplary in terms of challenge and diversity. But even full to capacity the Studio was uneconomic to run and in any case artistic success did not guarantee good audiences as the thin attendance for *Harvest* demonstrated. The relationship with the main house was to say the least problematic. An artistic policy which sustained small-scale radicalism with large-scale conservatism could create a damaging disjunction between the two spaces and their audiences with an inevitable knock-on effect on programming.

Since Simpson's experiments with *Up Spaghetti* and *Thingummybob* there had been no attempt to put the work of local writers to the test in the main auditorium. As the new plays flourished in the Studio in May 1981 Pryde ventured onto the big stage with the première of Stephen Bill's *Piggy Back Riders*: a continuation of the preoccupations of *The Old Order*, but with the focus on Birmingham life shifted from the factory setting to the suburban affluence of middle-class Hall Green as encapsulated by Geoffrey Scott's Victorian house set. Bill's acute ear for local speech idioms, which lightened a solidly-authentic exploration of the pressures of management with verbal comedy, was perhaps the play's greatest strength. Peter Sallis played George Newman, the retired small factory owner torn apart as Gareth Lloyd Evans put it 'by his own indecision, his daughter's left wingery, his son's ambitious tycoonery, his younger daughter's punkery and his wife's flapdoodley' (*G*, 9.5.81). Roger Sloman played Mike, the humourless, go-getting son/manager with 'a bald head and bald ideas', while Gillian Raine played Connie, George's wife obsessed with indoor plants and carpets.

The audience attendance of 44% of capacity was by no means disastrous given the vast disparity in size of the two auditoria, but for a directorate under pressure to maintain high box office figures the result would have signalled caution. By 1985 when *Naked in the Bullring*, the final part of Bill's trilogy focusing on different generations of the same family within the changing economic and cultural climate of Margaret Thatcher's Britain, was premièred on the main stage, the Rep itself had gone through a traumatic period of change.

1 Richard Eyre, *Utopia and Other Places* (Vintage, 1994) p.129

Exterior of the
**Birmingham
Repertory Theatre**
on Station Street

Exterior of the
**Birmingham
Repertory Theatre**
on Broad Street

As You Like It
1967
Brian Cox (Orlando),
Deborah Stanford
(Rosalind)

The Knack
1964
L to R: Simon Ward
(Colin), Celestine Randall
(Nancy), Christopher
Bidmead (Tom),
Colin Smith (Tolen)

98

Guys and Dolls
1973
L to R : Rosemary Leach
(Miss Adelaide), Patricia
Michael (Sarah Brown)

The Nailmakers
1973

**The Snow Queen
1985**
Paul Mulrennan
(Cobweb Spider),
Crispin Redman (Polar
Bear), Devon Scott
(Snow Queen), Iain
Glen (Reindeer), Paul
Kiernan (Raven
'Scruff')

**Mary Barnes
1978**
L to R: Simon Callow
(Eddie), Katherine
Kitovitz (Beth),
Patti Love (Mary)

100

**An Inspector Calls
1988**
L to R: Dominic Letts
(Eric Birling), Jack
Smethurst (Arthur
Birling), Lorraine
Brunning (Sheila Birling),
Miles Richardson (Gerald
Croft), Angela Moran
(Sybil Birling)

**The Last Carnival
1992**
Back row L to R: Joseph
Charles (George),
Catherine Russell
(Aggie), Lorna Laidlaw
(Jean Beauxchamps),
Front row L to R: Trevor
Butler (Raphael),
Michael Bertinshaw
(Oswald Delafontaine)
Peter Woodward (Victor
Delafontaine)

101

**The Tenant of
Wildfell Hall
1995**
Janice McKenzie (Helen
Huntingdon), Ian Targett
(Gilbert Markham)

**All That Trouble
That We Had
1999**
L to R: Paul Bradley
(Oliver), Rachel Smith
(Hannah), David
Hargreaves (Vaughan)

The Snowman
1997
Kaspar Cornish
(Snowman),
Drew McOnie (James)

Hamlet
1998
Rakie Ayola (Ophelia),
Richard McCabe
(Hamlet)

Interior of the
auditorium of the
old Rep in the late
1960s

Interior of the main
auditorium of the
new Rep after the
refurbishment in
1999

8. The City Intervenes

The Tenth Anniversary

As the Rep reached its tenth birthday in the 'new' building what kind of company had it become? Clearly the Old Rep faithful who had accompanied the journey from Station Street to Broad Street no longer had the opportunity to watch actors grow and mature out of the old-style ensemble base. Also the vast expanse of the main stage had radically altered the experience for artists and audience alike. Actors were certainly challenged as they attempted to establish a compelling stage presence and this could be difficult for the inexperienced. Indeed Jane Freeman who continued to perform at the Rep from time to time stated firmly that the main stage was for 'grown-up' actors. If the criteria for challenge, however, revolved round innovative writing and performance opportunities then obviously the focus had to be the Studio space which the more conservative work of the main stage had effectively maintained.

Some ex-Old Rep actors like Rosalind Boxall performed at the theatre on a regular basis moving between the two spaces. She played Lady Bracknell in Perry's very popular 1981 production of *The Importance of Being Earnest* and in the autumn of 1983 she was cast as Mrs Dudgeon in Shaw's *The Devil's Disciple*. David Ryall had never worked in the old theatre but with every performance in Broad Street he seemed to enhance his personal standing. He was singled out as the First Player in *Rosencrantz and Guildenstern are Dead* in 1978. As King Lear in 1980 he managed to convey the confusion and frailty of extreme old age with moving power even though he was by no means old. Peter Sallis became a familiar face in both homegrown and commercial co-productions while David Suchet continued his creative partnership with Peter Farago.

Alan Rickman, Simon Callow, Lindsay Duncan and Timothy Spall were given early opportunities at the Rep before they achieved greater prominence, but what was gone was the nurturing environment where actors could test and develop their skills over an extended period of time. Of course some actors-especially those who were locally-based like Sheila Kelley and Terry Molloy formed an on-going relationship with the theatre. But actors were no longer members of a family, as it were, but regular visitors instead. The wider professional context had changed. Whereas in the early 1960s John Harrison brought in actors who had worked in television but who were happy to commit to a permanent company, by the 1980s the financial advantages of television far outweighed the attractions of regional short-run theatre and if anything the pull of London and the national companies was even stronger. The glamour which had once surrounded Birmingham Rep had evaporated and actors' agents predominantly based in London exercised a powerful influence. It was going to get harder to get actors of stature to play the roles which were needed to power the main stage and attract enough punters. Furthermore with Arts Council grant-aid in the early 1980s chronically set at below the level of inflation, the financial balancing act got even trickier.

The Stars Policy

Perry tried to woo mainstream Birmingham audiences with well-known actors, more often than not in productions directed by guest directors, but set and dressed by the Rep workshops and wardrobe and destined thereafter for transfer to London. In April 1980 Frith Banbury directed Margaret Lockwood in *Motherdear*, a sumptuously-dressed play by Royce Ryton based on the life of Queen Alexandra. Immediately afterwards the continuing collaboration with Triumph Apollo enabled the world première of a Ben Traver's farce *After You With the Milk* which featured Julia Foster directed by Frank Hauser. In 1982 Peter O'Toole gave a barnstorming performance as Jack Tanner in Patrick Dromgoole's production of *Man and Superman*. The following March Robert Chetwyn directed Peter Ustinov in the actor-writer's own play *Beethoven's Tenth*.

But the policy was fraught with danger. The Ben Traver's première built on the earlier success of the 1979 Frank Dunlop production of *Rookery Nook* was an embarrassing demonstration of the elderly decline of a once-great farceur. Plays geared to glossy West End production values like *Motherdear* were also artistically unsatisfactory. Stars like O'Toole gave performances which made little concession to the principals of ensemble acting. Ustinov, however, went down well with the Rep staff. He treated them to an impromptu stand-up comedy show to enliven the longeurs of a technical rehearsal. Even this production created a major planning headache when Perry was forced to agree to delay its appearance by several months from the previous autumn. The substitute, in October 1982, a new play by

Michael Pertwee called *Do Not Disturb* had a small cast, was relatively cheap to mount and starred Tony Britten directed by Clifford Williams. Robin Thornber's acid review undercut any potential appeal to economic exigencies: 'it is the sort of would-be commercial rubbish that used to tour the seedier sort of circuit without benefit of the massive public subsidy that is implied by a première at B'ham Rep' (*G*, 27.10. 82). Audiences were very poor.

The biggest drawback was the lack of final control over the product. All theatrical ventures are an act of faith and a speculative risk but when the principal agents: directors, actors, producers are outside the company, especially those operating from outside the subsidised sector, the inherent risk becomes greater. Perry was constantly having to react to enforced changes which in turn could alienate much-needed subscribers entitled to expect reliable programming. For the tenth anniversary season October 1981 audiences had been tempted with the prospect of Derek Jacobi playing in *Cyrano de Bergerac* and *Henry VIII* directed by Robin Phillips with, it was hoped, Maggie Smith and Paul Scofield in supporting roles in the Shakespeare. When Phillips withdrew and a suitable replacement could not be found, Perry was forced to inform subscribers that his own Edinburgh production of *As You Like It* would follow *Candide* and that a completely new production of the old, if much-loved war horse *Hobson's Choice* directed by David Wylde would follow.

A year later in September 1982, Perry informed the Board that he and Jeff Kitto had flown to America to negotiate bringing over the original New York cast for the UK première of the musical *Sophisticated Ladies,* to launch a tour that would culminate in London. The trip had been paid for by the American management; there would be no loss to the theatre; higher seat prices would be required but subscribers would not be affected. The play would open on 19 April. By February the deal was off, a letter had to be sent to subscribers; there was yet more embarrassing press coverage, and yet another substitute courtesy of Duncan C. Weldon and Triumph Apollo had to be found. The result, in the midst of a heatwave in June and July 1983, was the regional première, prior to touring, of Peter Shaffer's *Amadeus* directed by Paul Giovanni with Keith Michell in the key role of Salieri. This should have been an attractive prospect in its own right but audience figures of 53% were part of a downward trend.

Moreover the theatre had moved into 1983 with an obvious homegrown disaster on its hands. Success at Christmas was vital to anything remotely resembling financial stability and *Worzel Gummidge* had carried on working for the Rep. The Rogers and Hammerstein version of *Cinderella* was advertised on the back of the *Worzel* programme and opened in Birmingham in December 1981 just as *Worzel* began a profitable run at the Cambridge Theatre in London. Directed by Bill Pryde, *Cinderella* was billed as both a lavish musical and a panto and featured popular local singer-comedian Don Maclean. It was by no means, however, vintage Rogers and Hammerstein and Perry was to discover to the theatre's cost that sumptuous staging was not in itself a recipe for success. To make matters worse the proposed production of *The Prince and the Pauper* by the Birmingham-based Second City Company which was to fill the children's play slot in the Studio had to be cancelled when the company collapsed.

For Christmas 1982 Perry attempted a two-pronged strategy to please children with daytime performances of David Wood's *The Gingerbread Man* and attract adults with a two month run of the musical *Call Me Madam*. The local actress-celebrity Noelle Gordon forever identified with the role of the motel owner Meg Richardson in the long-running television soap *Crossroads* gave a barnstorming central performance as the unlikely White House hostess Sally Adams in a succession of glittering frocks. For weeks the press was full of copiously-illustrated advance publicity. But the audience as Perry ruefully put it later 'stayed away in droves'. It was a financial disaster. Even sympathetic reviews of the London transfer failed to save the show from closure after only ten weeks at the Victoria Palace. Noelle Gordon, who had first played Sally Adams some thirty years before in the first touring version, died of cancer not long afterwards.

The City Intervenes

The discussion surrounding Perry's report to the Board on 24 January 1983 acknowledged that recent productions had 'not accorded with the theatre's objectives as originally founded' but Perry insisted that in the final analysis the role of the theatre was determined by the level of support which the theatre-going public and the theatre's sponsors were prepared to give. There was a conflict between the perception that the theatre's image was still 'too highbrow' and Arts Council and City Council views (which could also conflict) on what the role of the theatre should be. Furthermore the Arts Council was now adopting a confrontational policy to compel local authorities to fund theatres more generously while (as Marjorie Brown pointed out), local authorities were under yet more controlling, constraining pressure from the Conservative government.

Worrying signs throughout 1982 that a deficit was steadily accumulating despite (after much lobbying) increased grants from the City, the Civic Lottery and the Arts Council, were confirmed in February 1983 with the revelation of a projected net deficit of £159,692 which included a £36,886 deficit brought forward from the previous year. Failure to reach box office targets, especially the *Call Me Madam* fiasco, was inevitably blamed. But more seriously it was suggested that inadequate information was available about the true financial position, especially at the point of commitment to production expenditure. Matters had been made substantially worse by the heart attack suffered by Dick King in the summer of 1982. He continued to struggle on albeit intermittently but effectively the theatre was without a Financial Administrator for the next year. Perry admitted that his frequent absences from the theatre either rehearsing or negotiating with outside companies made it impossible for him to oversee financial controls. In May 1983 the Board together with the City's Chief Executive Tom Caulcott and the Deputy City Treasurer Brian Farrer resolved to make an urgent new managerial appointment to take over all the organisational control of the day to day administration of the theatre. In the person of the new Commercial and Financial Director the City effectively walked into the Rep's management offices and installed itself behind a desk.

Few Board decisions caused more public furore than the appointment in September 1983, out of some seventy applicants, of Clive Wilkinson, the former Labour Leader of the Council. As Commercial and Financial Director, Wilkinson had no accountancy training; his first-hand experience of business was confined to his early work as a self-employed carpenter, and perhaps most controversially he had no knowledge of, or indeed affection for, the arts beyond a liking for pop music. Proudly working-class Brummie he had gone on record as describing theatre in pejorative terms as a middle-class activity. Interviewed in late 1994 he still condemned the majority of theatre professionals as middle-class dilettantes whingeing about lack of money for their art. Inevitably there were dark suspicions about civic nepotism. But Marjorie Brown who delegated the final selection to her vice-chairman John Bettinson stoutly defended him as the best man for the job: a stance she maintained a decade later as did Clive Perry.

Clive Wilkinson exudes an aura of combative honesty, had extensive knowledge of the City's political and financial structures and understood the necessity for practical commitment to the Rep's well-being for the sake not only of Birmingham but the wider region which the theatre serves. He brought an incisive, not to say ruthless, approach to a deep muddle. Marjorie Brown retained comic-in-retrospect-memories of financial documents simply falling out of an over-packed safe. It was Wilkinson's job to delve and excise. Not for nothing was he dubbed Wilkinson 'sword edge'.

Wielding the Sword

Wilkinson set about ensuring that production budgets and schedules were adhered to. He identified lax working practices, especially time-wasting by production staff which then led to unreasonable levels of overtime payment. The most important priority was to get a tight grip on projected budgets and actual expenditure and curb the chronic tendency to make over-optimistic box-office estimates. A computerised accounting system which had been under discussion for some time was now installed, enabling the new accounts manager, Graham Collins, to provide more accurate and detailed figures for the artistic directorate and the Board. Dick King resigned in February 1984. It emerged that expensive set materials and properties went missing after shows and Jeff Kitto, the brilliant and long-serving Production Manager was dismissed and later prosecuted.

Several other administrative staff left. Christine Wilkinson, the publicity manager resigned while Colin Hurley, the box office manager was dismissed. Roger Popplestone left. The most significant casualty was John Greenwood who, marginalised and angered by Wilkinson's abrasiveness, chose to resign after sixteen years administering the theatre. At the time Clive Perry was yet again away from the theatre but this time caring for his dying mother. An added personal dimension to Greenwood's trauma was the decision to close the problematic hire department housed in the decaying instability of Pantomime House and run by his wife Silvia. New premises in Brasshouse Passage had already been located but now were simply used to store important sets and properties. Later a compulsory purchase order on the premises compelled a move to a building on Hurst Street.

Christmas 1983 was a success. The Board had balked at Perry's proposal to celebrate (with the assistance of Triumph Apollo) the festive season in the main house with Danny La Rue starring in *Hello Dolly*. This appeared to be taking star-laden vulgarity too far and would risk disappointing family audiences. The compromise hammered out between Director and Board resulted in *Hello Dolly* packing out the Rep between mid-November and December and then the safe but popular familiarity of *Toad of Toad Hall* through Christmas and the New Year which in box office profit broke the *Worzel Gummidge* record. The financial statement for 1983-4 recorded a surplus of £68,584 and the following year the City Council provided an additional grant of £20,000 towards relieving the accumulated deficit. Mark Everett, who in his capacity as Arts Council Drama Officer had sat in on Board meetings, became the new General Manager. Wilkinson also brought in as his assistant Wiff Maton, who after enduring initial resentment, rapidly earned a reputation for competence and reliability.

But there were other costs. Inevitably Wilkinson caused deep divisions amongst staff used to a more gentlemanly managerial style. Despite the respect he claimed for skilled workers, aggressive demands for stricter observance of factory-floor-style efficiency failed to understand the good will and creative zeal which is required to meet performance deadlines. The removal of Jeff Kitto left a yawning chasm in overall production capability because he had effectively created an empire based on unrivalled knowledge of technical processes and sources of crucial materials as well as the time-scale necessary for each aspect of production.

For several months the theatre was left without a Production Manager. Sebastian Barnes who was then Technical Manager recalled having to question van drivers to find out where materials had come from. Over the summer of 1984 a backlog of work accumulated creating delays on the build of *Great Expectations* which opened the autumn season and the realisation that the next show, a musical adaptation of Shaw called *Bashville* would not be ready in time. The day before what had to be designated a public dress rehearsal saw the entire theatre staff, including Wilkinson, on stage frantically completing the set. By November Nic Beeby was installed as the new Production Manager. Beeby, like Barnes had started as a young member of the stage crew.

The new team management team worked well together. Everett was very popular, understood public funding priorities and, because he had also worked with the Second City Theatre Company, had a commitment to innovative drama. The two Clives established a relationship based on mutual respect for their separate areas of expertise. But there were continuing problems about how Birmingham Rep was now perceived both locally and nationally. What was effectively Perry's last attempt to programme in an elegant, commercially-produced, West End-style vehicle for aging stars: *Aren't We All*, a play by Frederick Lonsdale featuring Rex Harrison and Claudette Colbert, had unlooked for consequences in more ways than one. In an interview before the show opened in May 1984, Richard Edmonds asked Rex Harrison what he felt about coming to Birmingham. The septuganarian actor, who had started his career at the Liverpool Playhouse in the 1920s, responded 'I don't feel anything at all…I didn't know I was opening in Birmingham. It's just a stepping-off point for West End productions these days isn't it? Not a bit like Sir Barry Jackson's day at all' (*EM*, 4.5.84).

Subsequently to add injury to insult the Rep found itself embroiled in protracted arguments with Duncan Weldon over royalties when the production eventually reached America. Of course it was mischievous to print a remark by an elderly, out of touch artist not noted for his tact, but it was nonetheless clear that very fundamental issues about the theatre's status and viability needed to be addressed. Could the artistic policy be revitalised? How were the constraints imposed by the building itself to be tackled? How was innovation to be managed and to what extent was the Studio's profile an index of the overall health of the company?

The Studio

It was very difficult to programme the Studio consistently. The Rep directorate was clear that financial stability was best achieved by concentrating all available resources in the main house, but the Arts Council effectively held a pistol to the theatre's head over any suggestion of cutting more radical work. But there were periods when nothing could be done. The run of premières inaugurated by *Harvest* in 1980-1 came after seven months of darkness. The Studio was also closed throughout the autumn and early winter of 1983-4. The more creative solution was to provide a home for visiting companies. October and November 1981 saw a clutch of women's work: the Traverse Theatre's production of Claire Luckham's *Trafford Tanzi*, Monstrous Regiment with Rose Tremain's *Yoga Class*, and Extraordinary Productions with Bryony Lavery's *Missing*. Bryony Lavery also wrote and promoted through Extraordinary Productions *Zulu!*— the entire Zulu wars of 1879 as performed by the two-man National Theatre of Brent. The following March and April Shared Experience, Lumiere and Son and Joint Stock came with plays. Also the Birmingham Youth Theatre continued to have a home there. Speakman and Nicholls directed an adaptation of Bill Naughton's *The Goal Keeper's Revenge* in January 1982.

The only homegrown Studio première of 1982 followed on from BYT. Bill Pryde's production of another Vince Foxall play, a gentle two-hander about W.H. Auden, *Strictly Entre Nous*, which divides the personality of the Birmingham-born poet between two actors was in fact a valedictory. In March he left the Rep to become director of the Cambridge Theatre Company. In the autumn in what otherwise would have been another closed period, Farago and Perry were able to stage small-scale productions of *A Man for All Seasons* and *Look Back in Anger* which were mounted for a British Council tour to Hong Kong.

Ironically while the Rep was struggling to ward off complete collapse in early 1983 the Studio programme regained a stronger balance of home-grown, co-produced and invited-in work which enabled a judicious mix of modern classics and brand new work. Female Trouble (as Extraordinary Productions had become) kicked off in January with Bryony Lavery's *Female Trouble*—Lavery, indeed, was beginning to consolidate what was to prove a long-term relationship with the Rep. In February, a week late through actor illness, Ian Brown directed a well-attended production of *The Caretaker* which was a co-production with the Cambridge Theatre Company. Ellen Dryden's *It's a Lovely Day Tomorrow* was premièred by Farago, relieved not to have to amplify her finely-nuanced dialogue for the main house. Farago also directed the British première of Stewart Parker's *Nightshade* while Foxall's play about Ruth Ellis *One Reputably Glamorous Woman* which had started life as a Rep commission was staged as a co-production following its première by the Sheffield Crucible. In July, before darkness descended again, Arnold Wesker came to direct the première of *Annie Wobbler*: three interlinked monologues which he had written specially to exploit the versatility and comic power of Nichola McAuliffe. McAuliffe was no stranger to the Rep or Wesker's work and this gave her an opportunity to give a virtuoso solo performance as three characters ranging from the elderly cockney char/bag-lady of the title, recalled from Wesker's childhood, to a scantily-clad high-flying student and finally a forty-year old novelist suddenly catapulted from obscurity to literary fame. For Wesker it may have served as a consolation prize for fact that Perry's plan to revive *The Kitchen* in the main house proved impossible.

When the Studio reopened six months later in January 1984, the BYT's production of Roy Mitchell's *The Walking Class* directed by Derek Nicholls inaugurated a powerful run of work. The première of Ellen Dryden's *Anna's Room* attracted the largest recorded Studio audience for a new play. In March there was a dynamic production of David Mamet's *American Buffalo* which brought a director –one John Adams—who was new to the Rep to work in the space. In April and May the home team resumed control. Pryde directed Roy Marsden and Barbara Jefford in the British première of Alexander Vampilov's *Last Summer in Chulimsk* which again brought in good audiences. Perry completed the season with Tom Kempinski's *Duet for One*.

Thus the nurturing of Ellen Dryden's development as a dramatist with three new plays staged between 1983 and 1985 took place within a context of diverse and wide-ranging work. The fact that it was a somewhat insecure working environment was also oddly appropriate to her artistic preoccupations. She commented at the time of *It's a Lovely Day Tomorrow* 'If one of my plays works, it works through creating believable, fallible, muddled people' (*BP*, 15.3.83). Certainly she had a gift for dialogue. *Lovely Day*, set in a Telford school hall, is structured round a two-strand narrative which shifts between the documentary recollections of wartime tragedy which form the basis of a play about the Second World War to be performed by a feminist fringe company, and the emotional battles fought out amongst the company members. Tessa Peake-Jones and Vivien Heilbron played Steph and Annie the two anchors of the company while Madeline Church played Louise the laconic drifter who turns up to challenge her father, the group director (Michael Harbour) who abandoned her as a baby. Fred Norris's review (*EM*, 18.3.83), complained that nothing happened, but Eric Shorter invoked Chekhov as he praised the naturalistic dialogue of players who 'ruminate, bicker, reminisce and philosophise in a provincial school hall' (*DT*, 6.4.83).

There was a very similar response to *Anna's Room* which Farago premièred the following year. Tessa Peake-Jones was cast again, this time playing a doctor and former school friend of the eponymous heroine Anna, a history teacher played by Petra Markham who is seeking independence from a former lover. The story of how Anna discovers a sense of identity and emotional depth while Prue reveals an unsuspected capacity for cruelty is intercut with 'visions' of other historical models for Anna all played by Mary Rutherford. Gareth Lloyd Evans praised the economical precision of dialogue which served a variety of emotional effects and indicated differences in age and class (*G*, 11.2.84). The perceptiveness and quiet humour were ideally placed in the Studio space. By 1985, however, the writing had shifted into a different register. in reviewing *Weekend Break* Irving Wardle acknowledged Dryden as a 'formidable practitioner of waspish point-scoring dialogue' (*T*, 14.3. 85), but there were also complaints about an overly schematic script and puppet characters. Mary Rutherford played Jessie, a wife saddled with an appalling chauvinist husband, who enrolls for a weekend course on 'Neglected Women Writers' and is inspired to rebellion by the example of the Restoration poet and playwright Aphra Behn. The designer Adele Anggard faithfully realised areas of an old house for the set but for a play which came across as a drawing room comedy possibly better suited for the main stage.

Coping with the Stage

There was always tension about how best to deal with the enormous stage—'a home which needs a celebration each time you do a production' as Perry put it. When he directed Wilde's *An Ideal Husband* in May 1983. Robin Thornber's review dwelt wearily on the opulent sets and ravishing costumes: the meticulous, painstaking good taste, lumbering scene changes and heavily-mannered acting. The 'real reason', he decided, for the production was the set 'The Birmingham audience seems to like spectacle' (*G*, 26.5.83). Perry was clearly trying to satisfy the 'worthy burgher' expectation but as audiences only reached 40% it seems that both men may have been wrong. Certainly Farago working a month before with Geoffrey Scott on the British première of Arthur Miller's *The American Clock* appeared to challenge that assumption when he made an epic stage accommodate the fate of a nation. Described by Miller as a mural for the theatre, *The American Clock* is arguably his most Brechtian play with an episodic approach to the impact of the Depression on American society. Fifteen actors played over forty characters on Scott's bare, wooden octagonal stage backed by a montage of pictures from the period projected onto five screens. The veteran variety entertainer Ben Warriss played the grandfather of the central family whose financial collapse Miller charts. Antonia Pemberton gave the most powerful performance as the mother whose eventual breakdown turns her from a piano-playing, graceful lady in a floating gown, to a slatternly derelict.

Just as Wilkinson was appointed, the production of *Dear Anyone* featured a set of awesome proportions. Directed by David Taylor with designs by Ralph Koltai and book by Jack Rosenthal, this new British musical charts the career-journey of insignificant New York newspaper-switchboard-girl turned-agony-aunt, Mercedes Taylor, played by RSC actress Jane Lapotaire, from caring confidante to cynical, self-indulgent bitch renamed Pandora. The American comedian/musical comedy star Stubby Kaye played Harry the mailman who becomes the newspaper's features editor. Critically it was a success with show-stopping central performances and an exceptionally strong chorus which belted out songs like the hilariously-raunchy 'Shortcomings' about the sexual disfunctions which form the basis of many of the agony-aunt letters.

It was clearly intended for a London transfer. Koltai designed a stunning two-level set. Surrounded by traditional dingy New York tenements, the office of the New York Globe was a futuristic perspex globe shining out of a revolving-doored entrance. The whole structure made from expanded metal mesh coated in perspex was exceptionally high. Terrified actors had to climb, in stiletto heels, up a vertical ladder to reach a cat walk to go through doors to reach levels which opened out some twelve feet above the stage floor. There was even a wheeled curved staircase on wheels to negotiate. It was difficult not to be impressed even though Tudor Davies as choreographer had little room for his dancers to manoeuvre. The show transferred for a run at the Cambridge Theatre.

The following March, *Hamlet*, Farago's final Shakespeare production was heavily encumbered with Poppy Mitchell's set. She used huge misty-grey drapes falling like fluted pillars to complement a mass of staircases which spiralled up to platforms, descended to some nameless pit and flew off at weird angles. With the help of light and sound the ghost seemed to appear on many different levels, or he did when the awkward sight-lines permitted the illusion its full effect. Actor-walkways were quilted with carpet-felt squares which was supposed to add an even greater sense of mystery and menace. The fatal weakness in the concept was that all the movement up and down stairs slowed the pace which tended to exacerbate the critical perception that the supporting cast were weak and undermotivated. That said, the publicity-attracting ploy of casting Simon Cadell best-known for his role in the popular TV series *Hi De Hi* proved to be a creative choice even though he had to endure schools' matinee cat-calls of 'hi de hi'. Martin Hoyle in his *Financial Times* review (11.4. 84) wrote of how the comedian's gift fed into Hamlet 'his tentative, trotting gait and sudden awareness of his own silliness are details in a portrait of emotional potential untapped'.

Audiences may have liked spectacular sets but it was also clear (pace Thornber) that they were not so easily persuaded into accepting shows that had little other intrinsic value or harboured sub-standard performance. Perry's production of *Treasure Island* for Christmas 1984 featured one of the most technically complex transformation scenes to the 'good ship Hispaniola' ever seen in the theatre. The scene-change utilising the under-stage lift combined with immaculately-timed flying of sails and rigging was greeted with gasps from the audience. The casting of guest star Jack Douglas as Long John Silver, however, was greeted with critical derision. By the actor's own admission he was a disaster.

Bill Pryde who returned to direct *Romeo and Juliet* immediately after *Treasure Island* in February 1985 spoke to Terry Grimley about the problem of getting his very detailed work with actors to project the full extent of the auditorium 'If you sit in the back row you can't even see the expression on the actors' faces' (*BP*, 9.2. 85). Three years earlier he had relinquished the responsibilty of directing on the main stage with some relief. In the event *Romeo and Juliet* was a great success with Douglas Hodge as a robust romantic Romeo with Tessa Peake-Jones 'round-faced and bright-eyed' (*FT*, 28.2.85), as Juliet. Shaun Irwin's design utilised the hydraulic platform which had assisted the rise of the *Treasure Island* ship but to much greater effect in a more satisfying production.

New Initiatives

By May 1985, however, there was a brand-new engineering and design concept which John Dove and designer Di Seymour were able to utilise for the première of Stephen Bill's *Naked in the Bull Ring*. Perry, for all his apparent capitulation to scenic elaboration had never ceased to hope that a more manageable main stage space might be achieved. As far back as 1978 he had contemplated creating a reduced-sized performance area by bringing down the safety curtain and seating the audience on the stage. Announcing ambitious plans to nearly double the number of future productions 'More for Less' in the programme for *A Man for All Seasons* in April 1985, Perry described a seven-year quest mounted by Christopher Morley and Jeff Kitto to 'design a new theatre within the theatre'. The idea as he put it was to reduce the number of seats, project the action closer to the audience and 'produce a whole library of plays which the very physical nature of the vastness of the big original stage had prevented before'. What came to be known as 'the Box' was a flexible multi-truck system which formed a motorised platform which rolled down to stop dead at the safety curtain line thus creating a reduced-size stage thrust out to row D at ground level. Occasionally for dramatic effect the set would literally roll down towards the audience at the start of a performance. The playing space, it was argued, would be less challenging for actors, contact with the audience would be enhanced, sets could be more economical, the turnaround between productions easier and thus more cost-effective. The City Council came up with an extra grant to help build it and even the Arts Council was impressed by the artistic and financial potential.

This was just one component of a bigger strategy for change. While the accumulated deficit was substantially reduced, Government economic constraints were threatening the level of Arts Council funding. Indeed Thatcherite ideology was hardly sympathetic towards the very principle of state funding for the arts. The Board meeting on 2 February 1984 had been forced to face the possibility that the Arts Council would not be maintaining its grant in real terms thus causing a serious shortfall which in turn would have a knock-on effect on the £1 for £1 basis of the City Council's grant. The publication in March 1984 of the National Arts Strategy *The Glory of the Garden* put external pressures on the Rep just when it was struggling to achieve something like financial stability. The document's rhetoric managed to combine romantic idealism about the value of the arts to the nation while adhering firmly to the market-driven principles which drove the government's agenda. While the document argued the case for more regional arts provision and a greater role for the Regional Arts Associations it also insisted on the need for increased partnership funding from local authorities and private sponsorship. It also suggested that regional theatres should commit to more educational provision and touring.

Perry was resistant to the idea of direct engagement in educational activity, but did respond with a small-scale touring initiative. In the autumn of 1984 his Studio production of a dramatisation of Raymond Briggs' *When the Wind Blows* toured locally with a guarantee against loss provided by West Midlands Arts. Inevitably some of the venues proved problematic but valuable lessons were learnt and the following spring the venture was repeated with *Dear Headmaster*, a double-bill of Rattigan's *The Browning Version* and a devised piece by John Baddeley called the *Rochester Sneath Version*.

The Board meeting on 24 January 1985 saw two more significant developments. There was a unanimous vote in favour of inviting David Edgar to join the Board, and the formal acceptance of a strategy which Perry had been contemplating for some time. Perry proposed to set up a Young Company in order as he put it 'to fulfill some of the aims and objectives of the late Sir Barry Jackson' a small group of actors in their twenties were to be engaged on a seasonal contract of some forty-four weeks to perform in both auditoria and to tour. The new stage format, it was argued at that point, would provide the necessary intimacy and flexibility to permit young artists of proven ability to develop their skills in a wide range of performance styles. Derek Nicholls, an Oxford graduate and former English teacher and the co-founder of the Birmingham Youth Theatre was invited to relinquish his job as Director of the Midlands Arts Centre to run the company. He took up the post in August 1985 eventually to be designated Resident Associate Director. Peter Farago, like Pryde continued to retain a relationship with the Rep as an associate director and advisor but was no longer resident.

The Young Company

Slap bang in the middle of the greed-is-good and value-for-money decade there were those who suggested that the Young Company concept was a way of getting ensemble performance on the cheap. The first company consisted of nine actors, six men and three women, some straight out of drama school who had been selected out of some 500 possible candidates. They included Iain Glen who had won the RADA gold medal the previous year and Devon Scott who was the daughter of the Hollywood film actor George C. Scott. What they all relished was the opportunity to return to something resembling the working conditions which their Rep predecessors had experienced in the 1950s and 60s and display the kind of versatility which had trained actors like Derek Jacobi. They rehearsed during the day and performed at night. They had to alternate between the challenge of the main auditorium and the intimacy of the Studio. They also toured in their very own Young Company mini-bus. By the time they performed *The Snow Queen* to packed morning and matinée houses for Christmas there had been two other productions seen in the main auditorium: *Wuthering Heights*, in an adaptation by Vince Foxall, which opened the autumn season, and a riotously-successful production of Dario Fo's *Accidental Death of an Anarchist* which attracted a visibly younger audience. In the Studio there was a production of Mike Stott's serio-comic play, *Dead Men*, about the pre-history of the Russian Revolution. Talking to Fred Norris, Devon Scott declared herself exhausted but happy 'I would never have missed this chance in all the world' (*EM*, 6.1. 86).

Sceptical souls were forced to admit that it was, after all, rewarding for audiences to see the same actors taking on a variety of roles. Also in Ian MacNeil the ensemble had their own designer who was able to establish a recognisable visual style forged out of the need to be infinitely flexible. For Stuart Patterson's adaptation of *The Snow Queen* the task was to achieve magic with economy in order to permit a swift turnaround each day for the evening performances of the more adult-friendly *Charlie's Aunt* which was designed by Tim Goodchild. After the technological complexity of *Treasure Island* there was approval for the refreshing simplicity of MacNeil's concept. The best moment scenically was when the ice palace of the Snow Queen seemed to float in the air. Devon Scott was a magnificently evil queen smiling implacably in the face of vociferous abuse from the audience. But there were also moments of quiet shock when Marc Culwick's Kay rejected his faithful friend Gerda who was played by Allison Harding. Richard Edmonds described the effect when Iain Glen as the Reindeer guided Gerda towards the snowy wastes of the palace 'apart from silencing a theatre packed with small children, Mr Glen brought a lump to this hardened old reviewer's throat' (*BP*, 12.12.85).

Glen was singled out many times during that year which must have brought back memories of the fledgling stars at the Old Rep. When Ann Fitzgerald reviewed Derek Nicholl's production of *The Recruiting Officer* she was not entirely happy about an approach which she felt lacked humanity despite a meticulous attention to the niceties of period style and speech. But she noticed Glen as Captain Brazen 'Taking the bare bones of the traditional stage fop which Farquhar's text gives him, to build a character of self-deluding silliness, the sort of man that consciously takes up the role of resident eccentric in whatever company he finds himself' (*PP*, May, 1986). MacNeil masked off the bulk of the stage to leave the simple hexagonal performance area on the apron stage. Shifting locations were indicated by little more than the odd flown window or strategically-placed chair.

What distinguished the company from the old-style Rep companies was its obvious youth and the fact that the contracts only lasted for a year when the selection and working process would begin again. Not only did audiences become accustomed to actors playing a range of roles but a range of ages as well. When the Company played Ibsen in Clive Perry's production of *The Wild Duck* in the Studio in May 1986 they inevitably had to age up to play the older characters. Iain Glen's ability to portray the vain, petulant middle-aged Hjalmar Ekdal created a curious sensation of time-warp back to 1945 when Paul Scofield played Dr Wangel in Peter Brook's production of *The Lady from the Sea*. Richard Edmonds praised the way that Crispin Redman handled Greger's speech about the dog trapped beneath the water and of Devon Scott's still, strong Gina Ekdal he wrote that 'when she leaves the stage you feel the terrors of the Nordic night closing in' (*BP*, 23.5.86).

Financing Change

Creating effective theatre required substantial money. Another sign of the times was the necessity to find commercial sponsorship to boost the core funding. Since 1978 there had been some sponsorship for Rep productions from the powerful T.I. Group but increasingly a generous financial commitment from industry for the arts was a way of raising corporate profile for donor and recipient alike. On the advent of the Young Company, P.J. Evans Trucks Ltd. were persuaded to donate a mini-bus for the touring programme. This sponsorship, shared with Freight Rover and worth over £12,000 meant that the business qualified for an award under the Minister for the Arts Business Incentive Scheme. In October 1986 the Arts Minister Richard Luce came to the Rep to present a commemorative plaque to the managing director of Ansells to pay tribute to the brewery's £15,000 sponsorship of an initiative to increase subscription sales as well as backing for the second phase of the Young Company and the 1986 Christmas production of *Peter Pan*. However Wilkinson also engineered one major commercial alliance which would have serious long-term consequences.

The problem of the catering franchise had never been resolved. In 1980 ARA Leisure Services took over the bars and the restaurant but the ongoing concern which crops up in the Rep Board minutes bear witness to chronic dissatisfaction. In 1985 Wilkinson brought in a partnership of Ansells and Iceford Catering which radically revamped the restaurant turning it into a wine bar and a bistro. A fifteen-year contract was agreed. The new operation became a magnet for local young people who came in droves to drink and listen to disco music which reverberated out into the theatre foyer. Eventually there were even bouncers. There was little or no linkage between the theatre programme and the enjoyment of the Café Bar patrons. Wilkinson was happy to see the building play host to local people especially the young, but it did not occur to him to entice them to see a show or consider the effect of the disjunction in ambience on regular theatre-goers.

The input of the Young Company gave the 1985-6 season two parallel programmes which virtually doubled the number of main stage shows. The policy of co-production continued for both auditoria but was deployed more flexibly, not only permitting an increased emphasis on new work, but altering the character of much of what was offered. The 1984-5 mainstage season ended with Bill Pryde's production of *Lost Empires* which was a musical adaptation of J.B. Priestly by Keith Waterhouse and Willis Hall (music by Denis King) mounted in association with the Cambridge Theatre Company. Described in one review as a 'cheerily sedate entertainment' (*ST*, 23.6.85), the show did not achieve the hoped-for London transfer. In October, however, Pryde returned with the première of David Pownall's adaptation of *Pride and Prejudice* which was a co-production with the Leicester Haymarket where the sets were built. The production with Peter Sallis as Mr Bennett later went to the Old Vic for a six week run. In the Studio for two years running from 1985 to 1986 there were fruitful co-productions with Foco Novo on Genet's *Deathwatch* and on a version of Gorky's *The Lower Depths* by Tunde Ikoli. 1985 also saw the Rep in partnership with Temba, the black theatre company, on *Mamma Decembra* by Nigel Moffatt.

The relatively modest regional theatre and small-scale touring production values were in complete contrast to the costly, hi-tech rock musical *Jeanne* based on the life of Joan of Arc which was a venture with Bill Kenwright Productions in September. It actually proved too dangerous to fulfil all the technical demands. The following June, a Theatre Projects co-production of Herb Gardner's *I'm Not Rappaport* which was finally to bring Paul Scofield to the theatre partnered by the black American actor Howard Rollins proved to be a public relations and financial nightmare. Scofield caused chaos when he decided that he needed two weeks extra rehearsal to perfect the première. Once again subscribers were disappointed and performances had to be cancelled. Sebastian Barnes recalled production values in a similarly perfectionist league. One member of the stage crew spent the entire performance solemnly dropping single leaves, at precisely-timed intervals, onto the stage below. The embarrassing tussle with Theatre Projects to get adequate compensation for the inevitable box office losses was to occupy Wilkinson for some considerable time after.

In September 1986 a brave attempt to put onto the main stage the radical work more usually associated with the Studio badly misfired. The Rep combined with Joint Stock to produce *A Mouthful of Birds* by Caryl Churchill and David Lan. This experiment based on *The Bacchae* by Euripides incorporated dance and mime choreography by Ian Spink and for many the production came across as a fragmentary, bewildering disappointment. Many members of the audience simply left at the interval and while there was some critical approval, the overall opinion was damning. What made the experience all the more unpleasant was that at least two national critics also chose to sneer at both Birmingham and Birmingham audiences. In the event the show went down little better with London audiences at the Royal Court. In fact dance audiences at the Rep were fully accustomed to radical performance. The relationship with Ballet Rambert which dates right back to the 1930s had continued with annual visits throughout the 1970s and 80s. Balletomanes had been able to the best of new choreography by major figures like Glen Tetley, Christopher Bruce, Lindsay Kemp, Siobhan Davies and Merce Cunningham.

The Final Phase

Despite the more contemporary and adventurous edge to the programming, and the warm critical response to the Young Company, audiences were still not performing as well as anticipated. Even when Timothy Spall, by 1986 well-known on television, came to star as the flamboyant nineteenth-century dramatist Dion

Boucicault in the première of Stewart Parker's *Heavenly Bodies* which Farago directed, the punters of Birmingham did not rise to the bait. Perry began to voice concerns that the policy of simplified staging was alienating audiences. The Box was not entirely problem-free. For certain kinds of built set design there were complaints about poor sightlines and when it rolled down towards the audience the effect could be unnerving. Indeed in a review of *The Perfect Defence*, a multi-layered who-dunnit by Charles Wood and Gary Bohlke which was encumbered by a large red-brick house set, B.A.Young (*FT*, 28.11.85), commented that the moment when the whole structure moved relentlessly downstage to stop dead at row D was arguably the only exciting moment in the evening.

Perry, along with Christopher Morley had been heavily criticised by Robin Thornber, of all people (*G*, 7.3.86) , for the ostentatiously simple setting for their production of *The Winter's Tale* staged in March 1986. Transparencies of branches projected onto huge grey right-angled screens signalled the movement from winter to summer while doors cut into the screens led onto the dappled octagonal stage out at the audience's feet. Most of the design elaboration provided by Morley's students at his theatre design school at Birmingham Polytechnic was focused on historically eclectic costumes: the court in jewel-like autumnal colours; the rural community in exquisitely-quilted and embroidered pastels.

There were several familiar faces in the cast: Peter Woodward who played Leontes together with Bob Grant as Autolycus and Antonia Pemberton as Paulina. Richard Edmonds welcoming the production reckoned it was like 'the real old repertory days' (*BP*, 5.3.86), when audiences came to see actors they knew. Woodward had begun to carve out a niche for himself at the Rep. First appearing as Cashel Byron in *Bashville*, he replaced an injured actor as Mercutio in *Romeo and Juliet* as well as directing the fights. He also played Lord Fancourt Babberley, the eponymous 'heroine' of *Charlie's Aunt*. At a time when it was vital that season programming should be contained within tightly-controlled budgets the prospect of showing off a popular actor's writing skills would have seemed attractive. Woodward's play *Outside Broadcast*, a comedy about a 1950s' radio broadcast of *Julius Caesar* was staged in June 1986 as the final production of the main season. Despite the fact that his 'amiably chaotic farce' was described by Michael Coveney as a structural mess (*FT*, 26.6.86), both Woodward and the Rep persevered. The following year he wrote and starred in *The Golden Years of Jack Buchanan* which proved highly successful and wrote *Wilfred*, a play about the war poet Wilfred Owen which was directed by Michael Meacham in the Studio.

A new, twelve-strong, Young Company, this time with two black actors, was formed for the 1986-7 season. The company still mounted its own independent main stage productions like the première of Fay Weldon's adaptation of *Jane Eyre* which Nicholls had commissioned, and Michael Meacham's production of Philip King's farce *See How They Run*. But the young actors were also integrated into the main subscription season which included *Peter Pan* at Christmas and Nicholl's production of *Julius Caesar* where Tam Hoskyns who played the title role in *Jane Eyre* was cast as Portia. While the directorate were concerned to preserve the company identity the decision to make use of actors for non YC productions was necessary if only to justify the increased salary costs necessitated by the increase in company size. There were other tensions. The short Young Company runs, the need for quick turn rounds and the demands of touring inevitably created technical and labour strains which were costly. No one, least of all the Arts Council with Anthony Everitt now Deputy Secretary General, wanted to abandon the Company and if anything the pressure for more innovation was even stronger. But it was equally clear that public funding was going to remain limited.

That said, the Young Company remained an exciting, if exhausting enterprise. Weldon's *Jane Eyre* which was only the third play by a woman to be seen on the main stage, went on to achieve considerable long-term success. Tam Hoskyns, in her first professional role, played opposite David Lansbury's Rochester in what was described as a profoundly erotic re-telling of Charlotte Brontë's story. Moving back through time in a series of flashbacks, Weldon focuses on the narrowness of women's lives and the particular powerlessness of the lone woman at the time Brontë was writing. Mark Lockyer played a proto-fascist Mr Brocklehurst while Gareth Tudor-Price played Jane's other suitor, St John Rivers. The multi-levelled set evoked a rambling, mysterious house with high walls, a steeply gabled roof and staircases disappearing into the flies. Back-lit gauzes which at first looked like dull brown wall coverings allowed particular rooms to come into focus for different moments in the narrative. A month later the company were appearing in the Studio in a fast and physically-energetic production of Ben Jonson's *The Alchemist* which Nicholls also directed. Alex Kingston played Doll Common with Mark Lockyer as Abel Drugget and Gareth Tudor-Price as Sir Epicure Mammon. The audience were thrust into the heart of a threadbare thieves' kitchen thick with bubbling vapours and incense and brooms, bottles and warming pans suspended from the ceiling.

There was a final flourish of new work in the Studio as this particular phase in its history drew to a close. The fortuitously titled and authored *King John's Jewel* was written by David Pownall and directed by Bill Pryde in April 1987. Set in 1212, the play revolves around two hours in the life of King John as he is camped in an ancient stone circle, fifteen miles south of Nottingham. Surrounded by the remains of long-dead civilisations, the king strives to weld a united kingdom out of the warring and disparate factions who also threaten his own life. Julian Glover played the king and Ian MacNeil designed the set which consisted of 200 metres of real grass which was maintained with copious watering, ultra-violet light, ventilation fans and insect repellent. The emphasis on the continuity of human experience and the ordinary concerns of everyday life which invariably accompany historic events, was reinforced by the smell of the turf just six inches away.

The Travelling Players by Chris Hawes which was premièred in May was the first (and last) commission by the Young Company. This was epic theatre crammed into a small space and played with all the vitality which had become the hallmark of the ensemble. A knowledge of *Hamlet* was almost essential to an understanding of the play which went even further than Shakespeare in manipulating the way art and reality merge. A group of actors, touring some unspecified East European state following a bloody revolution, are detained on suspicion of harbouring a fugitive member of the bourgeoisie who bears a distinct resemblance to Shakespeare's prince. Forced to play for their military captors, the actors' ability to take on new roles becomes the means of their survival.

For some local critics it came across as a teasing difficult play which lost its way in conceptual muddle. For Pat Ashworth writing in the *Guardian* (9.5.87), it was 'a pageant, interweaving brilliantly-costumed travesties of Shakespeare with swift and terrible tableaux of war'. Ian Judge directed, Peter Brewis added music, and designer Mark Negin exploited the height of the Studio to create the decaying grandeur of former royal stables with a classical bas-relief of horse and rider. The actors were dragged around on a big sledge. Julie Lloyd Barrie was singled out as a prima donna leading lady. Michael Brazier played the Prince while Ted Richards gave a lunatic performance as the ghost of Hamlet's father.

The Young Company proved to be a short-lived experiment although former members of the company would return to the theatre in future years. In *Wilfred*, Crispin Redman played the doomed war poet and it was fitting that a YC graduate should mark the end of an era. The ensemble had revived memories of Honer's early work in the Studio and of course reached back to the resident companies of the old theatre. The Studio space would now pass into a different directorial control with a very different agenda.

Looking to the Future

In mid-1986 Perry had signalled his desire to accept an invitation to go to Pitlochry and indeed directed little in his final season. He bowed out with a Young Company Studio production of *Entertaining Mr Sloane*. On the night of 5 March 1987 he went out onto the main stage to receive a farewell gift of a silver salver from the new Board Chairman John Bettinson secure in the knowledge that he and the Rep had survived through eleven turbulent years. All was not well, however, despite the excitement created by the Young Company and attempts at more innovative programming. Audiences remained very variable. There was still an accumulated deficit and for many theatre-goers in Birmingham, the Rep was no longer such a significant presence on the City's cultural scene. Marjorie Brown who had done so much to support Perry through his time resigned as Chairman in July 1986 although she continued to be a Board member until 1990. Although of a different background and political persuasion, Brown and Bettinson had worked well together. His memories of the Rep stretched back to childhood visits in the late 1930s. It was his job to co-ordinate the search for a new artistic director.

David Edgar was part of the selection team. He had become chair of the artistic sub-committee in the autumn of 1985. Ironically in view of past events, he was the only Board member ever to get a special article in a Rep programme celebrating his appointment. In the programme for *Naked In the Bull Ring* he reflected on the vital importance of new writing as well as the responsibility that theatres like the Rep had for its promotion. His polemic, however, was now more measured than in 1975 recognising the very real difficulties. In Board meetings he urged the creation of a recognisable company style and criticised programming which failed to promote a coherent artistic identity. The report which his committee tabled in October 1986 explored the theatre's record—especially the decline in audiences—against the background of regional industrial recession and demographic change—and gave detailed examples of work in both the main house and the Studio which had proved successful. The intention was to provide a framework within which Perry's successor would be appointed. No venture in programming, touring or co-production should 'sacrifice a clear Birmingham Repertory Theatre identity and spirit'.

It was considered important to develop the work of the now multi-racial Young Company and two further initiatives were signalled. The abolition that year of the six metropolitan county councils released funds from the West Midlands County Council which were to be used to set up the Sir Barry Jackson County Fund administered by the Sir Barry Jackson Trust. It was hoped to use grants from the fund to recruit small companies to tour small-scale plays to non-conventional venues. Associated with this venture, and in direct response to the Arts Council's imperative to all its theatre clients to upgrade their educational policies, it was proposed to appoint an Animateur who would promote and extend the value of community touring by further practical activity.

The Board advertised for a 'Grand Theatrical Inventor' to re-invent a theatre based in a great city of inventions. The man they got almost literally ran into the building.

9. Running a Marathon: John Adams

Marathon Man

John Adams had competed in marathons and loved to run. As artistic director of the Bolton Octagon he regularly ran to work and, presenting himself to the Birmingham press in March 1987 as both strong-minded and ebullient, he was clearly determined to hurl himself into the task of revitalising the Rep. He would not be content with the role of impresario; he would be an active stage director as well. 'There are some people who can do both' he insisted to Robin Thornber. 'It's my vision on stage that moves through the bricks and mortar and out into the city' (G, 6.3.87). In the course of the April Rep Board meeting when Marjorie Brown suggested that it was not part of his role to question the poor quality of the lunch-time sandwiches served in the Café Bar Adams replied that in order to make Birmingham Rep the best regional theatre in the United Kingdom he would need to consider all aspects of the organisation. It was a view endorsed by David Edgar on behalf of the Appointment Committee. This artistic director was to have a wider responsibility for the theatre and its work.

John Adams was forty-two and had been artistic director of the Bolton Octagon Theatre for three years before coming to Birmingham. He too was an Oxford graduate with a degree in English and history. After leaving university he served an apprenticeship in various practical aspects of theatre, including lighting design and box office management, before directing his first production at Dundee Rep. As co-founder, with the playwright David Pownall, of Paines Plough, the Writer's Company, which for a time was based at Warwick University, he had a proven record in the promotion of new writing. As a freelance director he staged several productions at the Belgrade Theatre and, in 1984, the Rep Studio production of *The American Buffalo*. He had been a great success at the Octagon broadening and increasing the audience base and enjoying a happy relationship with the local community. The Octagon could accommodate an audience of between four and five hundred within a completely flexible auditorium and the implications of the spatial contrast were not lost on local Birmingham journalists who made the usual invidious comparisons. But Adams refused to be daunted even as he acknowledged the difficulty of the challenge. What a big theatre needed, he claimed, was drama on the same scale: epic theatre. 'We're not going to pretend the stage is smaller than it is—we're pretending it's even bigger' (*BP*, 5.9.87).

While it was clear that Adams was temperamentally the polar opposite of Clive Perry, before he left Perry was prepared to accept and even support his successor's critique of company policy. Adams argued that there was a lack of logic in a budget which aimed for substantial box office income while deploying noticeably limited human and production resources on the main stage. It was vital to put more actors on the stage. Apart from the Christmas show only seven actors per show were planned. For Perry the problem lay in historic underfunding. A full programme in the main house, he stated, would require an additional £200,000 a year. As a preliminary move Adams proposed splitting the 1987-8 season into two so that only the first four shows until Christmas would be announced and then marketed on a '4 for the price of 3' basis. With an eye to past damage to subscriber confidence, this had the added advantage of reducing the risk that longer-term planning might have to be changed.

Out went Perry's proposed autumn season, out went the Box and the philosophy of reduced staging, and out went the constraint of small casts. Out also, and to considerable controversy, went the Young Company. In order for main stage productions to make a stronger impact it was necessary to cast actors of both proven range and experience. The Young Company, Adams declared, was the forerunner of the new Birmingham Repertory Company. The nineteen actors, including four black actors, who were cast for his opening production of Christopher Sergel's adaptation of Harper Lee's *To Kill a Mocking Bird* were to form the basis of a permanent company which could be augmented by guest stars such as Fenella Fielding and Christopher Benjamin who appeared in the second show *The School for Scandal.*

Outreach and Inreach

This policy could only be sustained by making economies on a home-grown Studio programme. Adams came up, however, with a creative rationale for the necessity of invited-in product. The autumn season was marketed under the general title of 'Made in the West Midlands' and largely revolved around local companies including Tic Toc, Theatre Foundry, Snarling Beasties and the Big Brum T.I.E. company. There were also two black companies: Temba and the new Midlands-based Third Dimension. Black artists in the Studio and the main house in greater force than ever before signalled a theatre policy which at long last was to address the multi-ethnic Birmingham community.

To Kill a Mocking Bird proved a hugely popular opening production and the theme of race relations in 1930s' Alabama naturally brought in black actors. Michael Buffong played Tom Robinson, falsely-accused of rape and defended by the white liberal lawyer Atticus Finch (Peter Needham), while Wabei Siyolwe played Tom's wife Helen. Morel Bernard played the Finchs' indomitable housekeeper Calpurnia and Ram John Holder played the Reverend Sykes. In The School for Scandal, the programme notes for Sheridan's play detailed the extent of the black population in eighteenth-century England thus justifying the more radical casting of black actors in an English classic play. Buffong and Holder played Trip and Mr Rowley while the Zambian-born Siyolwe played the key romantic role of Maria. For Adams' long-term impact on the theatre it was an opening move towards a policy of integrated or 'colour-blind' casting which would help break down barriers within the acting profession and, it was hoped, attract more diverse audiences.

The Rep was now fully committed to a policy of community outreach supported by the touring fund. Indeed the touring policy provided the only two Rep company productions which were seen in the Studio. Derek Nicholls, who directed both, was determined that the primary focus should be on the actors' physical skills. John Burrow's One Big Blow about a colliery brass band whose cornet player is suffering from pneumoconiosis, which was originally written for the 7.84 Company with music by Rick Lloyd, was launched in September at Hockley Port. The complete absence of set or props meant that the brass band had to be created from the actors' own voices. By mid-November some twenty-three assorted college and community centres had been visited. In February there was a tour of the Shared Experience version of Tales From the Arabian Nights. It was stripped-down in more ways than one. Billed as strictly for the over-15s, its exuberant retelling of the more erotic tales meant bare bottoms as well as a bare stage.

Mick Yates who had considerable experience of community playmaking and touring was appointed Animateur initially on a one-year contract financed by the touring fund. Before arriving at the Rep in September 1987, he had spent six months as playwright in residence in a Youth Custody Centre in Northumberland. During the first year at the Rep he was to run an extensive programme of pre and post-performance workshops in conjunction with the community tours. The emphasis was to be on extra-curricular, barnstorming entertainment with workshops reinforcing outreach and audience development. By the following summer in July 1988 outreach became inreach in the Theatre Focus fortnight when school groups were brought for free into the Studio to work with small theatre companies in devised performance pieces and watch presentations of work. The Birmingham Federation of Youth Theatres, set up that year to coordinate the activities of the network of locally-based youth drama groups, also benefited from a joint showing of sample work.

An Even Bigger Stage

From the beginning Adams' principal objective was to make the main stage the focus of attention and to celebrate its heroic scale with equally heroic design values. When the dusty timbered houses on Saul Radomsky's set for *To Kill a Mocking Bird* revolved to reveal a sweltering Alabama court house, complete with old-fashioned ceiling fans, the audience broke into spontaneous applause. A month later there were gasps and again applause when Simon Higlett's design for *The School for Scandal* was revealed. The scandal-mongers who open Sheridan's play gathered for the first scene, not in Lady Sneerwell's house, but in Hyde Park so the stage could be filled with greensward and surrounded by an engraved cut-out panorama of London.The programme note about the French fashion for manned hot-air balloons came vibrantly to life when a full-sized two-dimensional balloon descended and whisked away Mr Crabtree and Sir Benjamin Backbite in pursuit of the scandal-hating Maria. Lady Teazle enraged her husband crossing the park with a barrow-load of flowers to embellish the black and white classical pretensions of their town lodgings—the architect's instruction for 'white marble' was written on the wall of the interior set. There were cardboard cut-out sedan chairs and a roll-on, roll-off cut-out chamber orchestra.

At Christmas, Derek Nicholl's revived *The Wizard of Oz*. With designs by Terry Parsons, the show was an orgy of colour and 1930s Art Deco style. All the sets were contained within a rainbow-shaped frame which incorporated the orchestra pit. The Munchkin town was made up of lollypops and ice cream-cone houses and sweet-dotted streets. Oz itself was like a 1930s hotel lobby all marble and majolica, pillars and chandeliers and coloured green, gilt, turquoise and ultramarine. The girl dancers looked like Ziegfeld lovelies in plumed fan-shaped headresses. The Jitterbugs wore pink spectacles over black stocking masks, white gloves and shoes and bopped in pink zoot suits. Dorothy encountered her three new friends in a landscape of stylised hills and trees. Sue Devaney played Dorothy avoiding a quasi-Judy Garland performance and relying instead on what Martin Hoyle in the *Financial Times* called 'a warm voice with a hint of throaty plangency' (15.12.87). There was praise also for Tom Fahy's Tin Man and Aline Mowat's vigorous Wicked Witch of the West. In terms of audience approval, the production broke all records since *Worzel Gummidge*.

A Renaissance Event

Given the limited seating capacity in the Studio there was no way an influx of audience could generate a large income, but it was certainly possible to generate excitement and welcome publicity. Kenneth Branagh, at that time the golden boy of British theatre, had set up the Renaissance Company with David Parfitt in 1987 as a response to the growing discontent amongst actors about the power and dictatorial dominance of the director. The company's spring 1988 residency in the Studio was very much a pooling of resources by the Rep and Renaissance to create an ambitious and exciting project. Judi Dench, Geraldine McEwan and Derek Jacobi were invited to direct fifteen actors in some seventy roles in productions of Shakespeare's *Much Ado About Nothing, As You Like It* and *Hamlet*. Each production opened in succession from March to May and finally played in repertoire.

Audiences flocked to see the glamorous visitors and sit on three sides of Jenny Tiramani's simple evocative sets. Visually they were moved from an early romantic Napoleonic era for *Much Ado*—all sun-bleached wood, pale marble and white muslin—to dried leaves and arrangements of fern and grasses for a mid-Victorian *As You Like It*. Finally *Hamlet*, located at the decaying end of the nineteenth century, was played in a stark black box offset only by red velvet curtains. Branagh played a laid-back charming Benedict to Samantha Bond's husky-voiced, rather melancholy Beatrice. Bond then turned up as a voluptuous Phoebe in *As You Like It* while Branagh played Touchstone as a cheekie-chappie blend of Max Miller and Archie Rice dressed in a dreadful red and orange-checked suit. Tam Hoskins, a Young Company graduate, played Rosalind/Ganymede as a bouncy street urchin in baggy trousers. The climax of the project was reached with Branagh's Hamlet: pale, intense and sunk in an emotional distress which bordered on madness from the beginning. Sophie Thompson played a nervy, pre-Rahaelite Ophelia who degenerated into lank-haired lunacy fishing not flowers, but bits of twig and bone out of an ugly modern coat.

A Strong Start

In his Chairman's statement in July 1988, John Bettinson was able to report a gratifying level of achievement. By the end of the financial year in March there was a surplus of £59,181 which enabled the previous year's deficit to be cleared and money put towards a proposed capital renewal programme. Bettinson wrote warmly of the change in style which Adams represented, but also paid tribute to the good housekeeping maintained by Clive Wilkinson who had resigned at the end of January. Whereas Clive Perry had kept a discreet distance from the day-to-day running of the theatre, Adams insisted on being involved in everything. He and Wilkinson would have found it difficult to work in harmony.

The new policy seemed to work although, as Adams and Nicholls had discovered, the main house audience needed careful handling. Nicholl's raunchy production of *Privates on Parade* and the sex and violence cocktail offered by Adams' production of *No Orchids for Miss Blandish* in April and May visibly upset some patrons. The ground had been safer with guest director Michael Meacham's pre-Christmas production of Aykbourn's *Chorus of Disapproval* which he successfully relocated from the North to the Midlands, and then *Death of a Salesman* which he directed in March. In February Adams' production of Stoppard's *The Real Thing* was his first attempt with designer Roger Butlin to mount an essentially chamber piece with the kind of visually innovative approach normally reserved for larger-scale plays. Nicholl's production in July of *The Railway Children* which deployed a breath-taking train effect designed by Simon Higlett did well at a notoriously difficult time of the year.

The honeymoon continued. In September Robin Midgley's production of *A Midsummer Night's Dream* set a modern Bottom's dream in an elaborate Victorian-style fairy world again designed by Higlett. With the added attraction of rock singer/actress Toyah Wilcox as Hermia, this was the best-attended Shakespeare since *King Lear* in 1980. Nicholl's production of David Storey's rarely-performed *The Contractor* did less well but the stage was ideal for the construction of the huge marquee which is the play's dominant image. At Christmas, *Alice in Wonderland* which again Nicholls directed, attracted even larger audiences than the previous year. Adults were also happy to go to the Studio for some seasonal spine-chilling in Adams' production of *The Woman in Black* which ran for six weeks in January and February. Ian MacNeil as designer turned the whole space into an atmospheric recreation of a furniture and props-cluttered back-stage area of a Victorian theatre.

Where Adams really came into his own, however, was with precisely the kind of chamber drama theoretically least suited to the big stage. J.B. Priestley's 1946 play *An Inspector Calls* sends an apparently prosaic police inspector to a wealthy Edwardian family in the North Midlands with news of the needless death of a young girl which it is clear the family's class attitudes and industrial practices are responsible for. Despite its apparently naturalistic setting the play is closer to an expressionist parable. The Inspector moves outside time with a supernatural mission to expose the corruption and callousness of the society represented by the Birling family.

As the 1988 pre-Christmas production, Adams took on the melodramatic quality of the play, abandoned realism and shifted into operatic gear as he choreographed the relationships across Roger Butlin's huge banqueting hall set. A corner of the hall was constructed out of colossal pillars and marble walls with the confident Edwardian values *Peace, Prosperity, Progress* emblazoned across the top. As Harold Innocent's Inspector probed beneath the surface of the family's complacency so the bricks and floors of the set literally loosened and cracked.

At the end of the play, as time reels back, so smoke as from hell fires billowed up through the fractures in the tiled floor.

Two months later in February 1989 the same artistic team worked on the intimate soirée from hell in *Who's Afraid of Virginia Woolf*. Adams cast Sylvia Syms and James Bolam as Martha and George who expose the tortured underbelly of their marriage in a night of mutual flagellation and guest-baiting. Their horrified guests, ultimately compelled to reveal their own marital inadequacies, were played by Syms' daughter Beatie Edney and Jerome Flynn. Pat Ashworth writing in the *Guardian* (9.2.89) commented that the two halves of Butlin's raked, circular dark blue set looked as though they had been pushed apart by continental drift. Black central doors straight out of a Greek tragedy operated like sluice gates only just holding back the torrent which split the arena. The messy jumble of books redolent of George's academic failure were pushed to the perimeter of a lounge dominated by a huge drinks table and a larger-than-life stature of Martha's father which loured over the proceedings. The dark operatic ambience, combined with Paul Byant's brutal lighting and Adams' vivid directorial choreography, elicited powerful performances from all four actors. Syms came across as a younger, more attractive Martha than usually played as she counter-balanced the character's manipulative arrogance with increasing drunkenness and desperation. Michael Schmidt in the *Daily Telegraph* (13.2.89) much admired Bolam's skill. He was, he decided 'an architect with Albee's language: his sentences unfold in all their baroque banality'.

Adams' final flourish of the season was grande guignol writ large. Thomas Middleton's *Women Beware Women* is a revenge play from the 1620s which rejoices in such juicy plot details as clandestine marriage, forced seduction, incest, adultery and multiple murder. Adams and his designer Paul Brown updated the Florentine setting to the nineteenth century so the whole production seemed more like an opera by Verdi. The balconies and stairs provided ample spying places while the art treasures shown to the central female victim Bianca were kept in glass cases: objects to be confined and contained just like Middleton's women. Bianca's poor husband Leantio and his mother played by Mark Jax and Brenda Dowsett lived in a subterranean hovel under the stage. The dominant images of Roman Catholicism masked a corrupt society. Indeed the wicked Duke emerged from a huge statue of the Madonna to trap the hapless Bianca. Adams added an extra-textual Master of Ceremonies moving in and out of the action and played by David Moylan with a ghastly white shaven head and a demoniacal laugh. Patricia Quinn played Livia the wealthy widow whose machinations destroy innocence and love. In the murderous masque of the final scene she descended as Juno seated on a gigantic hand which provoked laughter from the audience. The production ended as macabre farce.

Theatre with the Community

The annual report for 1988-9 took on a new format. Glossily-produced and with numerous illustrations, this public statement clearly set out to celebrate the work and boost the corporate image. Alongside the precise details of production results there were the names of all the theatre staff as well as the actors who had performed during the year. There were some familiar names. Nicholls directed Jane Freeman as Miss Prism in *The Importance of Being of Earnest* and Paul Henry in *The Contractor* and *Privates on Parade*. But it was noticeable that relatively few actors had appeared more than once. The dream of the permanent ensemble had, as before, disappeared. There was, however, a great emphasis on community involvement. All the young people who had taken part in *Railway Children*, *The Dream* and *Alice* were named. Also named were members of Rep Youth Workshop which provided theatre-based activity and performance for young people aged between thirteen and twenty-five.

What was now known as the Community Department had expanded considerably. Mick Yates was now Community Drama Director working with Julia Smith as Community Projects Administrator and a number of independent workshop leaders who ran the Youth Workshop groups. Performances were given both in the Studio and at the Midlands Arts Centre. In addition corporate sponsorship from Ansells had permitted the launch of the XXXX Cabaret Season which presented stand-up comedy at three local pubs. Adams deliberately programmed the Autumn Studio 'Compact Theatre' season of visiting companies to appeal to the 16-30 age group. Tic Toc returned and other companies included Women and Theatre, Gay Sweatshop and an Asian group Urban Turbans. The October Community tour of Willy Russell's *Blood Brothers* directed by Maggie Ford played to nearly four thousand people in forty venues. Gwenda Hughes, the new Associate Director, directed the next Community tour of *On the Plastic*, a play about the credit card culture by Julie Wilkinson which went out in March 1989.

Gwenda Hughes, appointed just before Christmas 1988, had a degree in English and modern history from Liverpool University and began her career as an actor before being awarded an Arts Council Trainee Director's bursary to work with Theatre Centre in 1982. Subsequently she spent three years as Artistic Director of Watford Palace Theatre in Education Company. Further work as a freelance director with such companies as the Women's Theatre Group, Unicorn, M6 Company and Red Ladder gave her a strong political commitment to collective artistic values and the primacy of the woman's experience. Accustomed mainly to small-scale performance, it would be over a year before she directed on the Rep's main stage. However she advised the Board that the Community tour should pay more attention to younger age groups and as a result the tour in December 1989 of Lisa Edwards' *Stamping, Shouting and Singing Home* had a wider family appeal.

Gwenda Hughes brought a whole new female orientation to a theatre which had virtually no record of women's directorial input into artistic policy. Anyone could watch her rehearsals, chip in ideas and assist in the active development of the product. Her first two productions were both written and designed by women. *On the Plastic* deals with a serious social issue but uses the structure of a musical farce. Paul Herbert directed the music. Jane Linz-Roberts designed the set which was split down the middle of neighbouring houses with numerous necessary exits as the confusions and dilemmas created by two sets of debts multiplied. *Stamping, Shouting and Singing*, originally commissioned by Hughes for her Watford company and set in the southern states of America in 1937, tells the story of four generations of women who can trace their collective memory back to slavery. Amanda Fisk's design—sunlit porch, rocking chair, patchwork quilt and tin bath— counterpointed the hopelessness of the black predicament in 1940. All the performers were women and all sang unaccompanied (Herbert directed) negro spirituals. Jenny Jules played the child Lizzie Walker who grows into a young woman determined to fight for freedom.

In June in between the two tours, Hughes initiated the 'Worlds Apart' educational project for children with severe learning difficulties: an activity which had been part of her work in Watford. Based on the theme of a desert island, the complete experience was devised by her with her designer Jane Linz-Roberts and lighting designer Michael Jarvis together with a company of four women teacher/actors: Julie Wilkinson, Janice McKenzie, Tricia Wilcock and Vinny Dihillon. All had experience of community drama or T.I.E and McKenzie, who had worked with Hughes in Watford, had particular experience of this kind of enterprise. With the aim of developing sensory perception and simple communication skills, some 200 pupils from local special schools were encouraged to take part in co-operative activity, problem-solving and decision-making. The seating in the Studio was removed and the whole space was transformed into a desert island complete with sand, rock pools, trees, a pirates' den and two lady pirates. In a warm, safe atmosphere children learnt to touch, appreciate different textures and articulate their experiences.

Heartlanders

'Worlds Apart' was a well-nigh invisible enterprise which was nonetheless of immense importance in terms of the theatre's wider responsibility. *Heartlanders*, the community play staged in the main house in October 1989 was about as visible as it was possible to get. Some three hundred local people, nearly all amateur, took part in what was a vast logistical exercise co-ordinated over several months by Chris Rozanski of the locally-based Theatre of the Unemployed. As an attempt to bring the pluralistic Birmingham community onto the stage, and thereby broaden as well as increase the potential local audience, it was a good many steps beyond the *Up Spaghetti Junction* concept. Preliminary plans, which envisaged a kind of Birmingham version of a modern Mystery cycle with plays written by seven or more dramatists, were scaled down. The script was written collaboratively by David Edgar, Stephen Bill and Anne Devlin, the Belfast-born wife of the director Chris Parr who was then TV drama producer at BBC Pebble Mill. Parr had promoted and directed Edgar's early work in Bradford and had substantial experience in community theatre.

Heartlanders celebrated the town which became a city in 1889, but through engagement with Birmingham in 1989. Three strangers converge at Digbeth bus station: Aan (Jatinder Pal), straight from India looking for the beach and Katya (Denise Seneviratne) the girl he has dreamed of for five years; newly-redundant and ageing Tom from South Wales (Derek Demaine) looking for his lost love, and Margaret (Lynne Smith) from Shropshire, middle-class and bossy, looking for her runaway adopted daughter. Their journey through Birmingham gets them entangled with Joel (Sebastian) Jamaican by racial origin but Brummie by alienated birth, and Rose (Sian Smith) Northern Irish, heavily pregnant and alone. Rina Mahoney played Pushba, Katya's cheeky young sister, while Richard Thompson played Norman, Margaret's husband helping her come to terms with their past.

With constantly-shifting locations (café, pizzeria, hair-dressing salon, disco, high-rise flat, park, zoo, allotment, hospital and even the National Exhibition Centre) the play came across as essentially optimistic managing to suggest that Birmingham is inhabited by a multi-racial stew of good-natured eccentrics. The satire on the city and more generalised social criticism is very gentle. The set by Gavin Davies for a production where there were more than enough bodies to fill the stage, deployed the hydraulic lift combined with the sweat of the volunteer stage crew pushing and pulling unwieldy, steel-panelled trucks into various different configurations. The long-drawn out complexity of the technical rehearsal meant that John Adams had to announce to the first night audience that they were watching a dress rehearsal.

Chris Parr, however, kept his nerve, and the huge enterprise went off successfully if only to modest audiences. The play ended in reconciliation and Rose's new-born baby as the festivals of Christmas and Diwali came together for a candle-lit procession in a Hindu temple setting. Indian dancers led by Chitraleka mingled with a choir singing the Coventry Carol. There were four choirs including two Polish choirs which supplied yet another dimension to Birmingham's ethnic diversity. Robin Thornber remarked on the tension between the panoramic, fluid, filmic script and the real-time scene-shifting and remarked somewhat patronisingly that the play did not demand too much psychological depth of amateur actors (G, 21.10.89) But the playing was surprisingly convincing and the massive chorus of extras provided, as he acknowledged, the genuine feel of a bustling city. Multi-aged as well as multi-racial, *Heartlanders* was billed as the largest community-based play ever presented on a professional stage. It was an ambitious attempt to give the people of Birmingham a sense of ownership of the Rep, but despite the enthusiasm generated amongst the participants there was no follow-up exercise. The Community Department continued with more easily-controlled projects at a time when managerial control overall was about to become a major issue.

The City's Construction

The impetus for *Heartlanders* was the centenary of the City of Birmingham. The city was busily re-inventing itself yet again-there was, needless to say, another joke in *Heartlanders* about the constantly-changing urban skyline. This time however, the emphasis was shifting in the direction of the arts. The City Council was the first in the country to establish a Joint Arts, Culture and Economic Committee which consciously sought to use the arts for high-prestige economic advantage. Through the 1980s dynamic civic personalities like Bryan Bird, Chair of the Leisure Services Committee, fought to convince his colleagues of the value of the arts for quality of life. Sadler's Wells Royal Ballet (later Birmingham Royal Ballet) and the D'Oyly Carte Opera Company were encouraged to take up residence at the Hippodrome and the Alexandra Theatre. In 1989 Anthony Sargent was appointed to the newly-created post of Head of Arts and Entertainment.

The old dream of the Civic Centre had been revived. The stranglehold of the inner ring road was modified by sinking Paradise Circus under a wide pedestrian bridge. Chamberlain Square was now linked, via the glassed-over atrium of Paradise Forum, to the brand new Centenary Square which was built over the grassed area outside the Rep. Within yards of the theatre near the site of Bingley Hall where circuses had once flourished, and where Barry Jackson had mounted the British Theatre Exhibition in 1949, the International Conference Centre was to be built and behind that the huge National Indoor Arena. When the £180 million ICC was eventually opened by the Queen in June 1991, it housed a new concert hall for the City of Birmingham Symphony Orchestra which had achieved international status under the leadership of Simon Rattle. The Rep was no longer in splendid isolation.

Although their priorities were different, in 1987 both Wilkinson and Adams were agreed on the need for some kind of radical building initiative in response to the new developments. For Wilkinson it seemed clear that the theatre could not survive solely on audience-derived income. The insistent, if somewhat muddled signals which were coming from the Arts Council were that large theatres like the Rep could not rely on ever-increasing levels of subsidy and that other sources of revenue should be sought. The considerable technical and craft skills within the Rep could, with enhanced workshop facilities, service the display and presentation requirements of the ICC, undertake set building for other theatres and provide training schemes. What was envisaged was an industrial-style workshop extension which would finally remove the access difficulties created when Winteringham's original workshops were modified in the early 1970s. For his part Adams wanted to make the front-of-house area more welcoming and also provide potential space for informal performance. At a presentation to the Board in February 1988 Graham Winteringham proposed the conversion of the Café Bar to a new, more attractive central entrance from the civic square. The restaurant and bar would be rebuilt in front of the workshop extension thus harmonising the new and old façades. The new catering unit could provide a first-class restaurant service for patrons as well as a hospitality suite for sponsors and external conferences. There were even plans for a bookshop.

The snag was the contract with Iceford which was neither financially nor aesthetically profitable and which would be well-nigh impossible to break without serious economic penalties. The aspirations of Alan Satori, Iceford's managing director, to exploit the potential of the new civic environment was an added complication. In early 1989 Iceford, with Clive Wilkinson now acting as their consultant, presented an alternative private development strategy to the City Council which would have involved relocating the Colonnade—built with the Hall of Memory to honour the war dead—to form an entrance in front of an Iceford catering extension. In the process, a considerable area of the proposed site of the workshop assembly area would be taken up.

The Rep was faced with the fact that the City Planning Committee was sympathetic to this financially more attractive proposal despite objections both from the theatre and from West Midlands Arts to the implications of the City's intervention. Furthermore the City was adamant that the Rep development had to be completed by March 1991 before the opening of the ICC. Thus with a pistol effectively pointed at their heads, Bettinson and Adams had to make a rapid decision to embark on a revamped extension project in the hopes that the necessary additional finance could be raised. They had to be confident that the three-storey conference/hospitality suite, which was now to be built in front of the workshops, could be made commercially viable as a separate operation. Iceford and the Café Bar remained in situ, apparently immovable.

The Rep Board of management and indeed the artistic director were no longer simply running a theatre. They were now chasing Incentive Funding from the Arts Council, drawing up a three year Business Plan (which meant employing business consultants) and holding high-profile presentations to attract the necessary sponsorship. After *Women Beware Women* Adams proposed to delegate all play direction for the next eight months leaving him free to concentrate on the building scheme. At the Board meeting on 27 April David Edgar warned that the theatre appeared to be moving into areas of business which had little to do with theatre and that the role of the Artistic Director was about to change to that of Building Development Director. But, he was told, the Government now expected arts organisations to seek funding from the private sector through sponsorship and developing commercial activity. Bettinson assured the Board that theatrical production would always be the first priority but that supplementary income had to be sought.

Different Directions

These crucial decisions coincided with the departure of both Derek Nicholls, who left the Rep to become Director of the York Theatre Royal in March, and Mark Everett who took up his appointment as Executive Director of the Bristol Old Vic that May. The new General Manager who arrived in September was Bill Hughes who had been Theatre Manager at the Belgrade for five years before a further two and a half years as Administrator at the Contact Theatre in Manchester. Anthony Clark who was Artistic Director of the Contact was appointed in March as the second Associate Director but did not begin work in Birmingham until January 1990.

Like Adams, Clark came to Birmingham with an excellent record of running a theatre. The Contact Theatre had developed a formidable reputation for exciting work in both new and classic drama. In Manchester his European première production of *To Kill a Mocking Bird* and his production of Lorca's *Blood Wedding* had won awards and he had also achieved considerable success as a writer. *A Matter of Life and Death* had been written for the National Theatre, and his adaptation of Saint Exupery's *Little Prince* and Raymond Briggs' *The Snowman* had been staged in Bristol and Leicester as well as Manchester. He had worked hard to develop young peoples' theatre and that, combined with a commitment to Afro-Caribbean and Asian writing, made him a valuable new member of the Rep team. For his part he left the relative security and intimacy of the Contact and the more theatre-friendly ambience of Manchester for the greater challenge of the Rep and the opportunity of greater resources.

Clark's inaugural production of *The Seagull* in the Studio had an unusual provenance in the entrepreneurial energies of the ambitious young man who played Konstantin. Twenty-three year old Neal Foster had raised the money to set up Endless Theatre Ltd. by interviewing famous personalities like Judi Dench, Dustin Hoffman and John Cleese in front of a paying audience. The partnership with the Rep provided an opportunity both for a personal showcase for Foster, who clearly saw himself following in Kenneth Branagh's footsteps, and a generously-sized cast of twelve actors. In the event Clark's skillful direction of the ensemble came off best enabling the actors, as the critic Paul Taylor put it, to give off 'that distinctive Chekhovian sense of society as an orchestra composed of self-preoccupied soloists' (*I*, 23.2.90). Reviews were sympathetic to Foster's aspirations

137

if not to his performance. There were general misgivings about Liz Fjelle's design which set the play in a swirling, garishly-coloured landscape created from an enlarged woodcut by Edvard Munch. Terry Grimley decided that Clark had yet to get the measure of the Studio space (*BP*, 21.2.90). The acting revelation of the production was Emily Raymond in her first professional role as Nina. In 1992 Foster founded the Birmingham Stage Company based at the Old Rep.

The Seagull opened in the Studio on 16 February 1990 the week after Adams launched *Summer of the Seventeenth Doll*, his first main stage production for virtually a year. At best this period had conveyed an impression of artistic diversity. The autumn 1989 'Compact' Studio season had brought in a succession of dynamic experimental companies beginning with Snarling Beasties' *Punch and Judy* which was a physically energetic, blackly comic exploration of domestic violence. When John Adams took over the Christmas slot with *George and Harold*, a double-bill of Pinter's *The Lover* and Shaw's *Village Wooing* there was a palpable sense of relief in Terry Grimley's review which wistfully asked if the Studio could go on reviving miniature classics all year round (*BP*, 20.12.89).

On the main stage, however, there was a more damaging impression of fragmentation. Adams' great gift to the Rep in his first two seasons was a distinctive house style and a confidence that the big stage could be used effectively. The number of guest-directed productions in 1989 began to dissipate that confidence, despite potentially exciting shows like the musical *Damn Yankees* which Paul Kerryson directed in September. The significance of *Twelfth Night* which followed on from *Heartlanders* in November lay not only in the fact that it was directed by a woman, Pip Broughton, but it was set on a sun-soaked Caribbean island with delightful poster-paint designs by Jacqueline Gunn and had a predominantly black cast. Joseph Marcel played Sir Toby Belch, the rich-voiced, opera-trained Thomas Baptiste played Orsino while Judith Jacob well-known as Carmel from the television soap, *East Enders*, played Maria. Jan Ravens as Viola, and Matthew Kelly, playing Sir Andrew Aguecheek as a sweaty, Hawaiian-shirted German tourist, stood out as white faces.

But the end result was a disaster provoking some vicious reviews in the national press. A guest director unfamiliar with the Rep stage, combined with a heterogeneous cast brought together for the usual brief three-week rehearsal period, came up with a production heavy on slapstick and calypso but little emotional engagement with the text. There was a major public row provoked by a headmaster enraged by explicit sexual groping and a crude gag of urinating twenty feet into the onstage swimming pool. Puritanical protest paled beside the fact that for the most part the large schools' audiences were simply bored. Subsequently the co-production with Vanessa Ford Productions of an adaptation of *A Christmas Carol*, which was written and directed by Ron Pember, also attracted large audiences, but the sense of loss of ownership of artistic product was growing. The audiences for *An Evening with Harold and George* were well down on the previous Christmas and there was some concern voiced that Adams' direction lacked firmness of touch.

There were favourable local reviews for *Summer of the 17th Doll* despite divergences of opinion about the quality of the Australian television soap stars brought in to add extra authenticity. Audiences were moderate; a pattern which was repeated with Adams' production of *Flare Path*, a play by Terence Rattigan which had been a major hit in 1942 and now brought Nicky Henson back to the Rep in the role of a Hollywood actor seeking his lost love in wartime. The production was typical of Adams with a striking coup de théâtre when a backcloth of a Wellington bomber appeared to become a solid aircraft taking off on a flare path which lit up the stage. Another characteristic gambit was the use of Benjamin Britten's highly-emotive *War Requiem* to accompany the action—a device which some felt did not fit comfortably with Rattigan's restrained style.

Deficit Again

With the Studio closed for the duration of the building and refurbishment period, a lot now depended on the success of the main stage programme. To offset any potential losses, raise the theatre's profile and hopefully make money, the Rep management had also embarked on a strategy of major national touring. In the autumn of 1989 and the spring of 1990 the revived production of *The Railway Children* was taken to theatres around the country but the result was a significant deficit. Many of the venues were organised very late which resulted in disappointing audiences and a financial loss which was exacerbated by the impossibility of performing at Christmas. The fact that the show had to be effectively re-produced after the long gap since the 1988 performances proved costly. John Pitt, Production Manager since early 1987, had additional problems because the project also created delays on the in-house production schedule. However a co-production of Snarling Beasties' *Valentino* which toured nationally in early 1990 proved very successful.

But in his 1989-1990 annual statement, John Bettinson was forced to reflect on a deficit of £228,000. Part of the cause was perceived to lie in the generally gloomy climate of yet another economic recession. Higher interest rates had affected consumer spending which in turn led to a decline in audiences. It was particularly unfortunate at a time when the Rep had committed itself to the enterprise culture of the Thatcherite era to a hitherto unprecedented extent. The estimated cost of the development project was put at £4,500,000. The basic revenue grants from the two principal funding bodies had risen to £548,409 from the Arts Council and £530,250 from the City Council. The City had also agreed to provide the land and a grant of £2,160,000 for the development. There was an Arts Council Incentive Funding Award of £110,000. To separate the proposed additional commercial activity (including the national touring) from the work of the Birmingham Repertory Company, a new trading company, Birmingham Rep Enterprises Ltd., was set up. In December 1990 the Birmingham Rep Foundation was incorporated with Philip Couse as the Chairman and Dorothy Warner as the Director. The brief was to address the issue of major fund-raising which up until that point appeared to have failed. In May 1991, the Company secured a loan of £1,500,000 and a £600,000 overdraft facility with the Midland Bank to pay for the development.

That same month, the Rep Company took possession of their new extension. It was then officially opened by Princess Margaret at a Royal Gala performance of Clark's production of *The Threepenny Opera* on 21 October, almost exactly twenty years after the first opening ceremony. The new workshops included loading bays with an overhead crane, metal and woodwork shops and a huge set assembly area nearly seventy feet long and thirty feet high. Two full-size sets could be built simultaneously. There was now a light, spacious, much-needed rehearsal room near an equally impressive Green Room. Front of house, the original dimensions of the foyer area had been modified using plaster board and metal stud partitions. The architect Paul Burley, a senior partner in S.T. Walker, also designed the catering and conference centre complex. On the ground floor the Centenary suite provided a venue for large-scale receptions and banquets. The top floor had a flexible suite which could accommodate up to 200 people and an imposing Board room. Great panels of slightly-tinted glass looked over Centenary Square harmonising with the original glass windows and matching the tinted glass used in the ICC. At the time of the opening, the middle floor remained an empty shell until the necessary funds to complete it could be found while somewhere along the line the bookshop had disappeared. The costs to the Rep Company, and in particular to the Artistic Director, had been very high. Within a few months Adams resigned.

Reasons to be Cheerful

The sadness and sense of defeat which accompanied John Adams' departure from the theatre in the summer of 1992 cast a long backward shadow back over much that was achieved by the company during the second half of his directorate. The programming aspirations for the main stage remained strong, and during 1990 and 1991 directorial responsibility was evenly spread with the two associate directors working on a range of plays. For the first time in the Rep's history a woman was a leading member of the artistic team. Hughes' productions included *When We Are Married*, *All My Sons* and, in a calculated move to tap potential audiences in Birmingham's large Irish population, Brian Friel's *Translations*. Clarke directed *Of Mice and Men*, *Macbeth*, and with a cast of Shakespearean dimensions, Eduardo de Filippo's ebullient Italian comedy *Saturday Sunday*

Monday. Both directors followed Adams' example in strong design values and both stuck resolutely to the principle of integrated casting .

Adams came to be recognised as a significant regional figure in his efforts to get the theatre to reflect a pluralistic society. 'Colour blind' casting: that is casting which not only ignores the original ethnic provenance of a play, but also internal consistencies such as family racial characteristics, became a striking if controversial aspect of artistic policy. In Vanbrugh's late Restoration play *The Relapse* which Adams directed in September 1990, he cast two black actors as the young male leads. Colin McFarlane played the incorrigibly promiscuous Loveless partnered by two white actresses: Maggie Ford as his long-suffering wife Amanda and Amelda Brown as the duplicitous Miss Hoyden with whom he enjoys a brief fling. Genetic caution was thrown completely to the winds with Jude Akuwudike as Young Fashion, the black brother to the white 'stab me vitals' Foppington played by Michael Bertenshaw. Young Fashion's beloved Berinthea was, however, the dark and beautiful Caroline Lee Johnson.

Some critics and theatre practitioners, most notably the leading black director Yvonne Brewster were uneasy about casting 'that makes nonsense of life'. Interviewed for an article by Michael Billington which discussed the issue (*G*, 1.11.90), she said with reference to *The Relapse* 'There was no problem until you had the confrontation of the brothers. That's when the audience started to talk and me too. When you make nonsense of the possibilities I find it less challenging. It becomes tokenistic'. But Adams was unrepentant stating that audiences had in fact accepted this and other similar casting without demur. The problem he felt lay with critical perception: 'That is sad for two reasons. It confirms the prejudices of die-hard sections of the audience and it possibly deters potential black customers'.

There had been a few raised critical eyebrows in April when Gwenda Hughes, making her directorial debut on the main stage with J.B. Priestley's solidly realist comedy *When We Are Married*, cast the black actress Jenny Jules as Nancy Holmes, daughter of the prim-and-proper Edwardian household and courting the choirmaster of the local Methodist chapel. Hughes doggedly continued the policy with Michael Frayn's *Noises Off*. Not only did she update this farce about a farce performed by a disaster-prone traditional touring company to the 1970s, but she also cast the black actor Burt Caesar as the typically English thespian Frederick Fellowes. For *Hobson's Choice*, that best-loved of all the products of the so-called Manchester School of realist drama, Hughes chose Vivienne Rochester to play a black daughter of the white Henry Hobson and then matched her with a black suitor played by Haydn Forde as Fred Beenstock.

In his *Birmingham Post* review (26.2.92), an exasperated Terry Grimley enquired why it was necessary to bother with Lancashire accents if more fundamental principles had been ignored. He did concede however, that within the parameters of what was a non-naturalistic setting the ploy could be considered reasonable. Grimley would probably have preferred the time-honoured visual approach which emphasised the muck, brass and gloom of late Victorian Salford. The costuming was Victorian but the designer, Ruari Murchison created a surreal yellow setting of rows of shoe boxes which receded sharply upstage to a vanishing point. Robin Thornber was delighted by the departure from tradition and enjoyed the performances. Janice McKenzie played Maggie Hobson descending on Tom Watt's spindly, shock-haired, owlish Willy Mossop with gravel-voiced determination.

Exciting design was an important factor in the reconsideration of well-known texts as well as a means of making the stage come into its own. For *When We Are Married*, Paul Dart presented the audience with the usual ornate and cluttered Edwardian parlour within the substantial Clecklewyke home of Alderman Helliwell. But perched on top of the roof were the unlikely figures of a large ram and two ewes—the moorland basis of Yorkshire wealth—which stared out in woolly calm across the auditorium. As the comic plot unfolded with the respectability-shattering revelations about the couples' non-marriage, the house literally seemed to tremble and then shrink away as the chaos subsided.

Both Hughes and Anthony Clark directed in the classic American tradition in 1990 and both used women designers to draw visual inspiration from the dominant images of the American landscape. George S. Kaufman's dramatisation of John Steinbeck's *Of Mice and Men* was Clark's first main stage production. Designer Kate Burnett attempted to capture the spaciousness as well as the futile dreams and depressed reality of 1930s California. There was a symbolic sky changing colours over an expanse of open scrubland and a huge billboard promising California Paradise. In the farm where the tragedy of George and Lenny unfolds a long rambling dormitory seemed as Michael Schmidt put it in the *Daily Telegraph* 'to reek of male habitation' (15.6.90) Clark elicited powerfully moving performances. Tyrone Huggins as the crippled negro farm hand Crooks was singled out. Jeremy Flynn played a credible and shrewdly-observed George a full head shorter than Clive Mantle who played the gentle, doomed Lennie. Of Mantle Michael Schmidt wrote: 'I have not seen a performance as compelling as his for a long time. His clumsy movements, slurred speech and violent tenderness, and his complete social helplessness, give him a poignancy which rises to tragic proportions' (*DT*, 15.6.90).

When Hughes directed Arthur Miller's *All My Sons*—another tragedy of the American dream—in November 1990, Fran Thompson designed tall, white clapper-board houses grouped around a neighbourhood garden. A gauze curtain rose on the dawn of a hot summer's day with white clouds moving in a brilliant blue sky: a deceptively idyllic refuge from the betrayal and criminal culpability long-hidden by the central character Joseph Keller who was played by Del Henney. For Hughes

142

what was important about the play was not only that it was emblematic of post-war America, but that as a domestic drama it had great clarity of vision. For the Rep's first permanent woman director the domestic context, especially that which contains strong female characters, was no soft option conceptually but an opportunity to bring a woman's perspective on the largely-male domain of mainstream drama. As Kate Keller who has to endure the collapse of her husband's carefully-preserved probity, Collette O'Neil invested her role with powerful emotion, while Janice McKenzie was praised for her performance as Ann Deever, the daughter of Keller's sacrificed colleague.

Gwenda Hughes' final community production toured just as *When We Are Married* was nearing the end of its run in May 1990. Again publicised as suitable for children aged twelve and above, *Crime of the Century* set in Polstead near Ipswich in 1827, is Lisa Evans' reworking of the story of Maria Marten. Janice McKenzie played Maria, the daughter of a Suffolk mole-catcher, who was murdered by the gentleman-father of her two babies. The production clearly dispelled the image of community theatre as a poor relation of mainstream theatre. At a school in Small Heath it was observed that the packed, multi-racial, multi-aged audience was totally absorbed in a play more about rural poverty and the predicament of women in Maria's position, than the traditional murder mystery.

Where Hughes led other women followed. Teresa Heskins, awarded a bursary under the Thames TV/Regional Director Scheme, worked as assistant director on a range of main stage plays throughout the 1990-1991 season developing skills which would lead to her own productions. Julia Smith had emerged unexpectedly out of the Community Department where she had started work as a publicity assistant in 1988. In 1990, while *The Seagull* was occupying the Studio, groups from the Youth Workshop performed at the Midlands Arts Centre. Smith directed a small ensemble of older members in Stephen Berkoff's *Agamemnon*. Simply-staged on the raked platform made for *Village Wooing*, and with the young actors in evening dress, her production counterpointed the graphic brutality of Berkoff's language with stylised performances and elegant economy of décor. The production later won a Company Commendation at the National Student Drama Festival in Scarborough.

Subsequently she and Mick Yates formed a directing and writing partnership to dramatise the work of Angela Carter in productions of *The Company of Wolves* and *The Magic Toyshop* which were both staged at the Edinburgh Festival. Not only was *Toyshop* shown in the Rep Studio in December 1991 after winning a Fringe First, but Smith also directed the autumn season's community tour of Berkoff's adaptation of Kafka's *Metamorphosis*. Gary Sefton made his professional debut as Gregor Samsa who wakes up one morning to find he has turned into a giant beetle. As the audience entered the auditorium they were confronted by the cast, motionless apart from slow head movements, and watching them with expressionless, doll-like faces. The black set resembled both the skeletal structure of a turn-of-the-century doll's house and a gigantic climbing frame where Sefton scrambled and squatted. For this grotesque parable about the rejection of innocent suffering, there was no beetle costume, only movement and bestial noises to suggest his insect transformation. The so-called normal household carried on the functions of ordinary life and the betrayal of Gregor with terrifying mechanical speed.

Heskin's production of *The Turn of the Screw* was the ghostly alternative Christmas production which took the Studio through to the end of January 1992. Eve Lewis' dramatisation of Henry James' novella transposes the setting from a Victorian Gothic mansion in the Essex marshes to India under the British Raj. The idea was to increase the isolation and alienation experienced by the central character of the governess, who was played by Victoria Worsley, and make a more effective contrast between the rigid Victorian rulers and the relaxed depravity of the dead servants. The designer Shelagh Keegan created a multi-level set with billowing mosquito nets and rattan furniture. Reviewing the production, Fred Norris made an odd tendentious final comment on the woman writer and director (he forgot the woman designer) quoting from Henry James' The masculine tone is passing out of the world. It is a feminine, nervous, hysterical chattering, canting age' (*EM*, 20.12.91). Without any noticeable signs of hysteria Heskins almost immediately afterwards directed Guy Hutchin's *Island*, a strongly visual theatre piece based on the story of a native American woman abandoned on a desert island. Julia Smith, despite her departure from the Rep along with Mick Yates, returned in the summer with her own company The Mouse People with Berkoff's dramatisation of Kafka's *The Trial*.

New Work on the Main Stage

Adams' had come to the theatre with a significant record in the promotion of new work, and it was important to put new writing on the main stage despite the economic and artistic risk. *Heartlanders* was of course a major commission, and Adams directed two new plays in 1990 and 1991 which also had strong Birmingham affinities. *The Writing Game* by David Lodge, premièred in May 1990, attracted a good deal of attention as the work of the locally-based academic better known as a highly successful novelist. Lodge had, of course, contributed to the revues at the Old Rep back in the 1960s but this was his first full-length play. Three writers: a macho Jewish New Yorker, a popular novelist married to an absent-minded Oxford don, and a brilliant, trendy, ex-Cambridge bisexual arrive for a literary weekend at a seventeenth-century farmhouse converted into a centre for literary studies. Entertaining, if emotionally thin and with a formulaic plot, the play is primarily a series of verbal duels, laced with sex, on the pleasures and pains of authorship. It pleased audiences and the impressive array of reviews were full of compliments for Adams' meticulous direction and the witty naturalistic performances by Lou Hirsch, Susan Penhaligon and Patrick Pearson as the three principals.

My Father's House, premièred in October 1991, was theatrically more substantial territory for Adams and written by his long-time collaborator David Pownall. Designer Paul Farnsworth re-created Highbury—the house of the title— built by Joseph Chamberlain as the Birmingham home of the political dynasty he fathered. Richly-decorated and carpeted, this house rightly dominated the stage. There was a great triple-arched staircase leading from a gallery, a mass of metalwork screens and most importantly the glasshouse where the famous orchids, which Joe always wore in his button hole, were grown. The play begins mid-air raid in 1940, when the house had become a residential home, and then travels back to 1906 and the days surrounding Joe's seventieth birthday. Finally in a surreal reworking of Munich, the house becomes the place where Neville Chamberlain meets the dictator he so fatally misjudged and encounters a now comatose Joe. Adams used extracts from Tippett's Triple Concerto to link the discontinuous narrative.

The house then, is the symbol of Joe's empire-building ambitions and the source of his dominance over his children which, Pownall implies, Neville is still attempting to overturn when he goes to Munich. The production was generally well-received, but just missed convincing critics of the conceptual merit of Pownall's attempts to subvert naturalism. Some were simply baffled by the encounters with Hitler and a sweaty, gymnastic Mussolini. But the performances were much praised with Dermot Walsh as the dynamic Joe, and Chris Hunter, in the early scenes, an unexpectedly lively, mischievous Neville. Michael Bertenshaw played Austen as a pale imitation of his father with Tamara Ustinov, Amanda Boxer and Hazel Maycock as Joe's terminally unmarried daughters.

Even in the period after Adams' resignation was announced, Birmingham audiences were given more opportunities to see new work and judge for themselves whether a risk had been worth taking. Arguably the most ambitious, *Biko*, a chamber opera based on the life and tragic death of the black South African political activist Steve Biko, was in the event the most problematic. Premièred on 29 May 1992 to an audience consisting of many of the leaders of the city's ethnic minority and religious communities, the production was unconvincingly directed by Wilfred Judd and the piece itself, by composer Pritti Paintal and writer Richard Fawkes, was critically damned. The other experiment, a new version of *Beauty and the Beast* by David Holman, which Gwenda Hughes had commissioned as a summer children's play, had to be entrusted to Teresa Heskins when Hughes became ill. Heskins, however, seemed unable to get to grips with the big stage or instill much dynamism into the performances. Holman's script came across as bland and at moments rather ineptly concerned with environmental issues.

The Director's Burden

The model of theatre organisation which lays the greatest executive burden on the shoulders of the artistic director is fraught with difficulty. The strains created by the building development were enormous and Adams had thrown himself wholeheartedly into an enterprise which financially had got completely out of hand. Faced with the artistic problems which arose when he did not direct himself, he was forced to juggle both activities and he was not a man who found delegation of responsibility easy and there were tensions with Bill Hughes. For the associate directors' areas of responsibility were insufficiently defined and artistic policy decisions could be erratic. Clark had come to the Rep with a specific brief to develop new writing and introduce more European drama. Although he set up a writers' group which was aimed at developing new work, he had, not thus far, directed anything new. *Saturday, Sunday, Monday* is an agreeable, but lightweight product of the European repertoire, and Clark had been irritated by the sudden decision to replace a planned production of *The Caucasian Chalk Circle* with *The Threepenny Opera*.

Actors were finding it difficult to work in an increasingly tense atmosphere, although there was the much deeper-seated problem of attracting suitably high-calibre actors to come to the Rep which had been dogging the theatre for years. As always the need for actors to gravitate towards London, the lure of television, and the limitations of the short-run system with relatively short rehearsal periods, all make regional theatre casting difficult. Adams had worked very effectively with Sylvia Syms on *Who's Afraid of Virginia Woolf*, and in April 1991 he proposed to give her the opportunity to play Shakespeare's Cleopatra. It proved very difficult to find an actor of national repute to play Antony. Ultimately Malcolm Tierney, more well-known as a television actor was cast. The critical consensus was that the partnership lacked the necessary physical and emotional dynamism. Simon Dormandy, however, who was and remained staunchly supportive of Adams' ability to direct actors for a big stage, was given credit for his performance as a coolly duplicitous Octavius Caesar.

The Arts Council was about to deliver a body blow. Between February and May 1991 a team which included Genista McIntosh, Executive Director of the Royal National Theatre, Bill Farr, the Financial Director of the Crucible Theatre, Joan Knight, the Artistic Director of the Perth Theatre, and Anthony Sargent undertook an appraisal of the Rep as part of a long-term strategy adopted by the Arts Council in 1986 to evaluate the work of revenue clients. Their conclusion that there was a lack of clear artistic vision and identity had very serious implications. Managerial weakness and inconsistencies were noted. It was recommended that Board membership should be broadened to reflect the local community, and fixed terms should be introduced.

The role of the Artistic Director and his relationship with his associates required clarification, and more time was needed for research and creative reflection on productions. The work of the Studio, which had only just re-opened after a year's closure, was thought to lack a clear identity. The Community Department, although lively and innovative was too diverse and there was too much emphasis on the XXXX Cabaret programme. It was also felt that there was insufficient co-ordination with the main artistic policy and no firm educational strategy.

Deficit was accumulating and the fact that at least £500,000 would have to be raised over the next five years to cover the cost of the new development was very worrying. The Business Plan formulated in 1989 was now perceived to be unrealistic, as were the aims behind the national touring programme. Here, however, it was admitted that these ventures had been encouraged initially by the Arts Council Incentive Funding Scheme. Clark's production of *Cider With Rosie* which was scheduled as the next national tour was already in performance.

The Appraisal Report which was presented at the Board meeting on 19 June by Ian Brown, the Drama Director of the Arts Council, inevitably sent deep shock waves through the management. John Bettinson had already signalled his intention to resign to the Appraisal team. At the City Council's instigation he was replaced by Bryan Townsend, the Chief Executive of Midlands Electricity Board and completely new to the Rep. It was under his auspices that the response to the Arts Council was prepared. But arguably much of what had happened could be laid at the door of the Arts Council itself and the compromises and misguided thinking which had been forced on that institution by central government. David Edgar called the report a deeply hypocritical document. Of course Barry Jackson's belief that art has no possible relation to money was illusory. But the Birmingham Repertory Company was established to fight the primacy of the commercial purpose which at this point in its history had nearly destroyed it.

The Last Carnival

John Adams struggled on until the end of the year, but resigned in January 1992. The final season of main stage work was characteristically bold, but flawed, including as it did *Biko* and *Beauty and the Beast*. But there was also significant success which amply demonstrated the artistic strength and talent which continued to shine despite the trauma. Audiences enjoyed the visual eccentricities of *Hobson's Choice*, while Clark directed Louise Yates, Janice McKenzie, Christine Mason and Margery Mason in a moving and delicately-nuanced production of Charlotte Keatley's *My Mother Said I Never Should*. Clark had originally commissioned the play, which shifts through time in an intimate exploration of the lives of four generations of women, for the Contact where it was first directed by

Brigit Lamour. Now on the unlikely space of the Rep's main stage, Fran Thompson's evocative design of a towering forest of piled-up luggage provided the secret places needed by the women to create their own private worlds, and was satisfyingly emblematic of emotional luggage. When opened the suitcases and trunks revealed flowerbeds, family photographs, baby clothes and deceptively insignificant knick-knacks. The final image was a huge rose blossoming triumphantly at the back of a stage.

As for Adams, it was as though the relinquishing of what now seemed the impossible job of running Birmingham Rep had released his creative energies. He directed two comedies: Alan Bennett's *Kafka's Dick* and a co-production with West Yorkshire Playhouse of Sheridan's *The Rivals*. Poppy Mitchell designed a wonderfully surreal set of extravagantly-sized books for *Kafka's Dick* which was hailed by Robin Thornber, mourning Adams loss and noting a healthily young audience, as a roistering good night out (*G*, 29.1.92). Ann Fitzgerald described Andrew Normington's bemused Kafka, suddenly transported to a suburban British home 'like a ballet dancer performing on a bed of nails' (*S*, 30.1.92). Amelda Brown, she decided, contrived to make Linda, the philistine, childless wife of a literary obsessive, equal parts of 'bimbo, mother figure…nurse, vamp and Ortonesque suburban hostess'.

The Rivals was a joyful, iconoclastic revisioning of the play with a confident, energetic cast which included the black actor David Harewood as the dashing Jack Absolute and Simon Dormandy as the terminally sentimental Faulkland. As the play is set in the era of the sentimental novel, the action revolved around the rumpled brass bed where Kate Duchene's voluptuous Lydia Languish lolled in book-fed dreams of romance. Love's arrow was accompanied by a music-box tinkle and the lovers' messages were conveyed by a gold-winged cupid. There were great gusts of classical music especially, *Don Giovanni*, reverberating around the auditorium mocking the excesses of passion. Patrick Connellan's set seemed to defy gravity with a three-storey inward leaning façade surrounded by builder's rubble—the debris from Bath's building programme which had even landed on the bed—and books. In one inspired moment Jean Fergusson's Mrs Malaprop literally broke through the wall of books to get at her niece. There was a bright blue spiral staircase leading out onto balconies, a sawn-off billiard table and a promenade ending in stairs which rose steeply towards the audience. There were squeals of protest from some of the more conservative local critics, especially Richard Edmonds objecting to 'a huge 1920s Bauhaus rumpus room' (*BP*, 7.5.92), but most were delighted.

Adams ended the season and his work at the Rep with the European première of *Last Carnival* by the Caribbean poet and playwright Derek Walcott. The almost simultaneous world première of Walcott's adaptation of *The Odyssey* by the RSC at the Other Place threatened to overshadow the Rep event, but for Walcott it was important that his original, and indeed much-revised play, should be successful in Birmingham. Aggie, the central character played as a young woman by Jill Brassington, comes to Port of Spain as a Marxist cockney governess to two motherless children determined to make them and the black colonised servants who work in the Delafontaine household more politically aware. The passage of time and the hypnotic influence of her French Creole employer and subsequent lover, Victor Delafontaine, played by Peter Woodward, changes her utterly from her accent to her political views. Catherine Russell played Agatha, the conservative woman she matures into. In 1970 it is her white-skinned former charges who espouse violent radical politics while the maid Jean Beauchamps becomes Minister of Housing. Agatha is 'invited' to leave.

The central visual image of the play and symbol of European cultural exploitation—exploited in turn by designer Roger Butlin in huge onstage panels—is one of Watteau's *Embarkation to Cythera* paintings. Aggie poses as an eighteenth century shepherdess for the deeply insecure Victor who identifies with Watteau as a cynical outsider and ultimately slides into madness. Michael Bertenshaw played his brother Oswald who manages the estate and is more politically and economically resilient. All the action referred to in the play including carnival exuberance and guerilla violence takes place off-stage. Adams used Cantaloube's settings of Auvergne folk-songs to enhance the play's tone of wistful perplexity. Walcott had been tinkering with the play for some years, but it was clearly still flawed despite the prestige of the author. Onyekachi Wambu writing a thoughtful review in the *Weekly Journal* pointed out that ideas and language make a poor substitute for action in theatrical terms and that a heavily celebral play should find new territory for debate. 'I am now impatient' he stated 'with dramas depicting the decay of an old order' (23.7.92). With hindsight Adams' production looks like a complicated emblem of the Rep's fortunes at that point in its history. The stage looked well and truly conquered, and despite the absence of a permanent ensemble there was evidence of a continuity of acting experience and commitment to radical casting.

There were old-established and new actors on the big stage. Bertenshaw had become familiar throughout Adams' tenure, while Woodward, back after a five year absence, was like a ghost from the past. Of the black actors Joseph Charles and Trevor Butler had appeared in *Twelfth Night* and Haydn Forde in *Hobson*. Lorna Laidlaw who made her main stage debut as Jean Beauchamps was a local black actress who had started in Derek Nicholl's Birmingham Youth Theatre playing in the Studio. A seed sown in the past had borne fruit. But by now Adams himself represented the old order and the play manifestly failed to address more immediate and fundamental issues of life in a multi-racial city. There was little press comment surrounding Adams' resignation and departure. He slipped away in the summer quietly. On the 6 January before, his resignation was announced, he gave

an interview to Terry Grimley for the *Birmingham Post* and talked about the
theatre he would shortly leave:

> The scale of the theatre is immense. It's the best
> place to be, in the most ambitious city, sitting
> right in the centre of a motorway network
> with Symphony Hall and the CBSO next door.
> But you can't do everything with six actors and
> that stage is so immense you have to keep dressing
> it, as we've learnt to do. When they built this
> theatre they built a Rolls Royce, but when times
> are hard it's easier to run a mini.

10. Preparing the Ground for Change: Bill Alexander and John Stalker

A Bleak Prospect

In October 1992 Antony Clark brought Frank Galati's epic adaptation of John Steinbeck's *Grapes of Wrath* to the main stage. With his designer Patrick Connellan, Clark transmuted Steinbeck's tragic narrative of 1930s' Depression-hit America into a series of symbolic images. Giant red, work-worn hands appeared to thrust through barren, mid-western soil and then became the hands of fruit-pickers in California reaching for huge oranges which turned into stones. There was an emblematic harsh yellow sun, a barbed-wire fence and a child's faded drawing of a house. The dead baby of the tragic character, Rose of Sharon, was launched on a blue silk river to be received by more hands. The action was accompanied by Galati's central image of the musical instrument-powered Joad family truck which takes them on their hopeless migration. Onstage tragedy reflected generalised gloom in the world outside the theatre where there was economic recession and burgeoning unemployment. The actors gave free tickets for the play to miners at the Trentham Colliery in Stoke-on-Trent which was threatened with closure. All this together with the Rep's own predicament made the production powerfully resonant.

Former RSC director Bill Alexander had been appointed as the new Artistic

Director in May, but was not due to arrive until November. Although Hughes' and Clark's joint application for the job had not been successful, they retained their status as associate directors. In the transitional period the two associates provided a caretaker directorate in the context of a financial crisis which appeared about as bad as it could be. In March 1992 the operating loss before grants was £1,741,673. By March 1993 the loss was £1,981,264. The Annual Reports show the difference in the Chairman's style. Gone were John Bettinson's surveys of the Company's artistic work and the celebration of achievement. Now there were simply bald statements of economic fact. In 1992 Bryan Townsend outlined the financial background to the Centenary Square Development. In 1993 he gave an explanation for further heavy losses. Birmingham Rep Enterprises Limited had experienced a very difficult trading year and the Birmingham Rep foundation had failed to 'maximise income from private sector sources due to the effects of the recession'. In addition the Company had sustained an exceptionally heavy loss amounting to £189,538 on the musical *Radio Times* which had launched the autumn 1992 season.

The proposal to première *Radio Times* in collaboration with the producer Alex Armitage, who had devised the show based on songs written by his grandfather Noel Gay, was predicated on the assumption that substantial profits could be made for all concerned when the show transferred to London. The popular television entertainer Tony Slattery was cast as a feckless comedian/director trying to broadcast a variety show during wartime. When Japanese and American backers pulled out and the production was threatened, the Rep decided to bear the major costs of the regional run, even though Hughes and Clark recommended cancellation. There were certainly some enthusiastic audiences in Birmingham, but the reviews were mixed and the production failed to recoup its costs in London.

It was necessary to have not only strong management, but also a strong, supportive Board. The Arts Council Appraisal had made recommendations about the composition of the Board, length of service and the extent to which it should reflect a diverse community. At Christmas 1992 it looked like a war cabinet with no less than five city councillors, including Peter Barwell, the Lord Mayor, and Sir Dick Knowles alongside Edgar, Judith Mackay, Philip Couse and Professor Ronnie Mulryne. Feeling the need for tough business acumen Roger Taylor, the City's Chief Executive, had twisted Bryan Townsend's arm very tightly to persuade him to take on the Chairmanship. Once again there was a Chairman with scant knowledge of theatre, but as Chairman and Chief Executive of a newly-privatised public utility he was accustomed to management on a grand scale and ultimately proved to be the right man at the right time. The primary concern was to achieve a sensible balance between the criteria for artistic excellence and the values of the market place.

In late 1992 the city gave a capital grant of £500,000 which enabled the completion of the empty middle floor of the development, but as Townsend's

152

1993 report emphasises there were serious problems with Birmingham Rep Enterprises and the Birmingham Repertory Theatre Foundation. In addition to the fact that neither commercial activity nor organised fund-raising were generating the hoped-for revenue, there were other issues which needed to be addressed. In particular there was a disturbing disparity between the earnings of individuals working for the Foundation and BREL, and other Rep senior management. Also craftspeople working on external set building for BREL were paid more for their work than those engaged on Rep sets because the profits from commercial theatre are higher. Inevitably this created tensions especially as success in subsidised theatre is so dependent on good will and artistic fulfilment rather than high financial reward.

There had been some profitable set building for popular commercial musicals. But despite the greatly increased size of the facilities, the workshops were still not large enough for a thorough-going commercial operation and inevitably there were pressures on the Rep's own construction needs, production schedules and manpower. Again there were heavy financial imbalances. A commercial set using much more expensive materials would have a budget quadruple that for a Rep production. The other catering and hospitality dimension of BREL would continue to be undermined by the Iceford Catering franchise and the noisy success of the Rep Café Bar. On all sides it looked as though attempts to sustain the Rep through commercial dealings were doomed to failure.

Interim Art

What was encouraging about this transitional period was the combination of artistic continuity and aspiration. Much of the programming up until Alexander's inaugural production of *Othello* in March was built on the strengths of the old regime as well as the need to launch new initiatives born out of the frustrations of the past. In late September Hughes repeated the Studio experiment with special needs children. This time it was a music project called *Travelling Light* which was funded by Sounds Like Birmingham as part of Birmingham's year as UK City of Music. The Sir Barry Jackson Community Tour went out in October and November with Teresa Heskins' production of *The Devil's Only Sleeping* by Nick Stafford. The autumn season in the Studio prioritised new writing. Gwenda Hughes directed the world première of Lisa Evans' dramatisation of *East Lynne* as the alternative Christmas production. Clark directed Rod Dungate's *Playing by the Rules* and Sarah Woods' *Nervous Women*.

Both Dungate and Woods had been students on David Edgar's MA in Playwriting course at Birmingham University. Both had also benefited from the relationship established by Clark in 1990 with the West Midlands branch of the Theatre Writers' Union. TWU members had regular joint meetings with the Rep directorate to discuss current Rep productions, read samples of work in progress and discuss approaches to playwriting. Ultimately another independent training agency for playwrights, Stagecoach, was formed which worked with a network of regional theatres and local companies, organising workshop festivals of new work in a range of venues including the Rep. Another important development was the New Writers Seed Monies scheme whereby £250 was given to selected writers to prepare—with supervision and advice—a scenario. If the result was promising, a further £250 would be provided to write a treatment which might then go on to a full commission. It was out of this process that Dungate and Woods emerged. In June 1993, Clark also premiered *Syme*, a play about a campaigning Edwardian police inspector by Dudley-based Michael Bourdages (another MA graduate) which had been selected by the National Theatre for co-production.

Taking as its theme male prostitution, *Playing By the Rules* tells the story of a young boy, Danny, who runs away from a local authority home and is befriended by a group of Birmingham rent boys. Enticed into their way of life by the lure of easy money, it rapidly becomes apparent that Danny has made a Faustian pact. The naïve and ever-obliging lad ends up a ruthless exploiter. Dungate wanted to highlight the way society fails the young and vulnerable by exposing an aspect of life which is virtually hidden from public consciousness. He described in the September edition of *Plays and Players* the experience of working with Clark on the play: hours of draft script meetings when the text would be shredded, the narrative clarified, a new character, a new scene added, the writer's imagination controlled—all leading to a leaner, more muscular play.

Dungate was also fascinated by the collaboration between the director and the designer Ruari Murchison which 'could encapsulate complex ideas when creating an environment'. Visually the result was a cracked-mirrored set with a roof-top cat walk and hung with the shells of wrecked cars. Despite the energy imparted by a rich vein of humour, there was no attempt to glamorise. Language was explicit and at times there was full nudity. Ian Pepperell, who was to become very familiar to Rep audiences, gave a totally committed performance as Danny growing from a gauche ex-care boy to a mobile-toting wide boy. James Dreyfus played a wildly funny, camp kleptomaniac called Sean with Michelle Joseph as his girlfriend Julie. Jason Yates was Tony, a black clubber and Robin Pirongs, the brain-dead skinhead, Ape. The production proved so successful, it was revived in the Studio the following April before playing a short season at the Drill Hall in London. Eventually Dungate won the Eileen Anderson Award.

Sarah Woods described *Nervous Women* as a post-feminist ghost story which parallels and intercuts the lives of two women, Ali and Celia, living a hundred years apart, but trapped in the same room of a Victorian house. In nineteenth-century Birmingham when suburban Yardley was in the countryside, Celia is confined to the room for a 'rest cure' by her doctor husband determined to control her passionate nature. A century later, agoraphobic Ali and her boyfriend Sam arrive complete with supermarket trolley to squat in a now semi-derelict house. Unable to cope with the bewildering pressures of society and a boyfriend who cannot help her, Ali dreams about exotic holidays from travel brochures and becomes aware of her predecessor in the room. Victoria Worsley played Celia and Peter Shorey her husband Jonathan, while Louise Yates and Robin Pirongs were Ali and Sam.

Patrick Connellan designed the set with a bed and a single grimy window which looked out onto a tree which both women can see. Realism, however, was boldly subverted in bright blue chairs fixed diagonally up a yellow wall which at one point Celia literally climbed. The play graphically contrasts past and present attitudes to female sexuality. Jonathan's horrified reaction to Celia's need to masturbate is contrasted with Sam's casual acceptance of Ali's 'wank'. Celia dies as a result of 'curative' forced feeding, while Ali chooses to go out to sit under the tree thus answering Celia's anguished need to know that 'it will not always be like this'.

Gwenda's Run

Apart from Ian Judge's Christmas production of *The Wizard of Oz*, Gwenda Hughes' productions ran almost end to end from early November until late February starting on the main stage with one of J.B. Priestley's 'time' plays, *Dangerous Corner*. Designer Robert Jones exploited the height of the main stage with an enlarged and distorted version of a 1930s' period drawing room. Helen Baxendale made her Rep debut in the part of Betty Whitehouse, and then went on to play Isabel Vane in *East Lynne*. Mrs Henry Wood's 1860 'sensation' novel of the oft-misattributed 'dead, dead, and never called me mother' fame, may have seemed an unlikely choice for a modern feminist director and dramatist. However Lisa Evans' adaptation reveals, rather like her version of Maria Marten, the societal codes which constrained and controlled women's lives. Isabel Vane is the daughter of the spendthrift Earl of Mountsevern, whose pitiful circumstances draw her into a worthy, but unexciting marriage which she abandons when tempted by the treacherous Captain Levison. Inevitably betrayed, she returns ill and disguised to be a governess to her own children and witness one of them die before she too dies.

In her time Mrs Woods was credited with showing unusual sympathy for the luckless Isabel despite the fact that she was mainly concerned to demonstrate the innate degeneracy of the aristocracy. The central chilly message that women must learn to bear—come what may—the life-long bond of marriage, and that Isabel deserved her fate, was explicitly rejected by Evans. Rod Dungate, reviewing the production (*PP*, February, 93) praised Baxendale's performance and the 'single bold statement of Kate Owen's design: raised wooden floors. louvred doors, a gravel area and colossal columns, all unnervingly skewed'. He quoted the play's concluding lines 'I stand then, as now, outside the walls of her church, her life, her judgement. And the snow falls on me and women like me. And we feel the cold'.

Post-Christmas Hughes returned to the theme of blighted marriage but in another production aimed at Birmingham's Irish population. This was the British première of *Big Maggie*, a play written in 1969 by the Kerry-based publican-playwright John B. Keane. Set in 1963, it is the heroic saga of a newly-widowed Irish matriarch's battle to keep her liberty, her farm and her shop at the expense of the freedom of her entire family and all who come into contact with her. In provoking appalled admiration for the central character, Keane makes a far from oblique attack on the power of the Roman Catholic church and the faith which inhibits personal sexual fulfillment. The designer Ruari Murchison evoked a bleak Irish farming community with lines of receding telegraph poles and an austere, wooded-boarded disc tilted and thrust out into the auditorium. The performance began with the funeral of Maggie's husband: the graveyard represented by a stage cloth of black silk and overlooked by a great cross cut out of the sky.

Keane's revised 1987 text ends in a half-hour monologue by Maggie which draws the audience into the story of her young blighted hopes in her loveless marriage and then triumphantly celebrates sensuality. Hughes retained just enough of this to permit Gillian Hanna who played Maggie the opportunity to show how a powerful actor can take on the Rep auditorium and win. Michael Coveney, who devoted nearly half of his weekly *Observer* review column (14.2.93) to Keane, the play and the production gave an ecstatic account of her 'wonderful' performance 'suggestive of a nation poised on the brink of change and confusion'.

Bill and John

No amount of artistic innovation could entirely assuage the managerial traumas which had been suffered over the past year, or indeed mask the terrifying prospect opening up as a result of the financial crisis trumpeted by the press in March 1993. Nationwide throughout that year it appeared that the whole regional theatre network was under threat. The government's decision to cut five million from the projected grant-aid to the Arts Council, the rumours of a hit-list of ten regional theatres (the Rep was not one of them), the resignation of Brian Rix as Chairman of the Arts Council Drama Panel and generalised howls of anguish from everyone who cared about the arts contributed to an ongoing state of emergency. In February 1994, just before the much-compromised Arts Council of Great Britain was to assume its slimmer role as the Arts Council of England, Anthony Everitt—his position now untenable—resigned as Secretary General. On a both micro and macro level the new Artistic Director of the Birmingham Repertory Theatre had been handed a poisoned chalice of quite monumental dimensions.

Bill Alexander did not apply for the job. It was suggested to him by David Edgar, aided and abetted by Professor Ronnie Mulryne of Warwick University who had been on the Rep Board since 1987 and had also been a member of the Arts Council Drama Panel. Alexander who was forty four at the time of his appointment, was born William Patterson in Hunstanton in East Anglia within three days of David Edgar. After a degree in English and Politics from Keele University, he started his theatrical career travelling around London suburbs in a Fun Arts Bus with a group called the Interactive Street Theatre Company. The change of name (his second name became his surname) was prompted by the discovery that Equity already had a William Patterson on their books. A two-year director training course and extensive experience at the Bristol Old Vic led to work at the Royal Court and then the Royal Shakespeare Company which he joined with the special brief to direct new plays. He introduced work by dramatists such as Stephen Poliakoff, Barrie Keefe and Howard Barker, and formed a particularly strong relationship with Peter Whelan directing *The Accrington Pals*, *Clay*, *Captain Swing* and, in 1992, Whelan's play about Christopher Marlowe *The School of Night* which was premièred at the RSC's Other Place.

He had an impressive record in RSC Shakespeare. He directed Anthony Sher's celebrated performance as Richard III in 1984, and went on to direct Sher as Shylock in *The Merchant of Venice* and Malvolio in *Twelfth Night*. His 1950s' style production of *The Merry Wives of Windsor* won him an Olivier Award as Best Director. As Alexander gave his first press interviews on the Rep job, his production of *The Taming of the Shrew* had just entered the RSC repertoire. He was arguably the most high-profile director to be appointed to run Birmingham Rep and no doubt it was hoped that his prestige would benefit the theatre and attract other distinguished artists.

He knew virtually nothing about Birmingham or indeed about the Rep where his only experience of a performance had been *Worzel Gummidge*. Now he seized the opportunity to have 'a home, a base from which to work' and where he could develop as an artist (*BP*, 14.5.92). He arrived in Birmingham to begin work on 5 November, exhausted and more than a little shell-shocked after travelling straight from Washington where he had directed a production of *Troilus and Cressida*. Accommodation was a problem. He did not move his family with children still in full-time education from Gloucester and so chose to commute at weekends. A miserable time trying to find a suitable home for the working week led to a decision to live in one of the theatre flats which Burman and Winteringham had designed so long ago. Birmingham Rep literally became his home for the next eight years.

Dubbed the 'gangly thespian' by Christine Barker in the *Birmingham Post* (24.7. 93) Alexander was soft-spoken, charming in one-to-one interaction and casually-dressed to the point of scruffiness. All this barely concealed a passionate seriousness about his work, an unashamedly intellectual approach to directing, and a kind of arrogance based on a firm commitment to his stated principles. For a company in dire need of strong leadership he seemed the perfect choice. One of his decisions on arriving at the theatre was to extend the rehearsal period to six weeks. This was an economically risky decision, but one which it was hoped would expand the possibilities for creative work on a production and crucially attract top-class actors. Six weeks for rehearsal was almost unheard of outside the national companies, but Alexander was clear that he wanted his Birmingham Rep to have national status. The emphasis was to be on the company rather than the theatre. Echoing Nancy Burman thirty years before, he did not much care for the term 'repertory theatre'. Like his predecessors he dreamed of some kind of permanent acting ensemble, and he fell in love with the Rep stage.

His best-known experience was with a stage which in its earliest days had been condemned as vociferously as the Rep's. In 1932, the new Shakespeare Memorial Theatre had been considered an alienating disaster. Only after determined efforts to break through the proscenium in the 1950s and 60s did the criticism die down although the RST stage and auditorium remained problematic. For the new director of Birmingham Rep it was important that he was used to large-scale work on a large-scale stage. In a *What's On* interview with Stuart McGill in November 1992, he claimed it was one of the reasons why he had taken the job on 'I think we need to lift it a little, in all its width and depth, it will be raked and extend further into the auditorium'. He had a very strong sense of how the space should be used and there was, in his view, an unexpected intimacy about the auditorium. Looking out from the stage it was possible to see it as a large studio space. The stage had been thrust out to row D in the past, but this was now to become the norm. Audiences could virtually put their feet on the playing space. The raking of the stage was achieved with the construction of individual steel deck units which could be bolted together to achieve the required gradations in height. Kit Surrey designed *Othello* with black pillars and huge black floor tiles which seemed to stretch out limitlessly to the darkness at the back and sides and towards the audience.

The new director put forward a very clear programming policy designed to raise the status of the Rep both locally and nationally. There would be a conscious avoidance of newly-available popular successes. The Rep would not be staging the latest Ayckbourn or Willy Russell: not because these were in any way inferior plays but because the Rep needed to be more distinctive. There was to be a three-pronged strategy based on three kinds of plays: great classic plays, new plays and what he dubbed 'discovery plays' i.e. plays from any period which deserved to be better known. In the midst of all the idealism, however, was a very strong consciousness of the economic obstacles which had to be overcome.

The 1991 Appraisal Report had suggested that the Rep should look at alternative senior management models on other theatres of comparable size. Clive Wilkinson had brought the Company's finances under control, but during John Adams' time both the role of the Artistic Director and the General Manager had been ill-defined. The model of a partnership of Artistic Director and Executive Producer with separate areas of responsibility but effectively co-equal and united in artistic vision seemed infinitely desirable. Before the end of 1992 John Stalker was appointed as Executive Producer. His role may have been much the same as Clive Wilkinson's but Stalker's background was entirely different.

Thirty one when he arrived in Birmingham, Stalker was born in Scotland and from an early age had shared his parents' love of the stage, both as an enthusiastic audience member at theatres like the Glasgow Citizens and the Edinburgh Royal Lyceum, and as an amateur practitioner. While reading politics at Edinburgh University he became involved in student drama, helped found a theatre, tried his hand at acting and directing and then ended up working at the old Traverse Theatre. A Scottish Arts Council bursary led to a Diploma in Arts Administration at the City University in London which then took him to the Dukes Playhouse in Lancaster. From 1989 to 1992 he was the Administrative Director at the Liverpool Playhouse. In the Rep's new double-act Stalker was the suit to Alexander's tracksuit and together they made a formidable combination.

Effecting Change

Like Wilkinson before him, Stalker had to adopt the axeman's stance. The two most significant redundancies were Bill Hughes and Wendy Malpass who had been head of Publicity and Marketing. Ros Robbins who had a background in community theatre and had spent four years as administrator at the Liverpool Everyman, became General Administrator. Kate Horton who had been Account Director for a large advertising company came initially with the job title of Head of Sales, but eventually became Head of Sales and Marketing in a department which united publicity and box office staff. By the autumn of 1992 Graham Collins had left the theatre and Chris Bolstridge was installed as Head of Finance. Wiff Maton retained the role of Casting Associate which she had held since 1989, while John Pitt and Sally Isern continued in the key positions of Production Manager and Company Manager. David Williams remained as a survivor from the earliest days of the building. There were now very few who had worked at the Old Rep. Albert Vale who became Technical Manager in 1992 had fond memories. There was a still a little group down in Wardrobe who could reminisce about another era. June Callear retired in 1992 and Sue (Tottie) Nightingale became Head of Department.

A new kind of professionalism had entered the theatre based on enhanced financial and commercial expertise united to a common artistic goal. Although no one underestimated future problems, what came across very clearly as the new regime consolidated its position was a confidence in managerial strength. Kate Horton's policy was characteristic of the new approach. Before her arrival communication between the two vital areas of Box Office and Publicity which have most to do with public relations was very vague. Rachel Foster, formerly the Box Office Manager, now known as Sales Manager, was fully involved in the marketing policy. Everything was discussed and agreed. On her arrival Horton proceeded to audit the entire marketing operation: stripping down a mailing list data base which had remained unchecked and out-dated for years, and ensuring that there was a corporate image in line with current commercial practice. Programmes and season brochures were given the same format to present a sense of Company identity.

Clearly the introduction of more firmly-structured working practices in the theatre reflected what was happening in all kinds of institutions nationwide. The relaxed industrial relations in Station Street which had contributed to the family atmosphere became in the bigger and more economically-pressured environment of the new building, the source of dangerous corporate incompetence. The Rep was now fully unionised and half the staff had carefully-defined job descriptions. Working hours were regulated and all-night marathons were rare. The turn round between productions which used to take three days at the Old Rep with staff working long, underpaid hours out of sheer good will, now extended from the set strike following a final Saturday night performance to the second dress rehearsal on the next Friday afternoon before the first preview. Training opportunities were offered for front of house staff in customer services and more plans were laid for extending similar qualifications in technical and stage craft skills.

As Chair of the Board, Brian Townsend was a key figure. But he, too, had to learn. He had to be told gently by Bill Alexander that the Community Department could not be axed to cut costs. But he was able to arbitrate when friction arose over the status and function of the Rep Foundation. The role of Director of the Foundation ceased by the end of 1993 when Dorothy Warner left. Also by the end of 1993 the composition of the Board had undergone a substantive change. The City representation had been reduced to two, while three new members: Cicely Berry, the distinguished RSC voice specialist, Dr Vayu Naidu-Banfield, an expert in Asian story-telling, and David Waine, Head of BBC Broadcasting, Midlands and East, brought in significant arts/media-oriented experience.

Education

The other key figure who came at the beginning of 1993 was Joanna Read who was designated Community, Youth and Education officer. Her experience, after a degree from Bristol University, included directing with the Young Vic Youth and Education Unit, and a period at the Crucible Theatre on a bursary from the Regional Theatre Young Directors Scheme. While her basic brief 'to create an imaginative programme of theatre, workshop and outreach material that supports, challenges and extends the work of the theatre' was essentially no different to that which underpinned the earlier work of the Community Department, there was a definite shift towards more direct educational activity.

The first year established a pattern. There were both in-school and in-theatre workshops tied to the season programme. A series of pre-performance 'spotlights' and post-performance 'after-dark' sessions were organised where audience members could listen to the Rep directors discuss their approach to production and answer questions. Resource packs were provided not just on plays which were part of the autumn season but also on school syllabus drama like *Antony and Cleopatra* which was workshopped as a 'Page to Stage' session giving school groups the opportunity to see an examination text approached by professional actors and directors. Also that summer, a new Youth Theatre was established for 16-21 year olds which, unlike Rep Youth Workshop, did not audition would-be members. Weekly sessions were held inside the theatre in order to give a greater sense of being part of the Rep organisation. An Open Day was held in May to allow some thousand members of the public to see all aspects of the theatre's work. John Stalker turned chef for the day, cooking breakfast for the Rep staff.

In the autumn of 1993, events and workshops were organised round the Studio programme of visiting companies. Read took over the direction of the Community Tour and with her first production of *Joyriders* introduced a further element of educational interaction. The rehearsal process became effectively a residency at Wodensborough High School in Wednesbury in which other aspects of the school's expressive arts syllabus were supported. Further links were created with local arts and youth work officers. It was an extensive, ambitious programme aimed at making the Rep matter in the community which it served; trying above all to create audiences for the future.

Bill's Vision

As the strategy unfolded over the next three years, there were inevitably some constraints in respect of new work, especially on the main stage, and blurring of categories. In the first twelve months there was a strong classical orientation. Alexander directed Jeffery Kissoon as Othello with Young Company graduate Alex Kingston as Desdemona. In September, Gwenda Hughes, directing her first Shakespeare, cast Damien Lewis and Josette-Bushell-Mingo as the lovers in *Romeo and Juliet*. In June, Alexander also directed Bernard Horsfall as Volpone and Gerard Murphy as Mosca in Ben Jonson's *Volpone*, a big stage revival of a play Alexander had tackled successfully in the Other Place in Stratford in 1984. In October he invited three very distinguished actors Estelle Kohler, Carol Royle and Tim Piggott-Smith to play in the first major revival of Pinter's modern classic *Old Times* since 1985. In February 1994 Gerard Murphy scored a spectacular success as D'Amville, the godless central character of Cyril Tourneur's *The Atheist's Tragedy*.

The Towards the Millennium Festival, Birmingham's annual festival launched in 1991 to celebrate the arts of each decade of the twentieth century leading up to 2000, provided a focus for discovery plays. John Adams' production of *The Ragged Trousered Philanthropists* had kicked off the Rep's involvement in the first year. In April 1993 Gwenda Hughes directed Patrick Hamilton's 1920's thriller *Rope*.

Not only was it set in the appropriate decade, it was designed to attract audiences familiar with Hamilton's better-known play *Gaslight* to see a macabre tale of two students who commit a motiveless murder, hide the corpse and then add to their excitement by inviting the dead man's father and friends to dinner. For the festival the following year Alexander directed Clifford Odets' passionate 1935 political drama *Awake and Sing!* first performed by the Group Theatre in New York. The Rep programme for the play which addresses the social and economic conditions of the Depression, was full of information on America's ethnic melting pot, the background to economic collapse and the history of the Group Theatre itself and the celebrated artists associated with it. Alexander's acting company which included Joe Melia as Myron Berger was largely new to the Rep but the casting of June Brown, last seen with Birmingham Rep in 1958, as the matriarch Bessie Berger was a means of generating publicity round a very well-known television soap star.

But audiences were not to be wooed by an *Eastenders* star. The audience average for *Rope* was 32%. For Alexander's immaculately-directed *Old Times* it was 22%. Throughout the whole of Alexander's tenure it proved virtually impossible to achieve any kind of consistency of audience support for the work in the main auditorium. Despite growing managerial professionalism and efficiency, and irrespective of levels of artistic and critical achievement, the pattern of attendance remained much the same. Predictably *Othello* as Alexander's first production played to a very respectable 69%. *Volpone* managed 40%. *Romeo and Juliet* was a play prioritised by the National Curriculum and attracted large school parties. But some of the more conservative young people seem to have been disconcerted by a beautiful but black Juliet. Robin Midgley's production of Noël Coward's delightful *Blithe Spirit*, programmed as a grown-up Christmas treat was an artistic disaster (it was updated to the 1990s) and was poorly attended. *The Snowman*, however, playing as the principal family Christmas offering struck gold. At Christmas 2001 a year after Alexander's departure from the Rep, the production received yet another revival in London.

Ravishing to look at and listen to, *The Snowman* is based on the best-selling children's picture-story by Raymond Briggs. Briggs' original work had been given further life by a wordless cartoon film which featured the immensely popular song 'Walking in the Air' by Howard Blake. Alexander abandoned an early plan for dialogue written by Antony Clark in favour of the language of music and movement. Blake composed a much-expanded score played by the English Serenata, while co-director Pat Garrett choreographed a series of enchanting dances for troupes of multi-national snow people. There was even a Fred Astaire Snowman.

Ruari Murchison designed a basic white box set which formed a dazzling background for constant movement whether from the family home interiors which seemed to slide of their own volition onto the stage, or the outdoor scenes glowing with brilliant colours and huge snow-laden trees. Dancer Perry Douglin played the Snowman with two boys—Justyn Towler and Oliver Ashford aged ten and eleven—sharing the part of the little pyjama-clad boy James. Their flight hand-in-hand through the atmospheric night sky, accompanied by the much-loved song, invariably provoked applause.

Golden Opinions

The audiences who did not choose to return in the spring and summer months of 1994, missed an ambitious, diverse range of work. Clark directed an exuberant, joyful revival of *The Playboy of the Western World* as well as *The Atheist's Tragedy* which won him the TMA/Martini Regional Award for Best Director. Hughes directed the European première of an all-black Broadway musical *Once On this Island* which won an Olivier Award for Best New Musical. Audiences were disappointing for both *Playboy* and *Island* although both were targeted at specific cultural interests within the Birmingham community. Ironically however, *The Atheist's Tragedy*, by far the most obscure and theoretically difficult of the season's choices, achieved at 41%, exactly the same audience response as a sumptuously-dressed, commercial co-production with Duncan C. Weldon of *Lady Windermere's Fan* which Philip Prowse directed.

The Atheist's Tragedy, both a classic and a discovery play which had received only one important revival in the twentieth century, was a conscious risk. D'Amville is a machiavellian, materialist villain whose unbridled desire to increase his family's wealth leads him to pack his nephew Charlemont off to war, marry his sickly son Rousard to Charlemont's wealthy betrothed, Castabella and then murder his brother Montferrers who is Charlemont's father. In the end after the deaths of both his sons and the attempted rape of Catabella, D'Amville dies, accidentally cracking open his skull, while swinging an axe at Charlemont. The part was tailor-made for Gerard Murphy and he appeared to relish every moment of it, especially when dying he pulled out a blood-soaked chunk of his brain to examine it.

The bizarre comic-book horror was accompanied by an onstage pianist (Dane Preece) complete with Liberace-style candelabra and in a set by Patrick Connellan which conjured up a world where love and desire, war and justice are reduced to the level of toy town games. The heroically-wronged Charlemont (James Simmonds) went off to war on a giant wooden horse; the virtuous Castabella (Katherine Rogers) was wooed by the repulsive Rousard (Michael Gould) while seated on an enormous high-chair. The judges at Charlemont's trumped-up trial were flown in seated on cushioned tasselled swings—playground scales of justice—while the executioner, with a fairy-light equipped stand, looked like a pornographic caped crusader in gold-lame bootees and a gold cache-sex. Jane Maud played the sexually-rampant Levidulcia with Mark Jax as D'Amville's hilariously lubricious other son. Languebeau Snuffe, a sex-obsessed Calvinist who ends up an inadvertent necrophiliac, was played by Jamie Newell with greasy hair, thick pebble glasses and sandals.

Once On This Island which was a co-production with Imagination Entertainments, was co-directed by Hughes with choreographer David Toguria whose previous credits included award-winning work on the National Theatre's *Guys and Dolls*. With the book and music by white writer and composer Lynn Ahrens and Stephen Flaherty, and an all-black cast which featured American rock-star P.P. Arnold and Lancashire-born Clive Rowe, cultural diversity was built into the experience. Rowe and Arnold were cast as Pape Ge, the Demon of Death and Erzulie, the God of Love, two of four Caribbean gods who influence the fate of Ti Moune (Lorna Brown), a beautiful peasant girl on a French colonial island. She falls in love with the wealthy mulatto whose life she has saved only to be rejected in favour of an aristocratic bride and dies, transformed into a tree which will shelter her beloved for ever. Playing for only ninety minutes without an interval, and with a small band of five musicians, the show was an exuberant feast of song and dance on a flamboyantly coloured set by Kendra Ullyart. Transferred to London to the Royalty Theatre which Imagination renamed Island Theatre and transformed to create a total Caribbean experience complete with steel bands, the show came in for some flak from critics like Michael Billington who was sceptical of a Broadway myth peddling phoney reassurance. Scepticism was overcome, however, by the golden glow of the Olivier award, and the team in Birmingham could take a little time out from the struggle to make ends meet to enjoy an unexpected triumph.

A Balancing Act

The business of maintaining financial stability alongside the commitment to Alexander's core artistic principles was very tricky. Alexander and Stalker knew that grasping the nettle of commercial co-production could provide much needed revenue but the risks concerning artistic ownership and integrity were high. The deal on *Lady Windermere's Fan* and *Once on this Island* had the gratifying outcome of two Birmingham Repertory Company productions running at the same time in London. But *Lady Windermere* was an example of the kind of show which came as a pre-wrapped package with its director, designer and star (Francesca Annis as Mrs Erlynne) already chosen.

Over the next two years partnerships were both financially and artistically more evenly balanced. In March 1995, when a season gap needed to be filled, the Rep was able to present David Thacker's production of Arthur Miller's *A View From the Bridge* in association with the Bristol Old Vic and Pericles Productions. There were heavy advance bookings with large groups of young people brought to see a play by one of Britain's favourite dramatists interpreted by a director who had formed a long-standing relationship with Miller. Bernard Hill returned to the Rep to play the tortured longshoreman Eddie Carbone. Co-production was of course not new to the Rep, but it was increasingly seen as a way of cost-sharing and extending the creative life of a production. In 1996, both Clark's Towards the Millennium production of Osborne's *The Entertainer* and Hughes' production of Rattigan's *The Winslow Boy* were mounted in association with West Yorkshire Playhouse.

The happiest experience of a guest-directed production backed by some commercial acumen was provided by the 1995 spring celebration of the centenary of *The Importance of Being Earnest* which was directed by Terry Hands. Designed by Mark Bailey, and with Roger Allam and Philip Franks as Jack and Algy and Barbara Leigh-Hunt as Lady Bracknell, it was a joyfully traditional production which brought packed houses to the Rep. A small financial investment from Old Vic proprietor David Mirvish bolstered the month's run in Birmingham and then paid entirely for a transfer to the Old Vic. The Rep earned a very satisfying £100,000 as a result.

The strategies for more diverse and revenue-raising use of the main stage included the Sunday shows of music, comedy and virtuoso star turns which had continued ever since they were first introduced in the early seventies. The fact that the stage is an ideal dance space also led to some innovative programming which brought dynamic new companies drawing on a wide range of cultural traditions. In October 1993 the Birmingham National Dance Agency presented the British première of *Colored Children Flyin' By*. The following April the Kosh came with *Klub Anima*, an exciting mixture of 'raw music', dance, cabaret and theatre. In the autumn, the vibrant Birmingham-based Afro-Caribbean company Kokuma premièred *Spirit of Carnival*. The Spring Fling Dance 1995 festival included a two-day visit from the celebrated Mark Morris Dance Group. Bill Alexander chaired a relaxed post-performance question and answer session with Morris to an auditorium bursting at the seams with dance enthusiasts from all over the region. In 1996, Candoco Dance Company which integrates abled and disabled performers, performed as part of the Barclays New Stages Festival. A revived relationship with the Rambert Dance Company brought large audiences.

There were two important managerial developments. A consultative process initiated in 1994 with advisors working under the Business in the Arts scheme, finally concluded that the disadvantages of the BREL commercial set-building activities far outweighed the modest financial rewards and the operation was phased out. Of more immediate public significance, the stranglehold of the Iceford catering contract was broken. The nadir of the relationship with Iceford had been reached during the run of *The Playboy of the Western World* when an altercation with members of the largely Irish cast led to one of the Café Bar staff injuring an actor so badly that two Saturday performances had to be cancelled. This small, squalid and expensive episode just about summed up the whole sorry history of the Rep's attempts to give their patrons a civilised night out. The City stepped in to help broker a deal with the National Exhibition Centre parent company of the ICC to enable the Rep's next door neighbours to buy out Iceford in 1995 and take over the whole catering and hospitality franchise. The handsome sum paid for the privilege also helped the Rep to reduce some of its debt burden. The new restaurant area was renamed Olivier's in early 1996.

What could not be ignored, however, was the problem of the reduced core audience and the difficulty of predicting what would prove attractive, which was by no means automatically linked to acknowledged artistic success. The orientation in the 1994-5 season towards well-known classics brought the success of *The Importance of Being Earnest* and exceptionally good audiences for Clark's Christmas production of *Peter Pan*. Audiences for Alexander's production of *The Tempest* dropped, however, and were very modest for a bold but interesting strategy of alternating the Joe Orton classics *Loot* and *Entertaining Mr Sloane* on rotating suburban house sets which Hughes directed. An attempt in the summer to capitalise on the *Peter Pan* family audience for Clark's expanded musical adaptation of *The Red Balloon* managed less than 30%. The production featured a touching, beautifully-sung portrayal of the little Parisian boy Pascal by Nicky Adams, accompanied by Malcolm Shields as the silently expressive Dream Maker operating the disruptive red balloon. A charming, slightly old-fashioned piece for today's hard-bitten, high-tech children, it nonetheless won a Regional Theatre Award for Best Show for Children and Young People, and went on to play for a short run at the National Theatre.

A National Company

National critical approval, awards, regular London appearances: all were indicative of a company which was establishing itself as an artistic force to be reckoned with. While there was no resident Head of Design—that role had long gone with Geoffrey Scott—designers like Ruari Murchison, Patrick Connellan, Kit Surrey and Nettie Edwards could work with directors who were prepared to enjoy and celebrate the resources of the stage. Tim Mitchell who became head of lighting and sound during John Adams' directorate began to build up a record of lighting design which in itself became a significant player in the overall visual approach. Of course the time-honoured jibes at the size of the stage continued. There were jokes about the length of time it took to reach the coffee table on the set for *Old Times* for example, and criticism of the dimensions of Nettie Edwards' evocative New York tenement setting for *Awake and Sing!*.

The six week rehearsal period permitted intensive exploration of text and characterisation which is where Bill Alexander really came into his own, working with great rigour and attention to detail. Actors had time to mature and develop their roles and the results in performance could be very satisfying. However, the huge stage could also become a trap for productions which had been allowed to become ponderous and too self-absorbed. Slowness of pace in *Volpone* and *Romeo and Juliet*, for example, was symptomatic of a weakness which the directorate needed to address as they tried to satisfy their wayward audience, and in particular the local newspaper critics who were all too quick to damn any obvious flaws. A policy for using local student actors as supernumeraries, which began with *Othello*, meant that grander and more active visual effects could be achieved for big plays. But this strategy had to handled carefully. The decadent nineteenth-century Venetian café society created for *Volpone*, peopled and repeatedly shunted on and off the stage by twenty supernumeraries, was distracting and time-consuming.

That said, national critics were prepared to respond seriously to obvious artistic ambition. Reviewing *The Tempest*, Michael Billington wrote that Alexander's production was 'as visually rich, strongly cast and meticulously prepared as anything you could hope to find in either of the national companies' (*G*, 15.9.94). He was particularly interested in the rationale behind the updating of the play which pointed up parallels between the early seventeenth century, and the mid-nineteenth century preoccupation with scientific investigation, fascination with the occult, and the accompanying crisis of faith. Jeffery Kissoon's Prospero was 'a mixture of Victorian magus and Darwinian explorer seeking to discover the roots of civilisation'. The so-called civilised courtiers were nineteenth-century aristocrats in frock coats and top hats. Geoffrey Freshwater played Trinculo the jester as a music-hall comedian in a loud checked suit making an entertaining double act with Andy Hockley's drunken Scots Stephano.

As the nineteenth century was the period of the most far-reaching European colonisation of black races, the integrated casting took on powerful resonances. This was a black Prospero with a black Miranda (Ginny Holder) and a black Ariel (Rakie Ayola). Tony Armatrading played a black Antonio. The wedding masque which Prospero summons became an Indian dance choreographed by Piali Ray. Caliban, however, played by Richard McCabe was not the usual half man/half animal grotesque, but a bewildered, shambling, moon-faced 'natural' at times touchingly in need of love and attention. Indeed Ayola's Ariel had an intense, fixated, childlike quality lending her kinship not only with Miranda but also with Caliban.

Some reviews found Kissoon too melodramatic and disliked a harsh barking delivery of the words. But Michael Coveney noted his brooding presence and the pain behind the unravelling of his plot for Miranda (*O*, 18.9.94). There were moments when he seemed to be part of the fabric of the island. Ruari Murchison's set filled most of the stage with what appeared to be black rock carved in the shapes of Prospero's books. The principal playing space was reduced to an austere circle of white sand constantly changing colour with the complementary circle of sky which reflected images of clouds and waves. Everyone agreed that the opening storm was stunning. The ship was no more than a black platform suspended over billowing white silk. The opening lines were spoken in an eerie quiet, punctuated by a slow thudding heartbeat and the occasional roll of thunder. When the full fury was unleashed, the tempest reverberated right round the auditorium.

The Servant, which Alexander directed a few months later is, like *The Tempest*, about human power relations. Robin Maugham's novel, published in 1948, was written in the context of post-war social reform and the real possibilities of political revolution. Best-known in Pinter's screenplay for Joseph Losey's sixties film version, the novel was twice reworked for the stage by Maugham himself and the Rep production was only the second since it flopped in Guildford in 1966. Programmed as the Millennium Festival play, and as a result back-dated to its original forties period, this was an authentic discovery play. Kit Surrey's set, a cut-away section of a Belgravia mansion, was stratified like society: velvet-piled, satin-sheeted elegance on the top floor above the utilitarian kitchen and servants' quarters: all resting on the corruption-carrying sewage system beneath. Everything was literally and symbolically shored-up against bomb damage.

James Purefoy played the weak-willed Tony manipulated into alcohol-drenched dependency by the man servant Barrett played by Paul Copley. The class divisions were clearly signalled in the pairing of the flat-capped, Yorkshire-vowelled, dead-eyed servant with the cut-glass accent and feckless charm of the doomed representative of the ancient régime. The underlying political implications of Maugham's story became much more complex, especially with the added presence of Tony's decently upper-class 'good angels': his girlfriend Sally played by Amanda Harris and his old friend Richard, who was played by David Phelan. The production which Robin Thornber considered an 'important, telling piece of theatre' (*G* , 16.2.95) was hailed across the press political divide and Copley later won a Regional Theatre Award as Best Supporting Actor.

The cultivation of the perception that the Birmingham Repertory Theatre Company and its actors were of national status was of central importance to Alexander. Both Jeffrey Kissoon and Gerard Murphy were designated RSC-style Associate Artists of the Rep and Alexander worked to develop Kissoon especially as one of the company's leading actors. In the autumn of 1995 Kissoon played both Macbeth, and a brutally sophisticated Fainall in Congreve's *The Way of the World*. By casting the same actors for both plays, Alexander was able to keep an ensemble together for nearly four months. Lucy Cohu who partnered Kissoon as Lady Macbeth also played the abused Mrs Fainall. Linda Spurrier, who gave a virtuoso comic performance as Lady Wishfort, was a sinister nurse in the Macbeth household who was later revealed to be Hecate. Amanda Harris played Lady Macduff and an icily elegant Mrs Marwood. Rakie Ayola and James Purefoy who played First Witch and Macduff were then teamed as Millamant and Mirabell. Their key scene, when Millamant delivers her conditions for marriage, achieved a magical rapport which held the audience transfixed, and more than justified the weeks of painstaking rehearsal.

Ruari Murchison's design for *Macbeth* was arguably the boldest statement ever made on the Rep stage. The play was taken forward to some grim, futuristic warrior-oriented society in the twenty-first century. The space was stripped right back to its furthest extremities so it resembled a concrete and brick warehouse with rusting iron grilles, shutters and staircases and was big enough for Duncan (Geoffrey Freshwater) to ride in on a jeep. At one moment of despair in the final battle scenes, Kissoon stood with arms outstretched as though nailed to the back wall, while a servant stood quivering at the furthest downstage edge of an otherwise empty set. It was an epic moment on what looked like an epic stage. But as a whole the production divided opinion. For some, it was slow, over-long and over-conceptualised and indeed that autumn marked the end of Kissoon's sustained relationship with the Rep. A lot of young people liked it, however, and that, under the circumstances, was not unimportant.

Making it New

A survey commissioned by the Marketing Department to analyse attendance for *The Tempest* and the Orton plays, came up with a picture of an audience which was predominantly white, middle-class and over forty-five. Indeed in the sample a remarkable one in five was aged over sixty five—many of whom would presumably have been drawn from Old Rep loyalists. A similar conclusion was reached in 1995 by the much more wide-ranging consultations chaired by David Edgar for the West Midlands Drama and Theatre Review. Nation-wide traditional audiences for regional theatre were literally dying out. Theatre had to be seen to reflect racial diversity and youth culture. A letter sent to the *Guardian* on 21 November 1994, and signed by eighty six dramatists including Edgar, attributed the decline to the failure, largely for financial reasons, to maintain a steady flow of new writing for the stage. A challenge was laid down to theatres to produce at least three new plays (not adaptations) a year, at least two of which ought to be on their main stages.

It was thus a priority that Alexander should fulfil his avowed commitment to new writing and that the Studio should regain its status as an important space for artistic innovation. Given the profound financial problems this was easier promised than done. During the autumn of 1993 there was no homegrown Studio production apart from the Community Tour. The work presented was largely new but from small-scale touring companies. Graeae, the leading theatre company for disabled actors, and The Sphinx, the women's company, both brought new plays by April de Angelis: *The Soft Vengeance of a Freedom Fighter*, and *Playhouse Creatures*. A plan to present three Rep productions of new work in the spring of 1994 had to be postponed and the Studio was almost entirely given over to the interests of young people. There was a week's run of daytime performances of Clark's Royal National Theatre production of *The Day After Tomorrow*, a translation of a play about coming to terms with a new baby aimed at four to seven year olds by the Dutch writer Roel Adam. Joanna Read directed the Community Tour of *Micky and Me!*, by local writer Alex Jones, which targeted the eleven to fourteen age group. The Rep Community team of six spent a fortnight working on the play and running workshops at Cradley High School.

By this time the Department had also initiated Write Now, a new young writers' group led by Guy Hutchins. In addition to devised performances in April by the Youth Theatre based on Schnitzler's *La Ronde,* the two groups came together in June for a two-day festival of new writing. The four-week-summer devised project saw performances of *Break a Neck,* a kind of am-dram version of *Noises Off* , which was devised, written and designed by the Youth Theatre company. Bridging the gap between enjoyment in youthful collaboration and long-term interest in the theatre meant input and commitment from the professional company not just in terms of directorial and technical support for performance. Young people went into press nights and enjoyed master classes run by actors and directors. For the spring half-term in 1995, the *Hot off the Page!* festival included classes run by the cast of *The Servant,* performances of original work by local sixth form college students, alongside rehearsed readings by Youth Theatre members. The group also staged *Disturbed,* a new play by Nicola Kay set in a local authority-run home for disturbed young people, which was directed by Ed Robson, then at the Rep as Assistant Director under the Regional Theatres Young Directors Scheme.

That 1994-5 season saw a much stronger, largely homegrown Studio programme. An encouraging range of new work encompassed regional interest, cultural diversity, and plays which offered a challenging exploration of complex relationships. In the autumn Clark directed the première of Kate Dean's *Rough. A Shaft of Sunlight* was a co-production with Tamasha Theatre Company about the strains of mixed Hindu/Moslem marriage in present-day India, written by Abhijat Joshi. Lorna Laidlaw performed a one-woman song and sketch show, *Getting It Straight*, written with Jon Trevor, which used the knotty problem of Afro hair to probe wider issues of black female experience. There was more new women's writing in April and June with the premières of Bryony Lavery's *Nothing Compares to You*, and Lisa Evans' adaptation of Anne Brontë's *The Tenant of Wildfell Hall*, which were both directed by Gwenda Hughes.

Despite the fact that the audiences were alarmingly thin, *Rough* won the John Whiting Award. The play had undergone a long gestation period. Commissioned by the Royal Court and then not staged, it was initially rejected by the Rep, and then revised and workshopped as part of the 1993 Stagecoach programme, by which time Clark began to have more confidence in the piece. Set in the Malvern area where Dean lived, it looks at the impact of the arrival of a young, middle-class, single mother on a group of big bike and heavy metal drop-outs living around a pub. Patrick Connellan created the fractured tarmac base for a ramshackle pub yard and the squalid room where Molly (Rachel Dean) ends up with her baby. The previous occupant Deakin (Antony Byrne) hanged himself and it is through his now detached, ghostly presence that the story of inarticulate, disenfranchised young people unfurls in the unlikely environment of the Malvern hills. The play served as a useful reminder that societal malaise is not just about urban blight.

Matthew Wait played Raggy, the dangerously manipulative leader of the pack, dressed to kill in ruffled shirt and leather trousers. Judith McSpadden was Gay, his rainbow-haired grunge-style girl-Friday, revealing unsuspected depths of sympathy for Molly. Daniel Illsley was the damaged drunken Mole with Ray Emmet Brown as the black cellarman and hopeless devotee of Molly. Kate Dean was praised for authentic, gritty dialogue which Clark reinforced with drunken brawls, flying glass and a heavy-metal sound track. At one point, the young mother trying to quieten her crying baby, was tortured by Raggy thunderously stamping on the roof of her room.

Although death is a dominant theme in Bryony Lavery's play, it was altogether gentler and agreeably surreal. There was another ghost, Mary (Sharon Muircroft) killed in a car crash and in Hughes' production, lying splayed against the fragments of Ruari Murchison's set. There were also two mute fylgia (Norwegian guardian spirits) played by Angela Clerkin and Vicki Pepperdine like prim Shakespearean fairies watching over their human charges until death overtakes them. The core story is intercut with strange brief interludes of the fylgia turning themselves into birds laying eggs or parachuting with the aid of a voluminous petticoat.

Hughes had originally commissioned a gothic, female Dracula story with (after Playing by the Rules) the opportunity to see girls kissing. What she got was very different. Lesbian relationships give the main narrative structure to the play. Lily who was played by Lorna Laidlaw mourns her dead lover Mary, who was about to embark on an affair with Rachel (Lou Wakefield) who has a fruitless wait in a hotel bedroom following the crash. But the supporting characters: a man raging because his wife has left him (Jamie Newall); young sympathetic dying Todd (Newall again); Lou Wakefield again as Miriam, an elderly woman anxious about her missing cat, and obsessively house-proud; Joy (Karen Parker) drowning her sorrows and finally her life in alcohol and nicotine. All create a rich pattern of human loss and need ('Nothing Compares 2 U' as Sinead O'Connor sang), counterpointed by the detached games of the immortals.

Hughes moved straight on to The Tenant of Wildfell Hall, renewing her partnership both with Lisa Evans, and Janice McKenzie, who played Anne Brontë's heroine Helen Huntingdon. Bringing the insights and preoccupations of modern society to reflect on women's lives in the past was of course familiar territory for this team. Evans strips away much of the problematic structure of the novel as well

171

as the religious elements to focus on the central story of a woman who flees from her drunken husband and tries to make an independent life for herself and her son by working as a painter. The fact that married women, up until 1882, were effectively the property of their husbands and had no legal rights of possession continues to resonate, as far as Evans is concerned, in the way women can still be economically trapped by abusive husbands.

Ruari Murchison created a simple, wooden-floored traverse setting dominated at either end by two huge blown up paintings by Turner and Holman Hunt. Not only did *Crossing the Brook* and *Our English Coasts* suggest Helen's rural, coastal refuge, but were also a silent, looming reminder of the pre-eminence of male painters over their female counterparts. Draped with curtains to suggest different locations, the pictures assisted the time shifts as Helen's past is revealed. Mark Jax played Huntingdon, her husband who appropriating her fortune, slides inexorably into drunkenness, debauchery and finally, nursed by Helen, a dreadful death. Ian Targett played the young farmer Gilbert Markham with whom Helen ultimately finds happiness. A not so well-known story by a Brontë, a romantic ending, period costumes and strong performances, especially from McKenzie, all combined to make this production a huge success. Towards the end of the run it was impossible to get a ticket and twelve months later it was revived 'by popular demand'. McKenzie returned, but with Mark Arden giving an equally powerful performance as Huntingdon.

Refusing to be Cowed

In September 1995, enabled initially by a special grant from West Midlands Arts, the Rep acquired a literary manager. Formerly Research Director for the New Playwright's Trust, Ben Payne's brief was to 'grow' new writers. Barry Jackson would perhaps have blinked at Ben Payne's earring, sweatshirt and shorts, but he would also have recognised a kindred spirit in the Literary Manager who spoke of a refusal to be cowed. The eventual award of core funding for a post rarely sustained outside the national companies, was a vote of confidence in a nurturing policy which built on the foundations already laid by the directorate. Repwriters, a support, discussion and workshop group for aspiring writers which was launched in January attracted some seventy recruits. Payne was especially keen to give confidence to those individuals who could not, or did not wish, to write within traditionally accepted dramatic conventions. New kinds of writers might bring the added bonus of new kinds of audiences.

The context within which he started work was encouraging. The Studio programme for 1995-6 included three world premières before Christmas, of which two were co-productions, and all were thematically linked. The Rep and Tamasha presented *A Yearning*, a version of Lorca's *Yerma* about a woman longing for a child, relocated to Birmingham's Punjabi community. *Jesus My Boy*, a one-man show which gave the long-suffering Joseph's perspective on the birth of his son, was written by John Dowie. As the Rep's Community Tour Joanna Read directed *Johnny Watkins Walks on Water*, a play commissioned from Debbie Isitt, about a lonely, motherless sixteen year old convinced she is about to give birth to the second Messiah. What followed in April and May, however, was the unprecedented opportunity to see two brand new plays in simultaneous production in the large and small spaces. *Swamp City* by Coventry-born Paul Lucas, which had been workshopped as part of the 1993 Stagecoach Festival, was directed in the Studio by Ed Robson. On the main stage Bill Alexander directed *Divine Right*, a play about the British monarchy by Peter Whelan.

Both plays in their very different ways addressed life in contemporary society. The wildly Absurdist *Swamp City* has a bizarre cast of characters: itinerant, jobbing pet-killers, a nervous waiter who defecates code-bearing letters, toilet-bombing eco-terrorists, and a manic police inspector pursuing a green balaclava-clad ex woman-solicitor, turned bank robber who was played by former stand-up comic Cassie Stuart. It was immaculately directed and performed on a composite set by Matthew Wright. Tower blocks loomed from behind the audience; a dingy hotel front accommodated both a blown-up toilet and a pink satin, heart-shaped bed headed bridal suite. All this combined with a visionary pub garden complete with rabbits and flowers complemented the verbal and physical comedy provoked by the squalor and hopeless dreams of urban life.

When Alexander commissioned *Divine Right* from his long-time colleague, he could scarcely have hoped that the issue of the monarchy could have reached such a peak of public concern fuelled, as it was at that time, by the divorce of the Prince and Princess of Wales. The critical interest in the production was intense although yet again the audiences were relatively small (31%) if enthusiastic. Kit Surrey's design framed the stage with a huge rusting crown, which enclosed blown-up pictures of monarchs past and present, and provided a dominating upper level representation of the House of Commons. Some of Whelan's prognostications for a play set in 2000 proved correct; others not. In the Britain of the play, the Queen still rules, the Prince of Wales is renouncing the throne, and a 'decaffeinated' Labour Party is in power. Real-life politicians are not named but Paul Connolly, Sally Knyvette and David Phelan provided enjoyable lookalikes for Tony Blair, Betty Boothroyd and Michael Portillo who, it seemed to Whelan, was destined to become the next Tory leader.

The two narrative strands juxtaposed a three-day anonymous journey of the eighteen year old heir to the throne through the English Midlands, with the story of the unlikely alliance of an old-style radical Labour MP, a smooth, self-made right wing Tory, and an eccentric millionaire all in pursuit of a republic. The second plot strategy, boosted by engaging performances from Mary Jo Randle, Ian Gelder and Joe Melia as the republican three, provided an opportunity for lively debating points on republicanism but what came across most strongly, as always with Whelan, is the warm, humane sensibility behind the arguments. Despite Whelan's own republicanism it was the young prince who emerged most strongly as sensitive, thoughtful and resourceful in a remarkable performance by the eighteen year old William Mannering. The relationship with his younger brother, played by Christopher Trezise, in part drawn from Whelan's own family memories, had a particular authenticity, while the important first scene of a televised phone-in enabled probing questions about the fundamental inequalities enshrined in the hereditary principle. The critic Charles Spencer who emerged from the experience still a convinced monarchist declared that it was 'marvellous to see a regional theatre putting on an epic state-of-the-nation drama on its stage—and with such panache' (*DT*, 25.4.96).

If Whelan looked forward to the Millennium, David Edgar, who finally made his solo debut on the main stage in June 1996, two decades after *Destiny* was rejected, looked back to the previous century. As Whelan's play tackles the political most effectively through the personal, so Edgar's retelling of a Victorian horror story focused on the tragedy of one man was also, at a deep level, political. Promoted as a new play, *Dr Jekyll and Mr Hyde* was in fact a reworking of Edgar's dramatisation of Robert Louis Stevenson's novel which was perceived to be problematic when the first version was premièred by the RSC in 1991. Both men were writing in the penultimate decade of a century: Stevenson, when the questionable triumphalism of industrial capitalism was generating dark fears, and Edgar, as the de-humanising consequences of the Thatcher era had become all too obvious.

Edgar's play emphasises the *fin de siècle* uncertainty, fears even, of the unknown future and the sense that human beings exist on what his character Utterwood calls 'a little dish of light', surrounded by darkness. There are no obvious parallels drawn, but references to the homeless camping out in Trafalgar Square, the increasing gulf between rich and poor, and resulting fears of a degenerate and sexually-uncontrolled underclass inevitably resonated. Above all, as Edgar emphasised in interviews given at the time (*BP*, 26.6.96) there is now a profound awareness of evil and the potential, made only too apparent in present-day examples of individually-perpetrated atrocity, for savagery within all of us. When Hyde mindlessly attacks an old man in the street; when a hapless fellow traveller is confronted by a monster in a railway carriage, and when a young woman becomes the victim of Hyde's violent lust, the play engages with modern neuroses.

Alexander's production with design by Ruari Murchison used twin revolves inside a gleaming, gold false proscenium. The ambience of a Victorian melodrama was created with a row of footlights and the pit opened up to accommodate Simon Murray on piano and synthesiser playing Jonathan Goldstein's atmospheric music. The revolves, with T-shaped walls, allowed swift transition in an almost filmic succession of scenes from the Dorsetshire home of Jekyll's sister, to the London streets, to a railway station, to Jekyll's drawing room and the dusty, glass jar-lined environment of his laboratory. For the most important transformation from Jekyll to Hyde, however, theatrical sleight of hand was rejected in favour of human virtuosity. Instead of the two actors cast for the original production, David Schofield played both roles. As an actor, he had made his name playing, without the assistance of makeup, the grossly deformed John Merrick in Bernard Pomerance's *The Elephant Man*. In this production, the simple act of removing the doctor's spectacles, signalled the contorted transformation from a respected, albeit tormented, pillar of society into what Paul Taylor described as 'a contemptuous, combative, working-class Glaswegian troll of a Hyde' (*I*, 9.7.96). Waiting for the change to come was genuinely frightening.

Artistically it was a strong end to the year. For the Rep as a whole changes to the company infrastructure and business operation had been managed with strong hands and an air of public confidence. John Stalker remained, as always, bullish about the future and determined to carry on working with Alexander to put in place more ambitious strategies. There was a retained deficit: as at March 1996 it was £401,089. But compared with the situation four years before it appeared manageable. The legacy of the £1,500,000 development loan, however, remained a heavy burden, and the audience figures would have made Alexander's predecessors blench. Was it possible to argue, as it was, that declining audiences were part of a national trend? In the dying fall of the Conservative ascendancy which had set out to change the national psyche, prime minister John Major earnestly desired a nation 'at ease with itself'. This was palpably not the case and everywhere there was anxiety and unease. In Birmingham Alexander and Stalker faced a daunting challenge.

11. Stabilising Innovation

The twenty-fifth anniversary of the Broad Street theatre in October 1996 came and went unmarked. Birmingham Rep, Bill Alexander insisted, was a company, not a building. But as always the capacity of the building to variously facilitate, challenge, or indeed frustrate artistic policy meant that the health of the building was inextricably linked to the health of the company. While it was said that some Brummies walking past the Rep in Centenary Square thought it was a restaurant rather than a theatre, the ambience of the front of house areas was now at least in sympathy with the artistic ethos. The bar area leading to the restaurant formed a pleasant meeting place for both punters and theatre personnel. Stalker and Alexander could be found there on many evenings sitting chatting over drinks. In fine weather it was possible to sit outside on the terrace. No one could claim ignorance of recent accolades. The awards won by the company were inscribed on the walls of the main foyer. Inside the performance spaces, however, on nights when audiences were painfully thin, the constraints inherent in the spatial disjunction between the two auditoria were all too obvious. Other more pressing problems were also beginning to loom. At twenty-five years old some parts of the theatre's physical infrastructure were simply wearing out.

In the high noon of the capital funding climate created by the proceeds from the National Lottery, arts institutions had been encouraged to think on a grand scale about major building and refurbishment projects. Indeed in some cases (most notoriously the Royal Opera House which scooped up £78 million) the award out of the British population's pursuit of the crock of gold at the end of the Lottery rainbow, had been enormous. In Birmingham, where the Hippodrome was awarded £20 million towards its Centenary Development Project, hopes were raised that chronic building-related problems could be solved through

Lottery cash. In particular, and ironically in view of the history of the Old Rep, the race was on to create a new middle-sized venue. 3-500 seats was now seen to be the ideal capacity to enable innovative home-produced work and invite high-profile touring companies like Cheek by Jowl or Theatre de Complicité which tended to by-pass Birmingham. In April 1996 the Rep secured a Lottery Award of £87, 500 towards the cost of a feasibility study into possible options. Could the Rep win enough money to remodel the whole building, rethink the main auditorium, improve the front of house areas and create a new smaller space for challenging new work but one which was bigger than the existing economically problematic Studio? Thoughts that summer included ridding the main auditorium of its more alienating features like the long back row and the cinema-style incline of the seats. The side seats might be gently turned inwards to achieve a more inclusive collective experience.

The company now had a new enthusiastic chairman of the Board to help drum up support in the corridors of power. David Waine had thirty years' experience with the BBC where he was Head of Network Production Centre and later Head of Broadcasting. As he stated in an interview published in *The Entertainer* programme in February 1996, he had extensive multi-media knowledge; he was accustomed to juggling annual budgets of £100 million and he brought 'some useful contacts and a few ideas for future commercial exploitation'. In his view it was unrealistic to expect funding from the public purse to grow substantially in the near future. It would be necessary to attract private business investment and, as with shows like *The Importance of Being Earnest*, find ways to extend the life of successful productions by touring and other media exploitation.

Waine was by far the most appropriately experienced chairman to articulate the aspirations of the theatre in what was seen to be a new era. 'Audiences', he declared, 'are more demanding today whether it be in the theatre, concert hall or multiplex cinema. People want more and more spectacular, high quality events because they are used to switching on their television sets and seeing the world's stage'. Conscious of the power of mass communication and 'naked market forces' he was passionate, however, about theatre because of its capacity to permit alternative voices to be heard. As far as he was concerned the quality of the work at the Rep was 'second to no other theatre in the country'. Certainly with Alexander,Hughes,Clark and Read forming an ambitious creative team the artistic vision was as strong as ever. But the company remained vulnerable. Any artistic lapse; any production which did not please and the local critics pounced and audiences stayed away. The other huge obstacle to confidence was the development loan debt: the legacy of the last time the theatre had embarked on a major expansive strategy.

Stabilisation

The introduction of a pilot stabilisation programme by the Arts Council appeared to offer a lifeline. It had become clear that the targeting of National Lottery cash solely at capital building and building enhancement programmes had created an ongoing situation where artists had bricks and mortar and equipment, but no additional revenue to service them or sustain the core artistic activity. After more than a decade of exhorting the 'cultural industries' to pursue sponsorship, partnership funding and extra-artistic commercial enterprises, it was conceded in the *Guidelines for Applicants* for the programme launched in August 1996 that 'the arts economy in the UK suffers from inherent financial instability'. Stabilisation represented an attempt to address the problem but within the prevailing ideological assumptions which emphasised self-help and independent managerial solutions. The strategy was intended to probe deep into the infrastructure of arts institutions. Once the causes of inherent weakness had been identified within the organisation, appropriate remedies could be put in place and all might be well.

As a concept, stabilisation had its origins in 1950s' America, with schemes introduced by the Ford Foundation to prevent the benefits of its patronage from being negated by long-term business failure. The English model offered a unique recovery package tailored to fit individual needs. Organisations were invited to compete for a Lottery award which, while it offered significant debt relief, would compel participants to 'undertake a fundamental reappraisal of their artistic mission and business operation'. Change was not an absolute requirement of programme participants but all applicants had to 'confirm their willingness to implement potentially far-reaching changes'.

There was no possibility that the £1.5 million development debt would be simply cancelled or that some beneficent agency would suddenly come forward to give the theatre the money without strings attached. Bankruptcy, however, was beginning to look like a very real possibility. The Arts Council was at that point in time offering the opportunity to be rid of an intolerable burden and the Rep board insisted that it should be grabbed as soon as possible. Putting any doubts aside—in particular that it might be better to apply for stabilisation after a proven strategy had emerged from the pilot—Waine, Alexander and Stalker were prepared to put forward ambitious plans on a scale commensurate with the scale of the theatre itself and the challenges for good and ill which it presented. The Rep was admitted to the stabilisation programme in January 1997. Experienced management consultants, Robert Cogo-Fawcett, then Director of Programming for the Ambassador Theatre Group, and Adrian Ellis of AEA Consulting, were appointed by ACE to supply the necessary 'technical assistance'. There was a further clutch of consultants from the theatre industry advising on financial management and control systems, marketing, workshop and production facilities. Out of the joint consultation process emerged the Rep's stabilisation strategy which was presented in its final form in June 1997 and agreed by the Arts Council in September. The award, the biggest to any organisation, was £5,773,000. In the course of the financial year up to March 1998 the Business Development Bank Loan was repaid and in July the accumulated revenue deficit of £1,192,000 was also cleared.

A Bumpy Ride

The promised respite came not a moment too soon. The 1996-7 financial year had proved bumpy and by March 1997 David Waine had to put his signature to a disappointing set of accounts. The retained deficit for the year which included the critically successful new work in the spring and summer of 1996 was £401,089. Viewed against the background of the development of the stabilisation strategy, the record for that period clearly demonstrated the possibilities embedded in the company's national and even international aspirations, but the potential faultlines and pitfalls were also very clear.

Not only did the 1996 autumn season kick off with a co-production with the Royal National Theatre of Ben Jonson's *The Alchemist*, but it was immediately followed by the only English performances of the Romanian director Silviu Purcarete's imaginative reconstruction of Aeschylus's lost tetralogy *Les Danaides*. Presented in association with Birmingham City Council and with a cast of 120, the visually stunning production was staged in the National Indoor Arena. Even the more familiar repertory fare of *A Doll's House* had a potentially more radical edge with Russian-born Irina Brown as the guest director. After Christmas Alexander's unsentimental, strongly-articulated production of *The Merchant of Venice* with David Schofield as Shylock and Cathy Tyson as Portia, went on a national tour which included Bradford, York, Richmond and Liverpool as well as the Royal Court where it was the first Shakespeare seen in twenty years.

Casting a black Portia and Antonio (Don Warrington) together with Jah-Man Aggrey who literally revolved as both Old and Young Gobbo, set up unusual resonances of ethnic and cultural boundaries which extended beyond the Jewish/Christian dichotomy. In the Studio also there had been creative synergy in programming two plays tackling issues round the British Asian experience, and some unexpected reflected glory emerging from the third co-production with Tamasha of *East is East*. Terry Grimley pretty much represented a critical consensus when he described the première of Ayub Khan-Din's play as sensational. Kristine Landon-Smith directed Nadim Sawalha as George Khan, the Pakistani fish and chip shop proprietor-cum-patriarch desperately trying to control the lives of the seven turbulent offspring of his mixed-race marriage. Linda Bassett played Ella his emotionally-torn, white English wife. Developed through workshops at the Royal Court, the play that eventually grew into a highly-successful film, came across in Birmingham as simultaneously comic, shocking, surreal and warmly sympathetic. Grimley was reluctant to pigeon hole the play within a specifically ethnic genre but he did suggest it marked the 'real arrival of a mature contemporary British Asian Theatre' (*BP*, 14.10.96)

Debbie Isitt's play, *Squealing Like A Pig*, which Joanna Read directed for the Community Tour typically packed a more uncompromising punch at its target teenage audience. They were confronted with the moral dilemma of a white working-class girl ostracised by her community for squealing on her violent, racist boyfriend. The young, charming 'Paki bastard' Sidhu who is kicked into a coma was played by Paul Sharma initially confessing to an embarrassing fear of flying on his package holiday which is echoed in his near-death experience hovering over his hospital bed. Written in verse, but with sharp, believable dialogue, it went down well with community audiences as wide apart as Handsworth, Wolverhampton, and rural Shropshire.

But this diverse programme also suffered from a degree of artistic misjudgement. *The Alchemist* enjoyed the largest audiences of the season averaging 73% of capacity. It was a high-profile collaboration benefiting from the additional resources and anticipated kudos of a second London showing and very much led by the Birmingham team headed by Alexander as director reunited with designer William Dudley. The actors proved the main attraction with Tim Pigott-Smith, Simon Callow and locally-born Josie Lawrence cast as the virtuoso con-artists Subtle, Face and Doll Common out to exploit the greed and stupidity of a gullible set of London grotesques. The Birmingham reviews were generally enthusiastic, especially from Fred Norris and Richard Edmonds, although there were passing references to the leg-numbing length of the evening and the clotted, difficult-to-access text. In London the response was less charitable. Dudley's exuberantly complex set designed to fill both the Rep and Olivier stages created a futuristic gothic junkyard – 'Gormenghast chic' as Benedict Nightingale put it (*T*, 18.9.96)—with looming doors, walls and a spiral staircase which tended to dissipate the comic energy of the text in needless and time-consuming activity. The superfluity of inventive comic business seemed to distrust the play's capacity to entertain on its own terms. There was agreement, though, that Simon Callow gave a series of stunning star turns as Face, luring the alchemist's victims in a series of disguises including bare-chested East End mugger, baton waving Sandhurst toff, Brummie stoker and Scottish butler.

At about 38% the audiences for *A Doll's House* reverted to the more familiar pattern and thus it was vital that Christmas should boost the theatre's coffers. Playing in tandem, Gwenda Hughes' production of Ayckbourn's *Season's Greetings* and Anthony Clark's own adaptation of *Pinocchio* offered a choice between grown-up and children's fare. The Ayckbourn for which Ruari Murchison created an ingenious Christmas gift-wrapped set went down well critically with adroit, comic performances by Linda Spurrier, Samantha Beckinsale and David Hargreaves, but attracted no better audiences than the Ibsen. Clark's *Pinocchio*, however, was no Christmas treat. More thoughtful reviews liked Murchison's dark fantasy world: the tall, drainpipe trees and sinister mirrored playground where children were turned into donkeys and everyone liked the giant killer whale which plunged down from the roof. Richard Edmonds was unequivocally hostile: a 'bleak, poorly-dressed, thinly designed evening' (*BP* , 5.12.96). It played to just over 50% thus making the ensuing deficit more or less inevitable.

Debt or no debt the company maintained a bold front with Hughes and Clark moving straight on to direct new plays, both of which had a political dimension. Andy de la Tour's *Landslide*, which centres around an imagined Labour Party victory, actually played in the main auditorium on the night Tony Blair's party swept to power decisively ending nearly two decades of Tory rule. In the Studio *True Brit*, which was a Rep commission, renewed a relationship between Clark and highly-successful radio and television writer Ken Blakeson which had begun in Manchester in 1988. Both plays are about lost idealism; both pose awkward questions about the moral values of the present in relation to the past; both take a quizzical, if not bleak, view of the future.

The central character of *True Brit,* ex-photographer Charlie Martin who 'went into exile' fifteen years before in 1982 to run a small hotel in rural Spain, mourns the lost optimism of the sixties which finally collapsed in the aggression and avarice of 'the greed is good' decade. Forced, however, to play host to an archetypal yuppie lout out to grab whatever he can regardless of the misery he causes, Martin has to confront the fact that the unacknowledged selfishness of his generation has caused equal and equivalent personal suffering. He discovers that he has literally spawned the unapologetic brutality of the present. With a cast of five actors entirely new to the Rep including Frank Grimes as Charlie and Guy Lankester as his son Mel, it was strongly and confidently played and directed and well-liked by the press.

Stylistically *Landslide*, which was a co-production with West Yorkshire Playhouse, is cut out of the same naturalistic mode set, as it is, in the home of an Alan Clark-style maverick Tory MP just ousted by a novice, female New Labour politician: the sort of young woman about to be dubbed one of 'Blair's babes'. Christopher Ravenscroft played opposite Jenna Russell as Fliss Anderson. She opens the narrative hoping to enlist the help of her defeated rival St.John Hewitt against a new development scheme, only to end up bedding the man and becoming soiled along with a corrupt 'old' Labour councillor in the sleaze of a bipartisan conspiracy. As in *True Brit* the more immediate victims are a wife and son.

Before coming to Birmingham where again the critical response was good, but the audiences relatively small for what was an enjoyable, topical night out in the theatre, Gwenda Hughes spoke in the *Yorkshire Evening Post* (10.3.97) about the way the play reflected the current feelings of her generation and political orientation:

I'm afraid there is an awful lot of us experiencing

A bitter cynicism about politicians and their motives

There's a feeling that some might treat us contempt-
-uously, expecting us to be stupid or ignorant enough
to swallow whatever line they push out and there's a
fear that a new set might not be any better.

Of the tragic denouement of the play and the mood it generated she said, 'Is it optimistic? No it isn't. Will it be alright in the morning? That's the point. Nobody believes it can be'.

The Strategy

Viewed from the perspective of six years on in 2003 when all the main protagonists in the long drawn-out drama of the next episode in the Rep's history have gone, Gwenda Hughes' words sound horribly prophetic, although she herself did not see the process through to the end. She left the Rep in early 1998 on her appointment as artistic director of the New Victoria Theatre in Stoke-on-Trent. In the final analysis stabilisation did not make everything alright.

Everyone concerned knew that this was an experiment; a way of completely rethinking the way a theatre company as a business enterprise should operate. Box office success was vital.

Initially the stated target was an average annual audience of 65% but this was reduced in the final strategy to a more realistic 58%. Inevitably the unstated worry, given the 45% average of the 1996-97 season, was that even this could not be achieved. The strategy document makes much of the national context of a gradual decline in the audience base and changing patterns of leisure activity. Country-wide, theatres had lost confidence and clarity of purpose trapped between the upward pressure of labour costs inherent in live art forms, and the downward pressure on grant awards exacerbated by the fragmentation of funding priorities. Asked to address the question of 'residual value' of any investment in stabilisation if the strategy failed to deliver, the response was characteristically forthright, 'the funders would be left with a re-equipped, modernised and debt free theatre and, perhaps as important, an opportunity to understand better the nature and future of subsidised theatre in the UK'.

The plan that was put forward was very ambitious but then as the strategy declared 'The Rep was established by Barry Jackson to lead, not to follow'. The example of the past was to stand as the foundation of Bill Alexander's artistic strategy to take the Rep forward into the 21st Century. It was risky, but the ability to take creative risks ought to be the prerogative of the subsidised sector. Also it was obvious that as the Rep functioned as the principal repertory theatre in the region and with national as well as local status, a successful outcome would spiral throughout the artistic community of the West Midlands. There would be opportunities for local actors, writers and craftspeople while audiences would benefit from a richer, extended repertoire. The intention to dedicate the main stage to fewer, but substantially better resourced, large scale productions, while simultaneously mounting seasons of completely new work in a new flexible 300-350 second space, lay at the core of the artistic strategy. Increasingly new work would also be mounted on the main stage and in general educational objectives would be more closely integrated with productions. Along with a new and dynamic relationship between the producing company and the venue, a more pro-active and strategic approach to co-productions and touring would be pursued. A greater priority would be placed on the distribution of the Rep's work by means of a network of key, large-scale partner venues such as the Newcastle Theatre Royal, Canterbury Marlowe, Nottingham Theatre Royal etc. Established links with producers such as the Royal National Theatre would be retained, as well as international links with the Royal Alexandra Theatre in Toronto and the Market Theatre in Johannesburg. There were also plans for a 'creative consortium' of producing venues which would work together to develop large-scale productions for children and young people.

The outcome of the proposed parallel application to the National Lottery Capital Programme was crucial for the plan to create the new 300-350 seat auditorium exclusively devoted to new work. 'The Royal Court of the north' or 'the Traverse of the south', as the strategy dubbed it, would build on the previous record of developing new writing to mount two, four-play repertoire seasons a year providing thirty-two weeks of new work production. Anthony Clark would be the overall director assisted by visiting artists and the Literary Department. A company of eight actors would be engaged for each sixteen-week season. The old Studio would be devoted to educational and community-based work. One way of facilitating this initiative which was built into the Stabilisation Strategy was that outsourcing the set building to an external provider working for a group of local venues (thereby reversing the thinking behind the construction of the enlarged workshop in 1991) could significantly reduce fixed labour costs and release that part of the extension for remodelling as a new Studio.

As with other elements in the capital building plan, this proved impossible. Consultation rapidly demonstrated that different patterns of production need meant that a consortium approach was not practicable. More fundamentally, however, the bids made to the Arts Council were now being made within the context of new government policy towards the deployment of the National Lottery proceeds. A sixth 'good cause' had been introduced. The days of the huge capital awards were over. In total the Rep's proposed capital bid was for a rebuilding/refurbishment project budgeted at £16-18 million of which 75% would take the form of lottery funding. In 1999 the award of £5.5 million made to the Rep was nowhere near the amount needed for a more radical reshaping of the building.

However what external observers of the Rep were not aware of was the desperate need of the theatre for some measure of building refurbishment. The possibility that the theatre would not be issued with a performance licence was, as was the threat of bankruptcy, very real. Ventilation in both public and work spaces was very poor. The main auditorium seats were infested, loose and in some cases dangerous—to children especially. The sound system needed completely rewiring. The stage built with poor quality timber was collapsing. The rented substage scaffolding holding it up was, according to the Arts Council Assessor's report in March 1999, not only a pointless expense but also two years old. Whatever anxieties the City Council felt about the public reaction to yet more costly assistance to the Rep, there was, as David Waine bluntly told the Chief Executive Michael Lyons, no option to do nothing. By late 1998, when the stabilisation process was well underway, the relentless pressure to drive down the size of the grant even lower than the £7 million identified for vital building works, precipitated a savage exchange of letters between Waine and the Arts Council.

Keep On Running

Keep On Running, the musical celebrating Birmingham's vibrant 1960s 'Brumbeat' pop scene which launched the 1997 autumn season, took its title from a 1966 chart topper by the Spencer Davis group. It might also have served as a mantra for the whole of the journey which lay ahead for the theatre. The company had to reach key milestones—273 of them—in order to draw down tranches of stabilisation cash. Milestones ranged from relatively trivial tasks like light bulb replacement to major challenges like redefining the corporate identity of the theatre. As the 1997-98 financial year began, the international dimension to the strategy was reinforced almost immediately. May saw a co-production with the Market Theatre, Johannesburg in a South African adaptation of *The Cherry Orchard*, which won Janet Suzman the TMA Barclays Regional Theatre Award for Best Director. In June, a revival of the 1995 *The Importance of Being Earnest* played to a reassuring 55 % and then went to the Princess of Wales Theatre in Toronto for six weeks.

But the autumn in the main house was disappointing. *Keep On Running,* loosely based on the novel/opera plot of *Carmen* but with Longbridge car workers as characters, was an attempt to create a rock musical with teenage appeal, but the critical response was very mixed and audiences little more than 30%. Clark's production of *Julius Caesar* fared little better. Updated to 1930s' fascist Rome with Rep stalwarts like Michael Cashman as a Mussolini-like Caesar, Ian Pepperell as Octavius, and James Dreyfus, interestingly cast as a passionate, pragmatic Cassius, it played to only 28%. Christmas came to the rescue with a solid six week revival of *The Snowman* which replenished the theatre's coffers.

The Studio, however, maintained artistic energy braiding together innovation, interculturalism and community relevance. For six weeks in October and November the emphasis was on global cultures. Tamasha, back in co-production with the Rep, staged *A Tainted Dawn*, an ambitious company adaptation of nine stories about the turbulent events surrounding the partition of India and Pakistan in 1947 and the parallel Hindu/Moslem tragedies. *Soulfires*, which followed, presented in repertory three rarely-performed one act plays which shift between issues of racial persecution and integration in America to black/white relations in South Africa. Robbie McCauley's *Sally Rape*, Amiri Baraka's *Dutchman*, and Athol Fugard's *Playland* were directed separately by Pauline Bailey, Martin Glynn and Michael Aduwali who had all taken part in a workshop for local black and Asian directors led by Bill Alexander the previous autumn. A programming policy which focused on a range of intercultural themes was also enabling an increasing number of black and Asian artists to explore them. For the community tour the following March, Nottingham-born Indhu Rubasingham directed Maya Chowdhry's *Kaahini* about an Asian teenage girl's obsession with football. It arrived in the Studio just after Jatinder Verma's cross-cultural production of *A Midsummer Night's Dream* had been presented on the main stage by his company Tara Arts.

The other two new plays, however, were both solidly out of the white British experience. Gwenda Hughes' final production in the Studio was of playwright-in-residence Nick Stafford's *The Whisper of Angel's Wings* which focuses on the bitter antagonism which erupts between two families in a poor Staffordshire farming community in August 1914. Jane Linz Roberts' traverse set evoked a drab, dusty, far from idyllic rural England for what proved to be a powerful snapshot of a society on the brink of catastrophic change. Ian Pepperell played the stuttering Amos Pearce, the despised eldest son of the brutally authoritarian Jacob Pearce (Andy Hockley) whose death in a tractor accident precipitates more violent destruction. The final tentative resolution of the warring passions which brings Amos to an assured inheritance is achieved in the shadow cast by the other, dreadful war to come. As so often in Hughes' productions, the women proved to be a source of strength especially Amos' mother as played by Tricia Kelly.

After the snowman had flown out of the main auditorium in January, Anthony Clark premièred David Lodge's play *Hometruths* which also had a rural setting, albeit the well-upholstered comfort of a Sussex retreat. As in *The Writing Game*, Lodge puts writers at the centre of his play but the plot revolves round the dangerous allure of the celebrity interview and the intrusive power of the journalist. Sam Sharpe, a toupéed egotistical screen writer (Cliff Howells) outraged by a damaging newspaper profile, calls on the help of his friend Adrian, semi-retired, once celebrated novelist (Brian Protheroe) to set a trap for the sharp-tongued, female journalist Fanny Tarrant who was played by Rachel Pickup. The triumph of exposing, in every sense, her sexual susceptibility is immediately undermined by the hurt caused to Adrian's wife and further revelations about the pain, sacrifice and failure which have cast shadows on her marriage. The play ends with a television broadcast of the news of Princess Diana's death which jolts all the characters into reconsidering their life values.

Despite a witty interrogation of contemporary culture, opportunities for deeper emotional engagement are under-exploited. The ending seemed trite even though it was said to be the first attempt to tackle the impact of Diana's death in the theatre. Designer Fran Thompson added a surreal cave of piled-up books behind the affluent drawing room set, but the generic resemblance to 1950s' style domestic comedy provoked some waspish comments from more than one metropolitan critic.Terry Grimley liked what he called 'an intricate and amusing play' despite the potentially 'soft-centred' subject (*BP*, 19.2.98). But Fred Norris roundly condemned the production complaining bitterly that the performance start on press night was delayed to allow the critics to reach the theatre 'putting the odd London critic before a loyal Birmingham audience' (*EM*, 19.2.98).

The audience, in fact, was not that loyal coming in at just below 37%. But even when the next big main stage strategy pulled in double the numbers, Fred Norris complained again. It was clear from his review (*EM*, 26.3.98) that he enjoyed the performances in *The Rocky Horror Show*, and was amused by the vociferous fans dressed to match the outrageous characters on stage. Michael Cashman played the pompous Narrator fending off audience heckles. Jason Donovan played the insatiable drag queen Frank.N.Furter strutting down an enormous red tongue-shaped carpet in platform heels and pearls. But Norris was adamant that this was not the sort of show Birmingham Rep should produce. He forgot its 1973 origins in the Royal Court Theatre Upstairs as a risqué spoof on 1950s' kitsch movies, and that it was the Rep's contribution to the Millennium Festival.

What Sort of Theatre?

In August 1997 Bill Alexander wrote an article for the *New Statesman* in which he deplored a statement of Sir Peter Hall's that regional theatres were needed to provide 'the seed-corn that should be feeding the West End and major subsidised theatres'; that, as Alexander put it, 'regional repertory theatre is the bottom rung on the ladder of professional success'. On the contrary he declared 'Every regional theatre worth its salt is a place with its own vision, character, identity and mission'. It was this kind of fighting talk that won the Rep the support of the key providers of public subsidy, and it was the vision of a big theatre of national status, situated next to the International Convention Centre in the second biggest city in the country which also drove the support of the City. The grand vision did not alter the fact, however, that the traditional perception of regional rep as a training ground to be discarded on the way up was still very deeply entrenched amongst actors. In addition local audiences had to be persuaded to sign up to the vision.

In May 1998 the ICC became the venue for the G8 Summit. The leaders of the most powerful countries in the world, including US president Bill Clinton, descended on Birmingham. The world's press was in town. Inside the Rep, and on the main stage, however, there was no attempt to exploit the money-making potential of the international conference. Instead Alexander presented what was probably his most audacious experiment in epic theatre and with a play which, as had become typical of his commissioning policy, spoke to a topic of public concern. *Frozen*, Bryony Lavery's three-actor play about child abduction and murder, would normally have been confined to the Studio where her work had been presented before. But, as she explained to Ben Payne in an interview published in the programme, '*Frozen* is about death, redemption, revenge. It's an epic play with a small cast. And it's a small cast because it's about people fighting battles on their own'.

The three characters emerged out of a black void through a stunning curtain of white light created by Tim Mitchell. Ruari Murchison's décor was little more than a chair or crate for seating and a table for prison scenes, all lit in pools of white light. The narrative spans two decades from the disappearance in 1976 of Rona, a ten year old girl, to the arrest of her paedophile murderer and the discovery of her skeleton in his 'centre of operations' shed close to home. Through the voices, initially in monologue, of Ralph, her murderer, Agnetha, the American criminal psychologist who studies him, and above all of Rona's mother Nancy, Lavery takes the audience on an emotional journey through minds frozen from trauma, abuse, false optimism and grief. Probing the possible physical and psychological causes of dreadful crimes reveals the essential banality of evil. Bringing together mother and murderer releases the capacity for remorse which results in Ralph's suicide. The two women decide that nothing is unbearable and that new life is possible.

For many journalists who wrote about the play, including Terry Grimley in the *Birmingham Post* (6.5.98), the production had a mesmerising impact. The *Guardian*'s Lyn Gardner hailed a 'big, brave, compassionate play'. There were some worries that the character of Agnetha, herself grieving for a dead colleague and former lover, was rather contrived, but the performances could not be faulted. Josie Lawrence mediated powerfully between the strong professional academic personna of Agnetha and her internal emotional chaos. Tom Georgeson played Ralph, delivering in virtual monotone the obsessive speech patterns of a rigidly pedantic, deeply damaged personality. Anita Dobson, still best-known for her television portrayal of a pub landlady in *Eastenders*, ranged from the twittering, aproned, suburban mum, to the desperately driven lost-child campaigner unable to relate to her other daughter and husband, to the steely presence in a prison quietly forgiving the murderer but forcing him to feel the human consequences of his crime. Her monologue describing the wonder of her dead daughter's skull: 'I'm *flooded* with its joy', was recalled by Lyn Gardner (13.5.98) as 'one of the most harrowing and hauntingly beautiful moments' she had ever witnessed in the theatre.

187

4,690 people saw the production: 24% of audience capacity. Obviously not good, but more in fact than would have been able to see it in the Studio. Riding on the crest of the stabilisation wave, Alexander could afford to make such a gesture with an important, immaculately performed and directed play. The press response however, revealed some very sharply different levels of critical expectation and sophistication which both influenced and reflected crucial differences in audience—especially local audience—reception. Local critic Bob Haywood writing in the widely-circulated *Sunday Mercury* (10.5.98) was clearly moved by the play but warned against 'stomach-churning details and the worst of foul language'. He also described the production as 'a directorial shambles with two stage-hands permanently in view to shift the furniture'. The *Evening Mail* review was not this time written by Fred Norris. Instead Deborah Summers acknowledged the play as a brave attempt but condemned the script as 'vulgar and gratuitous'. Some of the audience, she noted, had walked out, 'It is not "entertainment" ' (6.5.98).

What to do? Too much entertainment, too little art; too much art, not enough entertainment. For Fay Weldon's *The Four Alice Bakers*, staged a year later as the next main house première, there was an attempt to combine popular appeal with another issue of current debate. Effectively cloning her own novel and television play, *The Cloning of Alice May*, Weldon focused on the ethics of cloning, but within the context of a grotesque television chat show. David Hargreaves played biogeneticist Richie Baker who is forced to reveal to a television audience that he has cloned three daughters from the cells of his unsuspecting wife (Diane Fletcher). Michael Cashman gave a barn-storming performance as Harry Harper, the frenetic, banana-advertising chat show host who exposes the dark secret. Despite his heroic efforts the production was a misconceived disaster which drew smaller audiences than *Frozen*.

Opening the Door

In the meantime, stabilisation was enabling the major new work strategy in the Studio. Launching the programme of new plays in September 1998 which began with Judy Upton's *Confidence* and ended the following June with Paul Lucas's *All That Trouble That We Had*, Anthony Clark was all too aware of the battle which might lie ahead despite the financial cushioning. Of course the artistic policy had rock solid foundations in the new writing initiatives of the previous decade, but the strategy had been based originally on the rapidly disappearing dream of a new 350-seater auditorium which might enable production transfer to and from the main stage and a more viable audience base.

Despite the constraints the audience had to be cultivated. Renamed The Door, the venue was to be reborn as the entrance to an innovative experience of theatre which had the capacity to appeal to a wide range of cultural and generational interests. The installation of new, if rather cramped seating units, and a gallery which surrounded both actors and audience, created a greater sense of intimacy, enabled a second level of playing and viewing, and expanded the capacity. There was also a parallel expansion of the education programme energetically led by the new Head of Education, and former member of the Custard Factory Theatre Company, Rachel Gartside. In collaboration with the Literary Department, her team went into schools and colleges with a Page to Stage package of workshops linked to the productions, opportunities to talk to writers and directors, published copies of the texts and tickets for the performance. The fact that play texts, which could be studied as well as sold as programmes, had now been taken up by a range of publishers including Nick Hern, Faber and Oberon Books was part of a significant development in the national as well as regional ecology of new theatre writing.

The programme's concentrated newness also drew very substantially on previous initiatives, principles and relationships. Of the seven home-produced plays, four were written by women including Kate Dean and Sarah Woods who were familiar to Studio audiences. Woods' *Trips* and Declan Croghan's *Paddy Englishman, Paddy Irishman and Paddy…?* which Clark premièred in February, started life on the theatre's attachment scheme. Fraser Grace who wrote *Perpetua*, which was produced and directed in April in association with the Soho Theatre Company, was a graduate of the MA in Playwriting course and began to write while working for the Birmingham-based Back-to-Back Theatre. In 1996, the year *Perpetua* won the Verity Bargate Award, *Swamp City* had been Paul Lucas's first play.

The marginalised, the surreal and the distinctly anarchic were qualities which characterised a good deal of the first year's work. Ella, the central character in *Confidence*, is an eighteen year old natural-born rogue with an unusual sexual proclivity for ice cream and dreams of doing 'business' in Hollywood. Played in Clark's production by Jody Watson, she has to settle in the interim for a decaying seaside resort and persuading her gullible allies Dean and Ben (Zoot Lynam and Robin Pirongs) into conning tourists with a motorised dolphin scam. Alison Lyntott played plump, twenty-one year old Ruby miserably cleaning up the beach-side café for her devious boss Mr Baylis (Michael Mears) while mourning her deep frozen hamster.

The same core of actors moved between Upton's zany summery satire on the scruffy underbelly of the leisure industry, and Kate Dean's exploration of youthful dereliction and rural poverty centred round a disused sand quarry overlooking the bright Millennium lights of Birmingham in December 1999. The rag bag of characters include Monty, the eighty-year old watchman and ex-soldier (Michael Mears), the hopeless, violent, glue-sniffing Spider played by Matthew Wait and his pregnant girlfriend Bea (Alison Lintott) who are about to be evicted from their tied cottage, and Mouse (Neil Warhurst) hoping to survive as a musician with a battered saxophone. Jody Watson played Nessie an affluent, sexually precocious, Canadian teenager exploring the quarry with her cousin Joel in search of excitement. As the play ends with the dawn of the new Millennium and the sound of JCBs filling in the quarry, Bea has given birth in a woman's refuge while Spider has fallen to his death after a night introducing Nessie to both sex and glue sniffing.

For all the bleakness of *Down Red Lane*, some reviews responded very positively to Patrick Connellan's atmospheric set and the directorial energy which maximised the moments of black absurdist humour as well as the physical and verbal violence of much of the action. Terry Grimley, however, hated it, opening his review with a comment on the uncomfortable seating exacerbated by the tedium of the play. 'Relevance is a sorely overworked word in discussing the alienation of young people from the theatre, but is it achieved simply by putting alienated young people on stage?' In fact none of the first three plays attracted good audiences young or otherwise. *Twins*, which should have been a light, witty experiment with Amelda Brown and Anne White as impecunious sisters Mimi and Gigi, suffered from heavy-handed direction and was genuinely tedious in performance. *Confidence* did best with audiences 20% of capacity.

Gradually optimism began to dawn. At Christmas, a highly successful co-production with Tamasha of a joyful Bollywood spoof *Fourteen Songs, Two Weddings and a Funeral* packed the Door with enthusiastic Asian audiences and any other locals who could get a seat. Directed by Kristine Landon-Smith, it was an endearingly ridiculous story of love, death and arranged marriage complete with lip-sync songs. In the New Year two one-man prison pieces played in tandem courtesy of Moving Theatre. Malcolm Tierney presented *Just Not Fair*, an account by Jim Robinson of his experience of imprisonment as one of the falsely-accused Bridgewater Four. Corin Redgrave gave a mesmerising performance as Oscar Wilde in *De Profundis*, Wilde's letter to Lord Alfred Douglas written from Reading Gaol. There was also a series of Saturday morning children's shows and, as usual, the spring Community Tour. *Nightbus*, written by locally-based Peter Cann, featured Lorna Laidlaw as Donna, a super- efficient tour guide on a Birmingham open-top bus. The theft of her handbag by a street-wise chimpanzee takes her on a comic journey into the twilight world below the flyovers where all her confident life-style assumptions are overturned by well-connected beggars, moonlighting estate agents, and a thieving surgeon specialising in the trade of stolen human organs. Musical interludes were supplied along the way by Robin Pirongs as a cheerful, guitar-strumming busker.

Audiences for *Paddy Irishman* and *Trips* were good. Set in the dingy Kilburn bedsitter inhabited by two young Irish labourers Anto (Tom Farrelly) and Kevin (Michael Colgan) Declan Croghan's play begins with the comic hopelessness of a lifestyle consisting of drinking binges, hangovers and gigantic fryups, and ends asking challenging questions about Irish identity and loyalties. Bar-stool republicanism and attempts to impress Una, the intense girl upstairs (Annie Farr) trap the endearingly naïve Anto into an unwitting entanglement with terrorism after he offers the renegade Peter (Sean Connolly) an overnight couch. Confronted with the terrifying implications of actual commitment to the cause, Anto has to make decisions about what his beliefs and allegiances are. As Kevin literally distances himself by opting to leave Britain altogether, what emerges is the insistence that cowardice is only cowardice when the reason for courage is valid. In both Birmingham and in Kilburn where it transferred to the Tricycle Theatre, the appeal to local Irish communities was important for the production's success as was overall critical approval. Indeed the London run ensured a much wider press coverage than was typically given to the Door plays.

Trips incorporated many of the anarchic qualities of the other plays including another animal joke—a four and a half foot tall fur fabric cat called Princess Anne—but was far more consciously experimental with a heavy investment in technology. Offered a window into the drug and club culture of six young Brummies, who share a city house, the audience moved with the characters interacting with filmed sequences in multiple locations on large video screens. There was a simultaneous experience of live actors, vivid hallucinatory images, clips from popular television, light and sound all within multiple locations. Audiences came and enjoyed making The Door feel wide open at last. Fred Norris chickened-out of standing up for two and half hours and saw most of the play from the gallery. Michael Billington, however, reviewing the experience in the *Guardian* (18.3.99) felt he had been successfully transported into an unfamiliar world: 'Even in a more conventional space the play would feel like honest reportage. In the strangely sexy intimacy of The Door it is like going on a trip without the damnable expense or the undesirable after-effects'.

The Economic Driver

During that year given the range of work undertaken, punters could be forgiven for thinking that the Door was functioning as an autonomous enterprise. An appraisal of the artistic record could offset the variable audience figures with the growing perception that the only venue outside London to be completely dedicated to new writing was beginning to establish a reputation. Audience numbers slipped back for *All That Trouble That We Had*, but at 31% was still a considerable improvement on the autumn attendance. Yet again there was a surreal plot and a clutch of bizarre characters as David Hargreaves and Rachel Smith played a desperate father and daughter trying to raise enough cash to buy back an urn of 'Mummy's' ashes from the dastardly Leyton (Paul Barnhill) by salvaging the bodies of suicides who have jumped off the nearby bridge. Paul Bradley gave a strong comic performance as the bumbling little man and failed suicide Oliver whose accident-prone heroism finally brings redemption.

Lucas's ultimately rather endearing black comedy is about the human capacity for survival even under the most vicious circumstances. The trouble for the Rep as a business enterprise, however, was that The Door experiment had proved to be far more expensive than had been originally envisaged. The stabilisation strategy had assumed that not only would eight commissioned new plays be staged in the proposed larger second space, but that two seasons of four plays each with the same cast and a composite set would considerably reduce production costs. In fact stage management expenditure had been underestimated to the extent that the net cost of The Door had nearly doubled from the original projection. Moreover, as John Stalker made clear in the summer of 1999 when these costs were being counted, the main stage had to be the economic driver of the Door. As always in the past failure to meet targets in the main theatre impacted on the creative capacity of the smaller space.

At first it seemed that Alexander had struck gold. In September 1998 his production of *Hamlet* not only attracted large audiences, but brilliantly exploited the collaborative strength of a group of artists who not only knew each other well, but were entirely familiar with the challenge of the Rep stage. For those who remembered Richard McCabe's performance as Caliban and his comic success as Puck and Autolycus for the RSC, the role of Hamlet may have seemed unlikely casting. But what Paul Taylor in the *Independent* called 'that prankster-cherub face and those subversive gobstopper eyes' (28.8.98) contributed to a characterisation where acute intelligence and manic energy never entirely masked profound distress. In his 'antic disposition' he wreaked havoc prancing about the stage in a white nightgown and saffron scarf unhinging Rakie Ayola's vulnerable, teddy bear clutching Ophelia, goading Jack Klaff's verbose, tedious Polonius and even at one point lasciviously kissing Claudius who was played by Gerard Murphy as a ruthless, if mentally-tortured thug.

Alexander's decision to remove Fortinbras and the political dimension from the play provoked controversy, but everyone admired the way the court of Elsinore was evoked. The *Frozen* team of Alexander, Murchison and Mitchell used the same combination of cavernous darkness and minimal scenic properties to create a murkily claustrophobic environment lit by great walls of projected light. The guards on the ramparts at the beginning of the play stooped under the curtain of light which later the ghost walked rapidly through. 'To be or not to be' was delivered on top of a huge step ladder in what appeared as a gloomy library lit only by shafts of light. At times light was almost literally painted on to the stage. Whatever his textual reservations, Billington hailed a *Hamlet* Birmingham could be proud of. The matinée he attended was packed with both young and old. 'Something' he claimed, 'is stirring in Brum' (G, 26.9.98).

In line with the stabilisation aspiration for work of higher profile two other directors of national repute followed Alexander after *Hamlet* into the rehearsal room. Bill Bryden directed a new translation by Mike Poulton of Chekhov's *Three Sisters* with Charles Dance playing Vershinin. Michael Bogdanov directed his own adaptation of *A Christmas Carol*. The Chekhov achieved a comfortable, if unspectacular 55% while Dickens' seasonal favourite did well at just over 78%. The critical response was more problematic. Despite Bryden's prestigious record in large-scale epic productions, *Three Sisters* seemed emotionally underpowered and defeated by the Rep stage. Artistically *A Christmas Carol*, given somewhat bizarrely a post- Second World War austerity setting came across as eccentrically ill-conceived. Richard Edmonds went so far as to advise audiences to stay at home and read the book.

The Chairman's introduction to the 1998-9 annual statement, however, adopted a confident tone. An increase in income from ticket sales of £257,135 added to the benefits of the repayment of the accumulated revenue deficit and a substantial refund of National Insurance contributions had resulted in a 'robust financial position'. But as Waine signed off the statement in September 1999 he would have been all too aware that he was partway through a new financial year which had not got off to an auspicious start, and that the management were engaged in a close critical review of how the stabilisation process was progressing.

The Pajama Game, the 1950s' Broadway musical by George Abbot and Richard Bissell which ran for a month in April and May 1999 was the most expensive show ever staged by the Rep, costing more than £400,000. Strenuous efforts to market the production emphasised the prestige of all the artists involved. Simon Callow, indulging a long-held passion for the musical, directed with David Bintley, the artistic director of Birmingham Royal Ballet, as choreographer. Frank Stella, the important American avant-garde painter designed the sets, while the music supervisor was the nationally-acclaimed saxophonist John Harle.

It should have been a success. The wealth of creative leadership was boosted by some £200,000 in external commercial investment for a production which was projected to make money in Toronto and the West End. Simon Callow was engagingly enthusiastic about a romantic tale set in the unlikely context of an industrial dispute in a mid-west pajama factory, and he enthused about the life-enhancing qualities of songs like 'Hernando's Hideaway' and 'Steam Heat'. In the final analysis, however, the combination of a not-so-well-known musical, an assortment of brilliant individual artists insufficiently welded into a team, and perhaps most crucially the absence of star performers robbed the show of a genuinely dynamic must-see quality.

The Swedish ex- television weather girl and media personality, Ulrika Jonsson, was cast as Babe Williams the leader of the workers' grievance committee who falls in love with the management man sent in to break the strike. While undeniably beautiful and sexy, she was no Doris Day, and the kind of audience member likely to be drawn by Callow, Bintley, Stella et al would not be much drawn by a temporary icon of popular culture possessing only modest musical talent. Both Anita Dobson as Mabel the secretary, and the comic poet John Hegley as the manic knife-throwing time and motion expert Vernon J. Hines, gave enjoyable performances, but Birmingham audiences were not enthused. At the Rep it played to just 46%. The Toronto run with Canadian actress Camilla Scott as Babe went better, but the show did not survive for long in London where Leslie Ash played the role.

The aim to recruit high-status, crowd-pulling actors was a crucial element in the stabilisation strategy, but even the promise of enhanced salaries failed to overcome the reluctance of star performers to come to Birmingham. It was difficult as always to prise actors away from London; any risk of failure made the gamble well-nigh impossible. Bill Alexander even conducted a consultation exercise with leading actors' agents but to no avail. In June 1999, immediately after *The Pajama Game*, the problem effectively scuppered Alexander's attempt to mount a successful revival of Tom Stoppard's 1972 acrobatic philosophical farce *Jumpers*. Both artistically and intellectually it was a typically ambitious enterprise which required ambitious actors and also an equally ambitious, responsive audience.

A versatile, multi-doored, two-level set design by Ruari Murchison, musical arrangements by Jonathan Goldstein which included a song jointly written with Alexander and Stoppard; Cosmo Hardy as tumbling consultant for the troupe of logical positivist acrobats; excellent comic performances by Samantha Spiro, Christopher Ravenscroft and Andy Hockley: none of the production's many qualities could make up for the gaping hole at the centre which only a virtuoso star performance could fill. Even those like Terry Grimley who never saw Michael Hordern take possession of the role of perplexed moral philosopher George Moore wistfully longed for the physical presence of sublime dottiness which is necessary to release comic energy from the intricacies of the text. At the Rep Malcolm Tierney, try as he might, was 'too unremarkable, too ordinary' (*BP*, 24.6.99). Worse still was the nightmare of a half-empty auditorium when a generous, collective good-humoured response was vital for laughter. After the final performance on 17 July when the theatre closed down completely in readiness for the building refurbishment, the management had to reflect on yet another disappointment. *Jumpers* had played to little more than a quarter of capacity.

A Protective Cloak

The 1999 Chairman's statement emphasised that no part of the company's operations had been unaffected by the implementation of the stabilisation strategy. It was very much an internal process, however, with little emerging into the public domain of what precisely was happening, at every level, to the theatre's personnel. John Stalker described it as throwing a protective cloak over the company while it underwent what was termed a management of change programme facilitated with assistance from management consultants from the Bourten Group. With the company reorganised on a team-based approach, everyone was put under enormous pressure not just in the day-to-day tasks of sustaining a complex, demanding, production programme, but in the simultaneous process of collective self-examination. In some cases work-loads increased by twenty or thirty extra hours a week. Team meetings could be held early in the morning with many staff continuing to work until late in the evening.

The aim, based on the most up-to-date management theory, was to create a dynamic organism focused on the common goal of the company's stabilisation at a much higher level of operation. Outmoded working practices were to be challenged including rigid areas of labour demarcation which could cause pointless and damaging delays to production efficiency. Every aspect of the collective endeavour was to be valued and everyone had to be part of the corporate mission. For the Arts Council officers who imposed the milestones and monitored progress on a regular basis, this was a major experiment. No other regional theatre had been given so much money to transform its entire operation and, as John Stalker acknowledged, the strictures imposed by the agreement with ACE left little room for flexibility.

What became clear in what David Waine later called the Arts Council's scatter-gun approach to the stabilisation process, was that far too much was being attempted too quickly. Furthermore the simultaneous work on the building redevelopment was adding another equally pressured commitment of time and energy. Ros Robins was appointed Project Manager for this leading on the negotiations with the Arts Council Capital Lottery Unit and the application for additional grant aid from the European Regional Development Fund. In a report made to Rep Board in June 1999 weeks before the refurbishment was due to begin, Stalker pointed out just how much had been done. In addition to the launch of The Door, the commissioning of new work and the achievement of the capital award, a comprehensive new information technology strategy had been designed and implemented as had the new education strategy. A new production facilities strategy had been completed and new marketing initiatives had been launched. It had been a tough year, he admitted, for the key support staff in finance and administration who worked alongside the creative teams.

The report is blunt about areas of underachievement, in particular the failure 'to make significant strides in the development of a feasible, structured and focused audience development strategy'. It had been a difficult year also for marketing which had not only seen the appointment and then departure of a marketing manager, but also, and worse, the long-term illness and absence of Amy Smart in the key senior management role of Head of Marketing and Development. As Head of Education Rachel Gartside had been responsible for a dynamic and progressive new education strategy, but she too had announced her departure. Education was not only a major concern of the company's major funding stake holders but essential to the success of the whole stabilisation mission. Both

Trevelyan Wright as the new Head of Education and Sarah Ogle as Marketing Manager were in post by the time the theatre reopened in October. But it would be 2000 before Trina Jones was established as Marketing Director.

Such was the concern about the potential impact of a prolonged period of closure that the building refurbishment process was completed in a remarkable twelve weeks of twenty hour days, seven days a week. Architects Pawson Williams 'cleansed' the foyer area, removing the modifications introduced in 1990 to create a white airy mall with informal comfortable seating. The auditorium was stripped to a shell and rebuilt with new air conditioning and acoustics and a new stage floor. More controversially the vertiginous effect of the original seating rake was modified by the removal of the steep aisles which had divided the audience into three actor-accessible blocks. The new aisles of light beech stairs now enclosed a single unitary sweep of 824 green-black leather covered seats reconfigured to provide better sightlines lines and more leg room. The side walls were built out so that 'the audience can be encompassed in the dramatic human embrace of an actor on stage'. For the Rep staff it was a time of extremes: a deeply unpleasant time for wardrobe and workshop still functioning in the theatre; a period of unprecedented intimacy for the majority working together in a suite of offices on a single floor in Alpha Tower across Broad Street.

Moving to an End

The hopes which were pinned on the renewal of the company's fortunes along with the auditorium were quickly dashed. The first production of the 1999-2000 season was a version of Tennessee Williams' *Baby Doll* created and directed from drafts by Williams and Elia Kazan by Lucy Bailey who had initially proposed the project to Bill Alexander. Playing to just 28% of capacity for a relatively short run it was seen by fewer than had attended *Jumpers*. No matter that subsequently the production was taken up by the National Theatre where it was received with critical acclaim, it did little to boost confidence at home. Following what had been a late start to the season, the company moved straight to *Nativity*, a much publicised collaboration between Alexander and Peter Whelan on the story of Christ's birth. But the creative spark was missing. Worthy, but lacking dynamism, the play felt celebratory neither of Christmas nor indeed the dawn of the new Millennium and it played to just 55%. Even the rich vein of *The Snowman* showed signs of being worked out when it was revived in January.

Failure to meet audience targets at Christmas was, as always, very damaging. But overall the stabilisation vision of main stage seasons based on a smaller number of high-quality, better resourced, productions made the theatre vulnerable. There were fewer opportunities to compensate for disappointing results. Ironically the only production which brought in large audiences that spring was a toured-in production of Yasmina Reza's West End hit *Art*: precisely the kind of 'second hand' commercial success which Alexander had so forcefully rejected at the beginning of his directorate. As programming policy was debated within the directorate, opinions were beginning to polarise.

On the Board representatives of the City Council like Councillor Brenda Clarke were inevitably concerned that the theatre should 'pick winners', while John Stalker emphasised the importance of giving the audience 'a bloody good night out'. On the other side it could be argued, by theatre academic Professor Joel Kaplan for example, that the extra financial investment brought by stabilisation meant the bold artistic risks could and should be taken. Alexander, for his part, however, could be very pragmatic. The plays which occupied the main stage after *Art*: *Death of a Salesman*, *Saint Joan* and *Present Laughter* were an attempt to play safe with three classic titles, each strongly directed—especially by Di Trevis in an emotionally-charged production of Miller's great American tragedy. But as the disappointing audience response demonstrated yet again, nothing was 'safe'.

Matters came to a head over Alexander's proposal to commission the distinguished feminist playwright, Timberlake Wertenbaker, to write a new version of *Cinderella* for Christmas 2000. Determined to prioritise artistic innovation, he succeeded in facing down Board alarm at the prospect of another festive gamble, but was compelled to mount *Absurd Person Singular* as a companion piece. Not only did he rehearse Ayckbourn's black comedy over just three weeks, thereby abandoning one of the most cherished elements of his working practice, but *Cinderella-The Ash Girl*, which played to just 30%, fulfilled all the Board's worst fears. More damaging still the management was forced to refute exaggerated press reports about cancelled performances. It was a bleak end to Alexander's tenure at the Rep.

The Chairman's introduction to the 1999-2000 financial statement recorded a deficit of £498,748 and the fact that with sadness the Board had accepted Bill Alexander's resignation. The decision was made public in June 2000. What ensued however was a lengthy, and at times acrimonious, newspaper debate about Alexander's record. In a manner reminiscent of Barry Jackson's fulminations about Birmingham's ingratitude, Alexander had often expressed anger and bewilderment at local audiences' refusal to take the rich artistic opportunities he offered them. Complaining to Terry Grimley about the consistently negative *Evening Mail* coverage of the Rep, he targeted the 'one particular factor' of Fred Norris. 'If the job is to build the audience beyond the usual well-heeled middle class people, when you have a major theatre critic constantly lamenting the state of the theatre and giving the message out that this is not the place to come to, I would be mad if I did not regard that as a factor in why we struggle in this city' (*BP*, 20.6.00). Norris immediately counter- attacked 'the legacy of the man who emptied the Rep' with relentless statistics of poor audiences and empty seats. He vehemently denied that his newspaper or indeed any other could exert such an influence. 'The theatre is still in a mess' (*EM*,22.6.00) Bob Haywood in his aptly titled 'Sunday Shout' column in the *Sunday Mercury* (25.6.00), joined in the slanging match with 'good riddance'.

Wanting to Stay

Setting aside the unseemly mud-slinging, both Grimley and subsequently Michael Billington in an extended interview with Bill Alexander in July (*G*, 26.7.01), pondered the issues in more depth. Both critics pointed out that the core problems were by no means confined to Birmingham Rep and that nation-wide theatres were struggling to attract audiences especially the young. Both also recalled that in Barry Jackson's golden age the theatre was often half empty. Alexander was determined, however, to demonstrate the disparity between metropolitan and regional audiences. In a move which alarmed some of his colleagues, he made the worst of the Rep's statistics available to *Guardian* readers in order to show how much better an artistically successful production like *Baby Doll*, which played to 74% in the National's Lyttelton Theatre, could do in London. Interviewed in mid-December just before he left, Alexander declared vehemently 'People like Billington don't know…they don't know that as an artistic director you're very very close to how hard it is to get people into the theatre'. It was important that there was understanding of an intractable problem.

Billington described Alexander's final autumn season, including the Wertenbaker experiment, as 'creditably ambitious' as indeed it was. *Hamlet* was revived, and subsequently toured, in tandem with a new production of *Twelfth Night* which featured Rakie Ayola as Viola and Gerard Murphy as Malvolio. What followed was a joyfully inventive adaptation by Peter Oswald of the ancient Hindu epic *The Ramayana* which was both a kind of festive pantomime for Diwali, borrowing from the traditions of Kathakali theatre, and as Indhu Rubasingham (now Associate Director) made clear, a production about being in 21st century, multi-cultural Birmingham. Staged as part of the city's Forward Festival, the final flourish of the decade-long Millennium Festival which now focused entirely on new work, the ambition which drove *The Ramayana* project as a whole reflected not only what was best about the stabilisation vision but also Birmingham's cultural aspirations.

Rubasingham worked with Oswald and the internationally-known designer Ultz for some fourteen months bringing on board Piali Ray as choreographer and virtuoso tabla player Kuljit Bhamra as composer. The seventeen-strong acting ensemble with four supernumaries represented a wide range of ethnic backgrounds. A Year of the Artist residency, masterminded by the Education Department, enabled regional Asian artists to create community performance work around *The Ramayana* stories which culminated in a special performance involving some sixty local performers. A major marketing initiative brought together a twenty-strong panel of advisors drawn from the community to stimulate strategies for South Asian audience development.

In the event the Rep sold 6,537 seats: 33% of capacity. But those who came were treated to an exuberantly eclectic retelling of ancient myth which focused on the god Rama, played by television heart-throb Gerald Kyd resplendent in blue body makeup, and his beautiful, long-suffering bride Sita played by Ayesha Dharker. On what was effectively a bare stage, princely grandeur sat under a saffron yellow canopy, while the demons plotted on free-wheeling office stools. The ten-headed manifestation of the devilish Ravana (Andrew French) who abducts Sita was created by a rumbustious phalanx of red-crowned and gloved actors who later turned into a gang of white-jowled marauding monkeys creating mayhem amongst the audience. Miltos Yerolemou played the hairy, banana-skin wielding Monkey King Hanuman. Piles of plastic drinks crates represented the causeway of stones built across the sea. Billington hailed 'a totally charming show' G, 26.10.00). Pat Ashworth in *The Stage* recorded 'rapture all round from the many cultures represented in the audience' (2.11.00). When it transferred to the Olivier auditorium of the National Theatre 13,110 seats were sold: 94% of capacity. Yet again London audiences had responded in greater numbers to a Rep product.

In his *Guardian* interview, Alexander confessed that he could have given more attention to the extra-curricular life of the building. But through the Education Department under stabilisation different levels of community outreach, linked to both the main stage and the Door, had expanded as never before. Rachel Gartside had revolutionised the department moving away from a policy which had tended to prioritise the directorial interests invested in the community productions. Now the aim was management and facilitation of a programme of educational activity delivered by a small team of education associates and tutors working with a range of institutions. It was, in the words of her successor Trevelyan Wright, 'the most invisible aspect of the Rep's work', taking place in schools and community centres with the aim of developing skills and fostering self-esteem in the participants.

Apart from in-school or college introductory workshops and large scale Theatredays where a director like Di Trevis with actors and stage management staff would work with as many as three hundred students, there were extended education projects initially linked to productions but which encouraged further independent creativity. Two terms' work with three secondary schools on *Twelfth Night* culminated in short devised performances staged as a curtain raiser before the main stage production of the play. For *Cinderella Storybox*, fourteen primary schools joined professional artists to create 3 D visual landscapes inspired by Wertenbaker's play which were exhibited at the Rep. 2000-1 saw expansion into work with adults in collaboration with Birmingham Adult Education Service which added short courses on the production process and creative writing to the well-established Spotlight and Afterdark events and Discovery Days.

During The Door's first year in addition to launching Play Ups, a series of daytime shows aimed at very young children, Gartside promoted the ambitious *Ten Days in*

June programme of performances and workshops designed for young people aged 9-14. The centre piece, co-produced with the Traverse Theatre and presented on the main stage, was David Greig's *Danny 306+Me (4 Ever)* a fusion of text, music and live animation. As Play Ups became an established feature of the Door programme, there was a return to the annual Christmas show for young children with Moving Hands Theatre staging *The Ginger Bread Pig* for Christmas 2000.

Increasingly The Door also became the venue for creative expression by young people. Young Rep, the youth theatre, was some one hundred strong by January 2001 when there were showcase performances by each age group. Work was already underway on a specially commissioned version of Aristophanes' *The Birds* by Michael Punter. Most exciting, however, was the continuing success, and growing media coverage, of the Transmissions scheme launched in October 1999 to nurture the potential of young playwrights. Two groups of young people (11-16 and 16-25) were led by established writers Carl Miller, Noel Greig and Maya Chowdhry to develop initial ideas into scripts. In February 2000 professional actors and directors came to workshop the scripts which were then performed as completed plays during a two-week festival in July. In the autumn the cycle of development began again.

In an article written in February 2001, Wright suggested that the virtual doubling of participants in the Page to Stage scheme between 1999-2000 made a vital contribution to the growing strength of The Door as a new writing venue. [1] *All That Trouble That We Had* played to an audience of 905. Eighteen months later Clark's production of Paul Lucas' next play *A Slight Witch* was seen by 2102—65% of capacity. While the offbeat comedy, surreal plotline and quirky characterisation which is typical of Lucas' work remained a major element in The Door's house style, there was less relentless emphasis on the young and marginalised, and a broader spectrum of theme and experience was represented. In April 2000, Bill Alexander's production of *Quarantine* dramatised by Ben Payne from the novel by Birmingham-based Jim Crace was very much a local collaboration. The Crace/Payne imaginative reconfiguration of the story of Christ in the wilderness, and Alexander's attempt at a promenade-style interaction of actors and audience made it a bold experiment.

There was still plenty of women's writing and focus on women's lives, but the noticeable absence of women directors was addressed. Clark directed *Silence*, an end of the first Millennium comedy by Moira Buffini, and another, wickedly black comedy of former school days, *My Best Friend*, by Tamsin Oglesby. Indhu Rubasingham, however, worked on Charles Mulekwa's *A Time of Fire*, while Jess Walters' *Terracotta* was directed by Marianne Elliot. Annie Castledine was a powerful directorial presence in Roy Williams' *The Gift* which ended the second Door year in June 2000. It tells the story of Heather, played by Doreene Blackstock, returning home to Jamaica after an absence of thirty years in order to bury her murdered son. In what was a delicately humorous exploration of personal identity, loss and acceptance, Claire Benedict played her half-sister Bernice credited with the gift of conjuring the dead.

Annie Castledine returned in the autumn with *A Wedding Story*, another play by Bryony Lavery which focuses, albeit playfully, on the difficult topic of Alzeimer's disease. Both Lavery, and Kaite O'Reilly whose *Belonging* was directed by Clark in November, led workshops linked to their writing. For O'Reilly this included encountering an unfamiliar diversity of age and background in an adult education group in South Birmingham. *Belonging* inhabits a similar thematic territory to *The Gift* in that characters—this time in the Birmingham Irish community a year after the pub bombings—have to deal with the diaspora experience of dislocation and nostalgia while forging a new sense of belonging. As a way of introducing young people to the play education associate Juliet Forster conducted a practical exercise based on an imaginary map to discover that all the participants had some history of travel and migration within their families.

Both *Belonging* and *A Wedding Story* played to 65% of The Door's capacity. As Trevelyan Wright later wrote 'What is common to all the work that is inspired by The Door is that we are providing an individual connection for each person to the process of writing and producing new work. This I think is what we might have learnt over the past few years about engaging audiences'. Failure to engage with audiences on the large, as opposed to the small, scale in the end defeated Bill Alexander. For a large, complex organisation in a large complex city other solutions needed to be found to make the necessary connections and Alexander was 'empty of ideas'. Interviewed just before he left, he still loved the 'brilliant, beautiful theatre space'.

If I knew the answer I wouldn't be leaving. I do want to leave because I don't know the answer. But if I did know the answer I'd passionately want to stay.

---

1 Trevelyan Wright, *Writernet Bulletin*, 3, no.1 (February, 2001) pp. 7-9

12. Postscript 2000-2002: Sharing Taste with Jonathan Church

The Boyden Report

In August 1999 Peter Boyden Associates was commissioned by the Arts Council of England to undertake a review of 'The Roles and Functions of the English Regional Producing Theatres'. The final report was published in May 2000. As the introduction explains, the review started from the proposition that 'many regional producing theatres have experienced a level of sustained crisis over the last two decades which has changed the way many go about their business'. The analytic summary of the '20 years of strategic confusion and funding attrition' which had brought the ERPTs to their start-of-century beleaguered state demonstrates very clearly on the macro level what, as an individual case study, the history of Birmingham Rep bears out.

What was so sobering about the negative effects of the Rep's stabilisation exercise was that there was a real fear that the company had reached a deficit-stable position—a predicament which Boyden suggests many theatres faced. Everyone at the Rep knew that the 2001-2 financial year, which had to be survived without benefit of stabilisation funds, would be very difficult. Indeed it ended with an accumulated deficit of £926,562. But there was some light at the end of the tunnel. The previous year, as the result of the national Theatre Review, the Government decided to provide an additional £25 million to put English regional theatres on a more secure financial footing. The grant to the Rep was to increase by over £250,000 a year in 2002-3 rising still further by £500,000 a year in 2003-4. But the interim period between the end of the Stabilisation Programme and the arrival of the new funds would require, as the Chairman's statement for 2000-1 puts it 'imaginative and creative use of a significantly reduced resource base'. It was emphasised that over reliance on funds from the public purse was not a sustainable strategy for the long-term.

This statement, written while John Stalker was designated Chief Executive, begs the question of what kind of strategy is sustainable given the herculean efforts which appeared to have failed. Boyden argues strongly that funding bodies and managements have to tackle the 'downward spiral of declining expectations' which prevent theatres from attracting the best of creative talent. Ambitious theatre practitioners need a 'defended space' for research and development . Determined to stress the extent of historic underfunding and the 'tangled thickets' of authorities and schemes which had made sustainable development so difficult to achieve, Boyden declares that 'Building based producing theatres are among the most over-regulated businesses in the UK. Senior managers have less room to "manage" than their counterparts in almost any other context'.

Interviewed in July 2001 Stalker spoke of how 'enormously heartbreaking to watch, to witness' had been the personal pressures brought to bear on the Rep staff during stabilisation. In the bleak aftermath eighteen full time employees left the theatre with virtually no section left unaffected. The Rep had journeyed into uncharted territory and now he wished he 'hadn't been so rash'. But David Waine was quick to defend him insisting that there had been no option but to accept the poisoned chalice which had been offered. In any case stabilisation had not been a complete disaster given the success of The Door and the unprecedented expansion of education and community outreach.

What was important, Waine argued, was that the Rep had to become a more outward looking organisation. There was in some ways a contradiction here. Under Alexander and Stalker the Rep had more consciously looked out beyond Birmingham to national status as never before. But ironically that effort had made the theatre even more inwardly focused especially in the person of an Artistic Director, 'the poet of the rehearsal room' as Trevelyan Wright dubbed him, who was happiest engaged in the creative process; who had never run a building before, and who continued to live in his top floor theatre flat cut off from the city. After Alexander's departure some of his most successful work took on a further life. The Snowman revivals in London continued; in the summer of 2001 Hamlet was staged in Elsinore with actors drawn from the 1998 and 2000 casts. Best of all Frozen with the same actors was revived at the National Theatre in 2002 to critical acclaim. With 11,996 seats sold in the Cottesloe it played to 85% of capacity.

The New Regime

Andy Allan, who started his career as a presenter for ABC TV and became Chief Executive of Central Television, replaced David Waine as Chairman of the Board. At the end of 2001 John Stalker left to go to Edinburgh as Chief Executive of the Festival City Theatres Trust, while Anthony Clark relinquished the role of Associate Director. Both saw the beginning of the new regime under Jonathan Church. His background is completely different to his predecessors. He has not acted professionally and he did not go to university. Instead he took the other, equally time-honoured route of stage management. Born in Nottingham and with vivid childhood memories of the Rep stage set for *Charley's Aunt* in 1985, he started in theatre as an electrician, lighting designer and stage manager in a range of companies. At the Dukes Theatre in Lancaster he changed light bulbs over John Stalker's desk. Following his first directorial experience in the Sheffield Crucible Studio, his formative period as a director and theatre manager was at the Nottingham Playhouse and the Derby Playhouse. In 1995 as Artistic Director of the Salisbury Playhouse he took over a theatre which was bankrupt and dark. When he left in 1999 to become Associate Director at the Hampstead Theatre in London, Salisbury was back on its feet, a thriving success. Thirty-four years old on appointment, long-haired, boyish in appearance and deceptively unassuming, Church is more Adams than Alexander, hands-on and engaged in the whole corporate operation.

His work at Hampstead, one of the leading London small venues devoted to new plays, was an important factor for the Rep management determined to hang on, against all the odds, to the commitment to The Door and new writing. Ben Payne's post as Literary Manager was upgraded to Associate Director (Literary), while the Clark/Hughes model of Associate was for the time being, not sustainable. The work of developing new writers was to continue even though there were now more co-productions in The Door. Church's attitude to his London experience was revealing however. He missed, he said, 'the relationship with an audience that you have in a regional theatre. I had become used to that two-way dialogue that wasn't just fashion-led'.

His position on the audience was echoed by Trina Jones who as Marketing Director had come to the theatre at the tail end of stabilisation. For her it is important that the Rep talks to its audience and thus "get to grips with its customers" especially the first-time attenders. While the abandonment of the subscription scheme shortly before her arrival had provoked protests from older members of the audience the fact was that the list of subscribers had dwindled to some six hundred loyalists who paid an average of £4.50 a ticket. The discount schemes which replaced it were more economically realistic. Also more realistic in the light of the flawed stabilisation goal to increase attendance and ticket yield simultaneously, was the need to simplify ticket price bands and make the whole experience of coming to the Rep more accessible. Season brochures had been made less glamorous to look at but easier to read. There was also no point in adopting an embattled stance with local critics. A friendly pint of beer with Fred Norris was a good investment in public relations for the new director.

This in fact was essential given the damaging speculation in the press about the post-stabilisation deficit and emergency consultations with the main funding bodies. In an interview with Norris published in May 2001 Church was frank 'I am on a five year contract. I have drawn up my plans for the first season. It will need time to see how they go. But if they fail, I like to think I will be brave enough to go. I have no illusions about the task I have taken on' (25.5.01). He immediately overturned some of Alexander's most deeply-held principles. Long rehearsal periods and fewer, more expensive productions were no longer sustainable. Audiences had to be given the opportunity to see more plays and, in Church's view, a good many plays in the repertoire do not require more than three weeks' rehearsal. Shakespeare was to go on a back burner for a while and the problem of Christmas had to be tackled head on. Family expectations had to be satisfied.

Most controversial was his perception that Birmingham audiences had been somewhat starved of the best of contemporary drama. Alexander's insistence that the Rep would not stage recent successes generated by London theatres meant that much of the nationally-celebrated drama of the past decade had not been seen in Birmingham. For Church it was necessary on the main stage 'to take people with you' i.e. accustom the audience to contemporary trends so that the degree of shift to new work was not too abrupt. The opening gambit of the autumn 2001 season was an attempt to capitalise on the success of *Art* with the first out of London revival of the RNT's production of Yasmina Reza's *Life X 3*. Church's first work on the main stage was a bold coupling of Noël Coward's *Private Lives* with Patrick Marber's 1997 hit play *Closer* to reveal, with the same four actors, unexpected parallels in the sexual mores and tangled relationships of the 1930s and 1990s. He followed this with Steinbeck's *Of Mice and Men*, and at Christmas, a popular production of Alan Bennett's adaptation of *Wind in the Willows*. As Artistic Director he had to develop a relationship with the audience. In order to 'share tastes' as he put it, it was necessary to discover where tastes coincided.

The other Church strategy was to consciously reconnect the Rep to its roots. Apart from the fact that over the years he had seen a number of productions in Broad Street, he had also, in 1995, directed a highly successful production of *The Crucible* for Neal Foster's Birmingham Stage Company down at the Old Rep. A few months after his arrival the Broad Street building celebrated its thirtieth birthday with an enormous party. Invited to a gala performance of *Private Lives* many familiar faces thronged the foyer bringing together the different generations of Rep folk. June Callear was there as was John Greenwood and indeed John Adams as well as long-serving Rep audience members. Chief Usher Valerie Munday who had worked in the theatre since its opening in October 1971 cut a large birthday cake on stage. A small exhibition was mounted of production photographs from both Reps and there was a week-long series of talks and theatre tours.

The arrival of Stuart Rogers as Executive Director in January 2002 strengthened the Birmingham connections. Born and educated in Birmingham, where an enthusiastic English teacher stimulated a passion for theatre and led to involvement as an electrician and general helper at the old Birmingham Arts Lab, his first paid theatre work was at the Alex as Les Dawson's dresser. His first experience as an audience member was Michael Simpson's production of *Volpone* at the Old Rep and he was a regular attender at the Friday night alternative shows. He saw *First Impressions* in 1971. Management in a number of theatres including Chester Gateway and the Nottingham Playhouse with Jonathan Church had taken him to Teatro Kismet in Bari in Southern Italy. In an interview with Sarah Ogle in the Rep's Spring 2002 newletter he explained why he had left sunny Bari for not-so-sunny Brum. Apart from the opportunity to work with Jonathan Church again he 'couldn't resist the once-in-a lifetime opportunity to manage one of the best theatres in the country, and one for which I have a great deal of affection. In the short time I've been here, it's clear that that affection is shared by all the excellent staff at the theatre and many other people in the city'.

The newsletter also trumpeted a flying start to the new era. By comparison with the Autumn/Winter 2000 season audience attendance had nearly doubled. The average audience capacity percentage was 68% with *Of Mice and Men* playing to full houses. *Wind in the Willows* had been a great success, and Antony Clark's adaptation of *Winnie the Witch* for 4-7 year olds had sold out in The Door. Clark also directed Abi Morgan's *Tender* which had been developed on the Writers' Attachment Scheme and then went on to earn an Olivier Award nomination for Most Promising Playwright. Gurpreet Bhatti's debut play *Behsharam (Shameless)* which is set in Birmingham sold well in The Door and at the Soho Theatre. At 46% audiences had not flocked to the *Private Lives/Closer* pairing but, compared to some of the disappointments of recent years, the result was comfortable enough. The balance was redressed, in any case, by the other more consciously populist main stage options.

Nevertheless it was impossible to hide the fact that the theatre was back to fighting the threat of insolvency under very difficult circumstances and that co-production and collaboration had to be an important part of the survival strategy. With one notable exception none of the 2002 spring-summer shows on the main stage were stand-alone Rep productions. Triumph Entertainment was very much in evidence as a partner in a toured-in production of John Mortimer's *Naked Justice*, the British première of Timothy Findley's *Elizabeth Rex* which Church directed in May, and *Masterpieces*, a celebration of Noël Coward devised by Christopher Luscombe and Malcolm McKee. Alan Bennett's *Single Spies* was a Bath Theatre

Royal production, while Church's production of *Hobson's Choice*, with Tony Britton as the alcoholically-challenged Salford boot maker, was presented in association with the Arts Council-funded Touring Consortium and Theatre Royal Plymouth.

In an interview with Rogers published in the *Birmingham Post*, Terry Grimley suggested that the apparent success of the more-choice policy was being achieved partly by 'fudging' the issue of production provenance. Rogers responded robustly. While *Single Spies* was a production from another theatre it 'feels like one of our shows'. *Hobson's Choice* was home-produced but was to tour for twelve weeks. 'We're much more about blurring the distinction between what's our production and what's a touring show… This is something the West Yorkshire Playhouse has done very successfully. Most people outside the business don't understand the difference. It's a distinction we get obsessed with in the industry but that's breaking down' (11.3.02)

The policy did mean more constraints on the full exploitation of the Rep stage. But the impression conveyed was of considerable diversity. *Single Spies* did well. *Elizabeth Rex*, a romantic historical drama featuring well-known television soap opera diva Stephanie Beacham as Elizabeth I agonising between her desires as a woman and responsibilities as a queen on the eve of the Earl of Essex's execution, was potentially risky. But with an expansive Tudor barn set created by Simon Higlett, newcomer Alexander Brunati as a very engaging bear, old hand George Costigan as a sardonic choric Shakespeare figure and James Dreyfus as the dying male player of powerful women, Church's production attracted audiences of 60% and exceeded its target.

It was still possible to be ambitious albeit with greater pragmatism. No one wanted to see The Door close but the original purity of the new writing policy could not be sustained. One of the most successful post-Christmas productions was Shared Experience's revival of *The Clearing*, Helen Edmundson's passionate 1993 play about love, conflict and betrayal in Ireland under the Cromwellian occupation. Moira Buffini's *Silence* was revived as the Community tour. However the première, in co-production with Graeae, of Kaite O'Reilly's *peeling* incorporated the natural use of audio description and sign language into a play which literally peels away the outsize costumes of three actresses to reveal the bodies beneath. Directed by Jenny Sealey, the dialogue between the three women peels still further to expose along with petty rivalries and thwarted ambitions, deep desires and painful histories.

Alongside *peeling*, a parallel programme of performances, showcases and discussions aptly titled *Beyond the Boundaries* revealed more about the Rep's continuing mission to develop and promote the theatre voices of the future. The Transmissions Scheme continued as did the Young Rep. There were also two home grown productions. *No Sweat* marked the Attachment Scheme-developed debut of Birmingham-born Lloyd Withers. Set in a Midlands' car factory about to be taken over by a foreign company, and with a group of workers forced to consider their priorities, the play is raw-edged and vigorously funny. Very much in the tradition of popular television dramas such as *Auf Wiedersehen Pet*, the grimy authenticity of the factory set and the ethnic mix of the characters played by a company of young black, Asian and white actors gave it a locally-focused immediacy. By contrast Lisa Evans' *Getting to the Foot of the Mountain* was not only a play by a writer with strong Rep connections but a warm, nostalgic backward glance to a young girl's childhood and the feisty women who shaped it.

On the main stage there were six performances in April of Tara Arts' twenty fifth anniversary *Journey to the West*, an epic trilogy of plays charting the twentieth century migratory experience of three generations of characters from India to East Africa to Britain. Director Jatinder Verma wove his personal history into the memories of other British Asians in a project which also included community workshops at each stage of the company's tour. Local young people were given the opportunity to present their own devised work on *Journey* themes on the stage before performances. Unlike *The Ramayana* this was not a Rep production, but it played to 47% of capacity, and at the end of a Saturday devoted to the entire trilogy, the theatre was packed with a large South Asian audience. More disappointing, however, was both the audience and critical response to *Krindlekrax*, Philip Ridley's adaptation of his own story for children which Clark directed in a co-production with Nottingham Playhouse. That said some 3,750 seats were filled leaving hope perhaps for the stabilisation dream of large-scale work for children.

Given the long erratic history of trying to attract Birmingham audiences to Birmingham-based shows in the main house, the success of *Wallop Mrs Cox*, the one wholly home-produced production staged at the end of the season was unprecedented. Written by Birmingham-born Euan Rose and Laurie Hornsby, and first staged at the Crescent Theatre in 2000, it is not perhaps the most sophisticated piece of music theatre. But revised to add more ethnic diversity and presented with a cast of more than 50 local performers, together with local media personality Malcolm Boyden as the Narrator, it was directed with exuberant panache by John Adams. Cynical Brummies melted in misty-eyed nostalgia at the century-long saga of an extended working class dynasty of Bull Ring market traders. There were five incarnations of Mrs Cox taking her from a young girl falling in love in 1915 to death at the age of 97 in 2002. Nick Owen gave a heart-felt performance as her husband Lenny who is killed in the Second World War. Sharron Burns as the widowed, embattled matriarch sang as powerfully as she acted. Terry Grimley singled out Sheila Palmer delivering Mrs Cox's moving final monologue 'like an Alan Bennett *Talking Heads* in miniature'. Of the songs including a celebration of Redfern's tripe and 'New Skyline' which Grimley dubbed 'the ironic hymn to '60s redevelopment', 'Birmingham' came across as a joyful anthem to the city. There were house full signs outside the theatre, while inside there were standing ovations. Birmingham audiences applauding Birmingham actors on the stage of Birmingham Rep. ' Much more of this kind of thing' quipped Grimley, 'and Brummies really will be proud of their city'. A revival was immediately scheduled for 2003.

Andy Allan's statement for 2001-2 struck a note of optimistic realism. The year had been every bit as difficult as expected but a new six year financial plan had been approved and the Company could congratulate itself on beginning the recovery through increased earned income and expenditure control. Whatever strategies have to be put in place to enable the Rep to thrive in the city, the main priority is to retain control and ownership of the artistic product. The Touring Consortium of six large-scale touring venues, including Nottingham Theatre Royal and Wolverhampton Grand, who co-produce their work combines product exploitation with artistic autonomy. The 2001 *Of Mice and Men*, re-rehearsed and toured for twelve weeks in 2003, will be managed by the Touring Consortium and assisted by an Arts Council touring grant. The Rep has also just been awarded a National Touring Contract giving additional Arts Council funding for three years to tour work with particular interest to young people. Seeds sown in the stabilisation strategy have borne fruit.

And so the Company journeys on into a new century. How far the Church/Rogers regime succeeds in producing new solutions to old problems remains to be seen. The current approach at the Rep is pragmatic. The vision of national and international status is, of necessity, suspended for the time being in favour of a more direct Birmingham focus underpinned by regional collaboration. Bill Alexander had attempted to give the theatre 'character and definition'. He wanted, he said in December 2001, 'to make a theatre company that was original, not a provincial rep that lived off the metropolitan leavings'. In that he failed, as he freely admitted, just as others had failed before him. Alexander, not unlike Jackson, wanted to direct the taste of the city. In wanting to share taste, Church offers a more varied, but arguably less distinctive diet. In the long term this may prove more nourishing as well as more palatable. As this book goes to press in May 2003, Church and Rachel Kavanaugh have directed a triumphant revival of David Hare's 1993 'State of the Nation' trilogy of *Racing Demon*, *Murmuring Judges*, and *The Absence of War* which ended its run with full houses. If as Boyden hopes 'quality and access' could be made 'two sides of the same coin rather than incompatible aspirations' then the old dichotomies might be broken down. If diversity of access opportunity can make the theatre Barry Jackson gave to the city more representative of the multiplicity of the city, then Birmingham Rep could look forward to a creative future. To survive for the best part of a century is no mean feat. To exploit the best of the legacy of the past to creative dynamic, relevant theatre for the future would be a triumph.

Appendix I
Birmingham Repertory Theatre Company Productions

Station Street

*World première; ♦British première; ●London transfer; ★Lunchtime performance; †Late night performance

Play	Playwright
1962	
The Tempest	Shakespeare
Saint's Day	John Whiting
The Lesson★	Eugene Ionesco, trans.Watson & Stewart
The Rivals	R.B.Sheridan
Duel of Angels	Jean Giraudoux, adap.Fray
Walker London	J.M.Barrie, adap.Harrison & C.Whelan
Lunch Hour★	John Mortimer
The Keep	Gwyn Thomas
Getting Married	Bernard Shaw
Look Back in Anger	John Osborne
The Double Deceit	William Popple
A Marriage has been Arranged and The Bells	Sutro & Leopold Lewis
Alice in Wonderland	Lewis Carol, adap.Harrison
1963	
King Henry VIII	Shakespeare
Troilus and Cressida	Shakespeare
Titus Andronicus	Shakespeare
Photo Finish	Peter Ustinov
Two Stars for Comfort	John Mortimer
The Country Wife	Wiliam Wycherley
Thark	Ben Travers
The Good Woman of Setzuan	Bertolt Brecht
Next Time I'll Sing to You	James Saunders
Colombe	Jean Anouilh
Between These Four Walls	Lodge/Bradbury/Duckett
Toad of Toad Hall	A.A.Milne
1964	
A Midsummer Night's Dream	Shakespeare
The City Madam	Philip Massinger
Spring 1600	Emlyn Williams
The Easter Man●	Evan Hunter
All in Good Time	Bill Naughton
The Knack	Ann Jellicoe
The Quare Fellow	Brendan Behan
The Seagull	Anton Chekhov
The Beggar's Opera	John Gay
Charley's Aunt	Brandon Thomas

Play	Playwright
1965	
A Measure of Cruelty	Steve Passeur, trans.Mitchell
The Winter's Tale	Shakespeare
Heartbreak House	Bernard Shaw
Candida	Bernard Shaw
The Provok'd Wife	John Vanburgh
An Ideal Husband	Oscar Wilde
Design for Living	Noel Coward
On Approval	Frederick Lonsdale
Zoo Story	Edward Albee
The Lover	Harold Pinter
Doctor's Delight	Moliere,trans.Jackson
The Representative	Rolf Hochuth
Slap in the Middle	Lodge/Bradbury/Duckett
Treasure Island	R L Stevenson
1966	
Inadmissible Evidence	John Osborne
Twelfth Night	Shakespeare
Edward II	Christopher Marlow
Simpleton of the Unexpected Isle	Bernard Shaw
Private Lives	Noel Coward
Boston Story	Henry James, adap Gow
A Crack in the Ice	Ronald Eyre
Galileo	Bertolt Brecht
Little Malcolm and his Struggle Against the Eunuchs	David Halliwell
Who's Afraid of Virginia Woolf?	Edward Albee
The Birdwatcher	George Feydeau
1066 And All That	Arkell & Reynolds
1967	
Richard II	Shakespeare
As You Like It●	Christopher Marlowe
Hadrian VII●	Peter Luke
How's the world Treating You	Roger Milner
Entertaining Mr Sloane	Joe Orton
Events While Guarding the Bofors Gun	John McGrath
Long Day's Journey Into Night	Eugene O'Neill
Blithe Spirit	Noel Coward
The Circle	Somerset Maughan
The Doctor's Dilemma	Bernard Shaw
A Severed Head	Iris Murdoch, adap. Priestley

Peer Gynt	Henrik Ibsen
Death Watch♦⁹⁺	Jean Genet
Lunchtime Concert⁹	Olwen Wymark
Hans the Witch and the Goblin	Alan Cullen

1968

Fando and Lis♦⁹⁺	Fernando Arrabal
Romeo and Juliet	Shakespeare
Endgame⁹	Samuel Beckett
Othello	Shakespeare
Anticlockwise⁹	Jeremy Mason
St. Joan	Bernard Shaw
War & Dissector (double bill)⁹	Jean-Claude Van Itallie & Rae Davis
After the Rain	John Bowen
Beware of the Dog	G.Avout, trans. B. Mitchel
Investigation*	Leslie Sands
White Liars & Black Comedy	Peter Shaffer
The Merchant of Venice	Shakespeare
Prisoner & Escort⁹	Charles Wood
Police⁹	Slawomir Mrozek
Old Time Music Hall	
Miss Julie⁹	August Strindberg
The Rose and the Ring	John Dalby

1969

Hamlet	Shakespeare
Volpone	Ben Johnson
Keep Tightly Closed in a Cool Dry Place⁹	Megan Terry
The Government Inspector	Nicolai Gogol
Happy Days⁹	Samuel Beckett

The Glass Menagerie	Tennessee Williams
Pretexts for Plays⁹	René de Obaldia
Transending⁹	David Cregan
Waiting for Godot	Samuel Beckett
Quick, Quick, Slow*	D.Turner, M.Norman & J.More
The Italian Straw Hat	E Labiche, trans. M. Simpson
Saved	Edward Bond
The Hotel in Amsterdam	John Osborne
Destruction⁹	D.Rudkin, D.Lytton, D.Turner
The Window⁹	Frank Marcus
Henry IV, Part One	Shakespeare
Words, Words/Come and Go⁹	P.Ableman et al & S.Beckett
Toad of Toad Hall	A.A.Milne

1970

Hamlet	Shakespeare
In His Own Write⁹	John Lennon
The Sorrows of Frederick♦	Romulus Linney
The Maids⁹	Jean Genet
Three Sisters	Anton Chekhov
Pygmalion	Bernard Shaw
Staircase	Charles Dyer
Tonight at 8.30.	Noel Coward
Forty Years On	Alan Bennett
Heads & The Education of Skinny Spew⁹	Howard Brenton
Rosencrantz and Guildenstern are Dead	Tom Stoppard
A Midsummer Night's Dream	Shakespeare
After Magritte⁹	Tom Stoppard
1966 And All That	R. Arkell & A.Reynolds

Broad Street

*World première, ♦British première; ⁺European première; ●London transfer, Studio productions are in bold.
The list does not include toured-in productions, dance performances and music or comedy one-night shows.

1971

First Impressions	A.Burrows & H.Jerome
Roll me Over*	Bill Canaway
Good Time Johnny	J.More & J.Gilbert
Noggin the Nog	O.Postgate & P.Firmin

1972

Man and Superman	Bernard Shaw
Vivat, Vivat, Regina!	Robert Bolt
The Recruiting Officer	George Farquhar
Oedipus & The Critic	Sophocles & R.B.Sheridan
Dandy Dick	Arthur Wing Pinero
The Real Inspector Hound & After Magritte	Tom Stoppard
Caesar and Cleopatra	Bernard Shaw
Present Laughter	Noel Coward

Macbeth	Shakespeare
Grab	**Albert Lyons**
Death Story*	**David Edgar**
The Homecoming	Harold Pinter
Nick the Dragon	**Reg Stewart**
Treasure Island	R.L.Stephenson, adap. G.Case

1973

Endgame	**Samuel Beckett**
Up Spaghetti Junction⁹*	M.Totten, D.Edgar, J.Clarke & D.Turner
The Miser	Moliere, trans David Turner
Stage One, Skin One* & One Season's King	**George MacEwan Green**

The Homecoming	Harold Pinter
The Hostage	Brendan Behan
The Nailmakers*	M.Totten & J.Raven
Twelfth Night	Shakespeare
Measure for Measure	Shakespeare
Home and Away (BYT)	R.Speakman & D.Nicholls
Guys and Dolls	A.Burrows, J.Werling, F.Loesser
The Changeling	Thomas Middleton
The Seventh (BYT)	R.Speakman & D.Nicholls
After Haggerty	David Mercer
Hobson's Choice	Harold Brighouse
The Pope's Wedding	Edward Bond
The Adventurer's of Robin Hood	Victor Pemberton
Barney's Time Travel	C.Honer & R.Lancaster

1974

Hedda Gabler	H.Ibsen, trans.Jens Arup
No Title*	David Rudkin
Capture the Flag (BYT)	R.Speakman & D.Nicholls
Henry V	Shakespeare
Waiting for Godot	Samuel Beckett
You Never Can Tell	Bernard Shaw
The Canal Show*	Michael G. Jackson
Baker's Boy (BYT)	R.Speakman & D.Nicholls
The Caucasian Chalk Circle	B.Brecht, adap. Steve Gooch
Say Goodnight to Grandma	Collin Welland
The Nuns*	E.Manet, trans. R.Baldick
How the Other Half Loves	Alan Ayckbourn
Ghosts	H.Ibsen, trans.M.Meyer
Blues, Whites and Reds	R.Planchon, trans. J. Burgess
In Your Own Time (BYT)	R.Speakman & D.Nicholls
Simulation Games	Roger Lancaster
The Thingummybob that's going to win the war*	Stephen Fagan
Drums in the Night	B.Brecht, trans. C.P.Taylor
Barney and the Puzzlemaster	C.Honer & R.Lancaster
The Magic Island	Keith Dewhurst

1975

Boudoir Follies of 1975	Alexander Herold
Simulation Games	Roger Lancaster
Trinity Tales	Alan Plater
Waiting for Godot	Samuel Beckett
Arms and the Man	Bernard Shaw
Equus	Peter Schaffer

Mrs Warren's Profession	Bernard Shaw
Trinity Tales	Alan Plater
The Importance of Being Ernest	Oscar Wilde
O Fair Jerusalem*	David Edgar
Votes for Kids	C.G.Bond
The House Gang* (BYT)	Stephen Fagan
Jumpers	Tom Stoppard
A Flea in her Ear	Georges Feydeau
Ted 'n Eddy (BYT)	R.Speakman & D.Nicholls
Move over Mrs Markham	R.Cooney & J.Chapman
Ashes	David Rudkin
As You Like It	Shakespeare
Knuckle	David Hare
Barney Joins the Fun Brigade	C.Honer & R.Lancaster
Toad of Toad Hall	A.A.Milne

1976

When we are Married	J.B.Priestley
Events Following the Closure of a Motorcycle Factory*	David Edgar
Sleepers (BYT)	R.Speakman & D.Nicholls
A Man for All Seasons	Robert Bolt
Uncle Vanya	Anton Chekhov
The National Health	Peter Nicholls
A Man for All Seasons	Robert Bolt
Anastasia	Marcelle Maurette
Are You Now, Or Have You Ever Been ?*	Eric Bentley
Get Away* (BYT)	Joyce Cheeseman
My Cousin Rachel	D.du Maurier, adap.G.Frow
Pythagoras*	Dannie Abse
Measure for Measure	Shakespeare
The Devil is an Ass	Ben Jonson
Travellers on Foot	Alexandre Ostrovsky
Daily Bread	R.Sloman & S.Brown
Schippel	Sternheim, adap. C.P.Taylor
Sherlock Holmes	A.Conan Doyle, adap. W.Gillette
Loot	Joe Orton
Loyalties (BYT)	R.Speakman & D.Nicholls
The Magical Legend	C.Honer & R.Lancaster
The Wizard of Oz	F.L.Baum, H.Arlen, R.Harburg

1977

Macbeth! Macbeth!	David Beckford
The Norman Conquests	Alan Ayckbourn
Small Change	Peter Gill
Run Rabbit Run (BYT)	R.Speakman & D.Nicholls
Iniquity*	L.Tolstoy trans.P.Farago

The Devil is an Ass	Ben Jonson
Measure for Measure	Shakespeare
On Approval	Frederick Lonsdale
The Deep Blue Sea	Terence Rattigan
A Perfect Gentleman	Herbert Appleman
Pygmalion	Bernard Shaw
The Seed*	R.Speakman & D.Nicholls
Mother Courage	Brecht trans.E.Bentley
The Lady from the Sea	H.Ibsen trans.M.Meyer
Absurd Person Singular	Alan Ayckbourn
The Kingfisher Quest	C.Honer & R.Lancaster
A Christmas Carol	C.Dickens, adap. R. Hastings.

1978

Kings & Clowns	Leslie Bricusse
Small Change	Peter Gill
Othello	Shakespeare
3 Plays in 1 Evening	P.Gems, D.Edgar & J.Bett
Gestures*	Vince Foxall
Hay Fever	Noel Coward
Action Replay*	Fay Weldon
Rosencrantz and Guildernstern Are Dead	Tom Stoppard
The Servant of Two Masters	C.Goldoni, trans. M.Duncan
Mary Barnes*●	David Edgar
She Stoops to Conquer	Oliver Goldsmith
All's Well That Ends Well	Shakespeare
The Merchant●	Arnold Wesker
Husbands and Lovers	F.Molnar, trans.B.F.Glazer
Kiss Me Kate	C.Porter, B.& S.Spewack
The Careless King	Bill Pryde
Babes in the Wood	Alan Brown

1979

Somebody's Daugher (BYT)	Gavin Blakeney
The Father	A.Strindberg, trans.Meyer
The Merchant of Venice	Shakesperare
Action Replay	Fay Weldon
Saint Joan	Bernard Shaw
Idle Rich*	Sheila Kelley
The Misanthrope	Moliere, trans. T.Harrison
The Duchess of Malfi	John Webster
Hearing*	Louise Page
Rookery Nook	Ben Travers
Spring Offensive	R.Speakman & D.Nicholls
Misalliance	Bernard Shaw
The Elder Statesman	T.S.Eliot
The Beggar's Opera	J.Gay, adap. M. Read

The Old Order*	Stephen Bill
The Crucible	Arthur Miller
The Wicked Cooks	Gunter Gras, adap.David Porter
Bedroom Farce	Alan Ayckbourn
The Not-So-Sad Story of Hansel & Gretel	Bill Pryde
Pinocchio	C.Collodi, adap.J.Morley

1980

Private Lives	Noel Coward
The British Empire Part One*	John Spurling
King Lear	Shakespeare
Mother Dear	Royce Ryton
After you with the Milk*	Ben Travers
The Wedding Feast	Arnold Wesker
The Master Builder	H.Ibsen, trans. M.Meyer
The School for Scandal	Sheridan
Harvest*	Ellen Dryden
Whose Life is it Anyway?	Brian Clark
The Ghosts of Riddle-Me Heights	Brian Patten
Worzel Gummidge*●	K. Waterhouse & W.Hall

1981

Midnite at the Starlite*	Michael Hastings
The Importance of Being Earnest	Oscar Wilde
The Triumph of Death*	David Rudkin
Chips with Everything	Arnold Wesker
Haworth*	Beverley Cross
Piggy Back Riders*	Stephen Bill
Theatre Royal	George Kaufman
Hosanna◆	Michael Tremblay
Candide◆	L.Bernstein & H.Wheeler
As You Like It	Shakespeare
Hobson's Choice	Harold Brighouse
Cinderella	Rogers & Hammerstein

1982

Goalkeeper's Revenge (BYT)	B.Naughton, adap. Speakman & Nicholls
Strictly Entre Nous*	Vince Foxall
Major Barbara	Bernard Shaw
Design for Living	Noel Coward
Man and Superman	Bernard Shaw
Look Back in Anger	John Osborne
Do Not Disturb*	Michael Pertwee
A Man for All Seasons	Robert Bolt
Call Me Madam●	I.Berlin, H.Lindsay, R.Course
The Gingerbread Man	David Wood

1983

The Caretaker (CTC)	Harold Pinter
The Rough Edge	R.Speakman & D.Nicholls
*It's a Lovely Day Tomorrow**	Ellen Dryden
Beethoven's Tenth	Peter Ustinov
The American Clock•	Arthur Miller
One Reputably Glamorous Woman (CT)	Vince Foxall
An Ideal Husband	Oscar Wilde
Nightshade•	Stewart Parker
Amadeus	Peter Schaffer
AnnieWobbler*•	Arnold Wesker
Dear Anyone*•	D.Black, G.Stephens, J.Rosenthal
The Devil's Disciple	Bernard Shaw
Hello Dolly	J.Herman & M.Stewart
Toad of Toad Hall	A.A.Milne

1984

The Walking Class (BYT)	Roy Mitchell
*Anna's Room**	Ellen Dryden
One for the Road	Willy Russell
American Buffalo	David Mamet
Hamlet	Shakespeare
Last Summer in Chulimsk•	A.Vampilov trans. P. Thompson
Aren't We All	Frederick Lonsdale
Duet for One	Tom Kempinski
Silver Lady	Liane Aukin
Portland Bill	Roy Mitchell
Great Expectations	C.Dickens, adap. Peter Coe
Bashville	D.King & B. Green
When the Wind Blows	Raymond Briggs
Season's Greetings	Alan Ayckbourn
Origin of the Species* (MON)	Bryony Lavery
Treasure Island	R.L.Stephenson, adap. W.Hall & D.King

1985

Bakers Boy (BYT)	R.Speakman & D.Nicholls
Death Watch (FOCO)	Jean Genet
Romeo & Juliet	Shakespeare
Weekend Break*	Ellen Dryden
A Man for All Seasons	Robert Bolt
Dear Headmaster (Double Bill)	T. Rattigan & J.Baddeley
*Naked in the Bull Ring**	Stephen Bill
*Lost Empires** (CTC)	J.B.Priestley, adap. K.Waterhouse & W. Hall
Wuthering Heights	E.Bronte, adap. Vince Foxall
Jeanne	Shirlie Roden

*Pride and Prejudice**•	J.Austen adap. David Pownall
Dead Men (YC)	Mike Stott
Accidental Death of an Anarchist	Dario Fo
Mamma Decembra (TEM)	Nigel Moffat
The Perfect Defence	Gary Bohike
The Snow Queen (YC)	Stuart Peterson & Derek Watson
Charley's Aunt	Brandon Thomas

1986

Roots, Rules and Tribulation (BYT)	Andrew Bethell
The Lower Depths (FOCO)	Gorky, adap. Tunde Ikoli
La Bolshie Vita (YC)	Ken Whitmore
The Winter's Tale	Shakespeare
The Recruiting Officer (YC)	George Farquhar
Volpone	B.Jonson, adap. K. Morley
*Heavenly Bodies**	Stewart Parker
The Wild Duck (YC)	H.Ibsen, trans. M. Meyer
I'm Not Rappaport	Herb Gardner
*Outside Broadcast**	Peter Woodward
*A Mouthful of Birds** (JS/RC)	Caryl Churchill & David Lan
Jane Eyre (YC)*	C.Brontë, adap. Fay Weldon
The Alchemist (YC)	Ben Jonson
The Miser	Moliere, trans. C. Fettes
Outskirts	Hanif Kureshi
Peter Pan	J.M.Barrie

1987

Saved (YC)	Edward Bond
Welcome Home Jacko (BYT)	Mustpaha Matura
The Daughter-in-Law	D.H.Lawrence
Julius Caesar	Shakespeare
Entertaining Mr.Sloane	Joe Orton
King John's Jewel*	David Pownall
See How they Run (YC)	Phillip King
The Travelling Players*(YC)	Chris Hawes
*The Golden Years of Jack Buchanan**	Peter Woodward
Three Sisters	Chekhov, trans. M. Frayn
Wilfred*	Peter Woodward
To Kill a Mockingbird	H.Lee adap. C.Sergel
One Big Blow (BJT)	John Burrow
The School for Scandal	Sheridan
Chorus of Disapproval	Alan Ayckbourn
The Wizard of Oz	Frank. L. Baum

1988

The Real Thing	Tom Stoppard
Tales of the Arabian Nights (BJT)	Shared Experience
Much Ado About Nothing (REN)	Shakespeare
As You Like It (REN)	Shakespeare
Hamlet (REN)	Shakespeare
Death of a Salesman	Arthur Miller
Privates on Parade	Peter Nichols
No Orchids for Miss Blandish	J. H. Chase, adap. R.D.MacDonald
The Railway Children	E.Nesbit adap.Dave Simpson
Midsummer Night's Dream	Shakespeare
The Contractor	David Storey
Blood Brothers (BJT)	Willie Russell
An Inspector Calls	J. B. Priestlehy
Woman in Black	S.Hill, adap. Stephen Mallatratt
Alice in Wonderland	L.Carroll, adap. M. Sircom.

1989

Who's Afraid of Virginia Woolf?	EdwardAlbee
The Importance of Being Earnest	Oscar Wilde
On the Plastic (BJT)	June Wilkinson
Women Beware Women	Thomas Middleton
Worlds Apart	Hughes Project
A Small Family Business	Alan Ayckbourn
Our Day Out	Willy Russell
Damn Yankees	Richard Adler & Jerry Ross
Heartlanders*	S.Bill, A. Devlin & D. Edgar
Twelfth Night	Shakespeare
Stamping, Shouting and Singing Home (BJT)	Lisa Evans
A Christmas Carol	C.Dickens, adap. Ron Pember
The Lover and Village Wooing	Pinter & Bernard Shaw

1990

Valentino (BJT)	Snarling Beasties
Summer of the 17th Doll	Ray Lawler
The Seagull	Chekhov, trans. M. Frayn
Flarepath	Terrence Rattigan
Crime of the Century (BJT)	Lisa Evans
When We are Married	J. B. Priestley
The Writing Game*	David Lodge
Of Mice and Men	John Steinbeck
Oh What a Lovely War (RYW)	Theatre Workshop

Company of Wolves (RYW)	A.Carter, adap. Mick Yates
The Relapse	Sir John Vanbrugh
The Canal Ghost (BJT)	Nick Stafford
Macbeth	Shakespeare
All My Sons	Arthur Miller
Wind in the Willows	K. Grahame, adap. D. Conville

1991

The Ragged Trousered Philanthropists	Stephen Lowe
Saturday, Sunday, Monday	Eduardo de Fillippe
Anthony and Cleopatra	Shakespeare
Threepenny Opera (RYW)	Bertolt Brecht
V (RYW)	Tony Harrison
Antigone (RYW)	Jean Anouilh
Translations	Brian Friel
Cider with Rosie	Laurie Lee
Noises Off	Michael Frayn
The Threepenny Opera	Bertolt Brecht
Lady Day at Emerson's Bar & Grill (BRA/OP)	Lanie Robertson
My Father's House*	David Pownall
Metamorphosis (BJT)	Steven Berkoff
The Pied Piper	Anthony Clark
The Magic Toyshop* (RYW)	A. Carter, adap. M.Yates
Turn of the Screw	H.James, adap. Eve Lewis

1992

Kafka's Dick	Alan Bennett
Hobson's Choice	Harold Brighhouse
Island* (BJT)	G.Hutchins & S.O'Dell
My Mother Said I Never	Charlotte Keatley
Whale Nation and Falling for a Dolphin (RWY)	Heathcote Williams
The Rivals (WYP)	Richard Sheridan
Biko*	Richard Fawkes & Priti Paintal
Animal Farm (RYW)	G.Orwell, adap. Peter Hall
Beauty and the Beast*	David Holman
The Last Carnival*	Derek Walcott
Radio Times*	Abi Grant
Playing by the Rules*•	Rod Dungate
The Grapes of Wrath	John Steinbeck
The Devil's Only Sleeping* (BJT)	Nick Stafford
Dangerous Corner	J. B. Priestley
Nervous Women*	Sarah Woods
The Wizard of Oz	Frank L. Baum
East Lynne*	Mrs Henry Wood, adap. Lisa Evans

215

1993

Big Maggie	John B Keane
Othello	Shakespeare
Syme* (RNTS)	Michael Bourdages
Playing by the Rules	Rod Dungate
Rope	Patrick Hamilton
Bidding and Binding (BJT)	Sarah Woods
Volpone	Ben Jonson
Romeo and Juliet	Shakespeare
Travelling Light	Hughes Project
Old Times	Harold Pinter
Joy Riders (BJT)	Christine Reid
Blithe Spirit	Noel Coward
The Snowman●	Raymond Briggs

1994

The Atheist's Tragedy	Cyril Tourneur
Awake and Sing!	Clifford Odets
Playing Hamlet	Gwenda Hughes
Lady Windemere's Fan	Oscar Wilde
Mickey and Me (BJT)	Alex Jones
Young Writer's Festival	
The Playboy of the Western World	J.M.Synge
Once on this Island*●	L.Aherns & S.Flaherty
The Tempest	Shakespeare
Rough*	Kate Dean
A Shaft of Sunlight (TAM)	Abhijat Joshi
Mohicans (BJT)	Garry Lyons
Loot and Entertaining Mr Sloane	Joe Orton
Getting It Straight	J. Trevor & L.Laidlaw
Peter Pan	J.M. Barrie

1995

The Servant	Robin Maugham
Hot off the Page Festival	
A View from the Bridge	Arthur Miller
Nothing Compares to You*	Bryony Lavery
Pygmalion	Bernard Shaw
Nights in Darkness	Milton Godfrey
Seven* (BJT)	Richard Cameron
The Importance of Being Earnest	Oscar Wilde
The Tenant of Wildfell Hall*	A.Bronte, adap. Lisa Evans
The Red Balloon●	A Lamorisse, adap. Anthony Clark
Macbeth	Shakespeare
A Yearning* (TAM/LH)	Ruth Carter after F.Lorca
The Way of the World	William Congreve
Johnny Watkins Walks on Water (BJT)	Debbie Isitt
Jesus My Boy	John Dowie
Toad of Toad Hall	A.A.Milne

1996

The Entertainer	Joe Osborne
The Winslow Boy (WYP)	Terrence Rattigan
Bretevski Street (BJT)	Lin Coglan
Hot off the Page Festival II	
Divine Right*	Peter Whelan
Swamp City*	Paul Lucas
Gentlemen Prefer Blondes	Anita Loos
Trust Byron	George Costigan
The Tenant of Wildfell Hall	A.Bronte, adap. Lisa Evans
Dr.Jekyll and Mr.Hyde	David Edgar
The Alchemist (RNT)	Ben Jonson
East is East* (TAM)	Ayub Khan Din
Les Dainaides (National Indoor Arena)	Aeschylus, adap.S.Purcarete
A Doll's House	Henrik Ibsen
Squealing like a Pig* (BJT)	Debbie Isitt
Pinocchio	Carlo Collodi adap. A.Clark
Season's Greetings	Alan Ayckbourn
Think no Evil of Us; My life with Kenneth Williams	David Benson

1997

The Merchant of Venice	Shakespeare
Bonded (BJT)	Mark Davies Markham
Mourning Song (BMT/D)	Black Mime Theatre
Hot Off the Page III	
Misalliance (TC)	Bernard Shaw
Landslide* (WYP)	Andy de la Tour
True Brit*	Ken Blakeson
The Cherry Orchard (MTJ)	Chekhov/R.Martin, adap. J.Suzman
The Importance of Being Earnest	Oscar Wilde
Keep on Running	Bob Carlton
A Tainted Dawn* (TAM)	S.Bhuchar & K. Landon-Smith
Julius Caesar	Shakespeare
Soulfires: Sally's Rape, Dutchman & Playland	R.McCauley, A Baraka & A Fugard
The Road to Hell	Andrew Alty
The Whisper of Angel's Wings*	Nick Stafford
The Snowman	Raymond Briggs

1998

Home Truths*	David Lodge
Kaahini	Maya Chowdhry
The Rocky Horror Show	Richard O'Brien
Hot off the Page IV	
Frozen*●	Bryony Lavery
A Fool and his Money (NP)	Moliere, adap. J Sams

Hamlet	Shakespeare
Confidence*	Judy Upton
Twins*	Maureen Lawrence
The Oresteia	Aeschylus
Down Red Lane*	Kate Dean
Three Sisters	Chekhov. Trans. M.Poulton
The Snowman	Raymond Briggs
A Christmas Carol	C.Dickens, adap. M.Bogdanov
Fourteen Songs, Two Weddings and a Funeral● (TAM)	S.Bhuchar & K.Landan-Smith

1999

2 Pianos, 4 Hands	T.Dykstra & R. Greenblatt
Paddy Irishman, Paddy Englishman and Paddy…*●	Declan Croghan
The Four Alice Bakers *	Fay Weldon
Trips*	Sarah Woods
Nightbus* (BJT)	Peter Cann
The Rocky Horror Show	Richard O'Brian
Perpetua* (SOHO)	Fraser Grace
The Pajama Game● (TT)	R.Alder & J. Ross
All that Trouble That We Had*	Paul Lucas
Ten Days in June	
Jumpers	Tom Stpppard
Baby Doll●	Tennessee Williams
Silence*	Moira Buffini
A Time of Fire*	Charles Mulekwa
Nativity*	P. Whelan & B. Alexander
Balti Kings* (TAM)	S.Bhuchar & K. Landon-Smith

2000

The Snowman	Raymond Briggs
Young Rep Show Case	
My Best Friend*	Tasmin Oglesby
The Free State (FA/WYP)	Janet Suzman
Death of a Salesman	Arthur Miller
Terracotta* (HAMP)	Jess Walters
My Dad's Corner Shop* (BJT)	Ray Grewal
Quarantine*	J.Crace, adap. B.Payne
St. Joan	Bernard Shaw
The Gift*	Roy Williams
Present Laughter	Noel Coward

Transmissions Festival 2000	
The Birds (YR)	Aristophanes, adap. M.Punter
Twelfth Night	Shakespeare
Hamlet	Shakespeare
The Slight Witch* (RNTS)	Paul Lucas
The Ramayana●	Adapted by Peter Oswald
A Wedding Story* (ST)	Bryony Lavery
Absurd Person Singular	Alan Ayckbourn
Belonging*	Kaite O'Reilly
Gingerbread Pig	Moving Hands
Cinderella-The Ash Girl*	Timberlake Wertenbaker

2001

The Lady in the Van	Alan Bennett
Having a Ball	Alan Bleasdale
Musical Youth* (BJT)	Nigel Moffatt
Morning Glory* (PTW/CAT)	Sarah Daniels
Fourteen Songs, Two Weddings and a Funeral	S.Bhuchar & K.Landon-Smith
Travels With My Aunt (NP)	Graham Greene
Blues in the Night	Sheldon Epps
Transmissions 2001	
The Wedding (YR)	B.Brecht, trans. C. Jester
Private Lives	Noel Coward
Closer	Patrick Marber
Tender*	Abi Morgan
Of Mice and Men	John Steinbeck
Behsharam* (SOHO)	Gurpreet Kaur Bhatti
The Wind in the Willows	Kenneth Grahame
Winnie the Witch*	K. Paul & V. Thomas, adap. A.Clark

2002

Naked Justice	John Mortimer
Peeling* (GRA)	Kate O'Reilly
Hobson's Choice (TRP)	Harold Brighouse
Silence (BJT)	Moira Buffini
No Sweat*	Lloyd Withers
Elizabeth Rex	Timothy Findley
Getting to the Foot of the Mountain*	Lisa Evans
Masterpieces	C. Luscombe & M. McKee
Krindlekrax* (NP)	Philip Ridley
Wallop Mrs Cox	Euan Rose and Laurie Hornsby

Appendix II
Visiting Companies

Arc Dance Company
Ballet Rambert
Belt and Braces Roadshow
Big Brum TIE Company
Black Mime Theatre
Black Theatre Co-operative
Bahumutsi
CandoCo Dance Company
Chitraleka and Company
The Cholmondeleys
Cleveland
Theatre Company
English Music
Theatre Company
The Featherstonehaughs
Female Company
The Fetch Theatre
Company
Foco Novo
Foursight Theatre
Gay Sweatshop
Geese Theatre Company
The General Will
George Piper Dances
Ghana National Dance
Ensemble
Les Grandes Ballets
Canadiens
Lip Service
Lords of Misrule
The Irish Company
Jade Theatre Company
Joint Stock Theatre Group
Kaleidoscope Theatre
Keeping Mum
Theatre Company

Ken Campbell's
Road Show
Kokuma Dance Company
Krazy Kat Theatre
London Contemporary
Dance Theatre
Major Road Dance
Company
Major Road
Theatre Company
Mark Baldwin
Dance Company
Mark Morris
Dance Group
Michael Clark
Dance Company
Monstrous Regiment
The Mouse People
Moving Hands
Theatre Company
Mrs Worthington's
Daughters
National Theatre of Brent
National Theatre Company
National Theatre
of Craiova, Romania
The Network
Northern Dance Theatre
Nuffield Theatre Company
Paines Plough
Pentabus Theatre
Company
Pip Simmons
Theatre Company
Prospect Theatre Company
Random Dance Company
Red Shift Theatre
Company

The Reduced
Shakespeare Company
Renaissance
Theatre Company
Richard Alston
Dance Company
Royal Court
Young Peoples' Theatre
Royal Shakespeare
Company
Scottish Dance Company
7:84 Theatre Company
Shared Experience
Shobana Jeyasingh
Dance Company
Siobhan Davies Dance
Company
Snarling Beasties
The Sphinx
Staunch Poets and Players
Tara Arts
Temba Theatre Company
Theatre of the
Unemployed
Theatre Foundry
Third Dimension
Tic Toc Theatre
Company
Traverse Theatre
Company
Turtle Theatre
Vox Theatre Company
Welfare State International
Women and Theatre
The Wrestling School
Yorkshire Actors Company
Young Vic Company

Select Bibliography

Beauman, Sally,
**The Royal Shakespeare Company:
A History of Ten Decades**
(Oxford University Press, 1982)

Cochrane, Claire,
**Shakespeare and the Birmingham
Repertory Theatre 1913-1929**
(Society for Theatre Research, 1993)

Kemp, T.C.,
**Birmingham Repertory Theatre:
The Playhouse and the Man**
(Cornish, 1948)

Mackintosh, Iain,
Architecture, Actor and Audience
(Routledge, 1993)

Matthews, Bache,
**A History of the Birmingham
Repertory Theatre**
(Chatto & Windus, 1924)

Mulryne, Ronnie & Shewring, Margaret,
**Making Space for Theatre
British Architecture and
Theatre Since 1958**
(Mulryne and Shewring, 1995)

Rowell, George & Jackson, Anthony
**The Repertory Movement:
A History of Regional Theatre in Britain**
(Cambridge University Press, 1984)

Salberg, Derek,
Ring Down the Curtain
(Cortney Publications Luton, 1980)

Trewin, J.C.,
**The Birmingham Repertory
Theatre 1913-1963**
(Barrie and Rockcliff, 1963)

Upton, Chris
A History of Birmingham
(Phillimore & Co Ltd, 1993)

Index of Names